Leaders are the ones who run headfirst into the unknown.

They rush toward the danger.

They put their own interests aside
to protect us or to pull us into the future.

Leaders would sooner sacrifice what is theirs to save what is ours.

And they would never sacrifice what is ours to save what is theirs.

This is what it means to be a leader.

It means they choose to go first into danger,
headfirst toward the unknown.

And when we feel sure they will keep us safe,

we will march behind them
and work tirelessly to see their visions come to life

and proudly call ourselves their followers.

PORTFOLIO / PENGUIN

LEADERS EAT LAST

SIMON SINEK is an optimist who believes in a brighter future for humanity. His talk on TED.com is the third most watched talk of all time. Learn more about his work and how you can inspire those around you at StartWithWhy.com.

SIMON SINEK

LEADERS EAT LAST

Why Some Teams Pull Together and Others Don't

PORTFOLIO / PENGUIN

PORTFOLIO / PENGUIN

An imprint of Penguin Random House LLC
Penguin Group (USA) LLC
375 Hudson Street
New York, New York 10014

First published in the United States of America by Portfolio / Penguin 2014
This paperback edition with a revised chapter 24 and new appendix published 2017

Most Portfolio books are available at a discount when purchased in quantity for
sales promotions or corporate use. Special editions, which include personalized covers,
excerpts, and corporate imprints, can be created when purchased in large quantities.
For more information, please call (212) 572-2232 or e-mail specialmarkets@
penguinrandomhouse.com. Your local bookstore can also
assist with discounted bulk purchases using the Penguin Random House
corporate Business-to-Business program. For assistance in locating
a participating retailer, e-mail B2B@penguinrandomhouse.com.

"This Be the Verse" from *The Complete Poems of Philip Larkin,* edited by Archie
Burnett. Copyright © 2012 by The Estate of Philip Larkin. Reprinted by permission of
Farrar, Straus and Giroux, LLC and Faber and Faber Ltd.

ISBN 9781591848011 (paperback)

THE LIBRARY OF CONGRESS HAS CATALOGED THE
HARDCOVER EDITION AS FOLLOWS:
Sinek, Simon.
Leaders eat last : why some teams pull together and others don't / Simon Sinek.
pages cm
Includes index.
ISBN 9781591845324 (hardcover)
1. Leadership. 2. Corporate culture. 3. Organizational change. I. Title.
HD57.7.S5487 2014
658.4'092—dc23
2013039108

Printed in the United States of America
19th Printing

Set in Minion Pro

To the men and women I've met in the
United States Air Force—

You have taught me more about what it means to be human
than anyone who wears a suit ever did.

CONTENTS

FOREWORD

I know of no case study in history that describes an organization that has been managed out of a crisis. Every single one of them was led. Yet a good number of our educational institutions and training programs today are focused not on developing great leaders but on training effective managers. Short-term gains are viewed as the mark of success and long-term organizational growth and viability are simply the bill payers. *Leaders Eat Last* is an effort to change this paradigm.

In *Leaders Eat Last*, Simon Sinek does not propose any new leadership theory or core principle. He has a much higher purpose to his writing. Simon would like to make the world a better place for all of us. His vision is simple: to create a new generation of men and women who understand that an organization's success or failure is based on leadership excellence and not managerial acumen.

It is not an accident that Simon uses the U.S. military, and in particular the United States Marine Corps, to explain the importance of leaders being focused on their people. These organizations have strong cultures and shared values, understand the importance of teamwork, create trust among their members, maintain focus, and, most important, understand the importance of people and relationships to their mission success. These organizations are also in a position where the cost of failure can be catastrophic. Mission failure is not an option. Without a doubt, people enable the success of all our military services.

When you are with Marines gathering to eat, you will notice that the most junior are served first and the most senior are served last. When you witness this act, you will also note that no order is given. Marines just do it. At the heart of this very simple action is the Marine Corps' approach to leadership. Marine leaders are expected to eat last because the true price of leadership is the willingness to place the needs of others above your own. Great leaders truly care about those they are privileged to lead and understand that the true cost of the leadership privilege comes at the expense of self-interest.

In his previous book, *Start with Why: How Great Leaders Inspire Everyone to Take Action,* Simon explained that for an organization to be successful its leaders need to understand the true purpose of their organization—the Why. In *Leaders Eat Last,* Simon takes us to the next level of understanding why some organizations do better than others. He does this by detailing all elements of the leadership challenge. Simply stated, it is not enough to know "the Why" of your organization; you must know your people and realize that they are much more than an expendable resource. In short, professional competence is not enough to be a good leader; good leaders must truly care about those entrusted to their care.

Good management is clearly not enough to sustain any organization over the long term. Simon's in-depth explanation of the elements of human behavior clearly demonstrates that there are real reasons why some organizations may do well over a short period of time but eventually fail: The leadership has failed to create an environment where people really do matter. As Simon points out, organizations where people share values and are valued succeed over the long term in both good and bad times.

"If your actions inspire others to dream more, learn more, do more and become more, you are a leader." In this quote, often attributed to John Quincy Adams, a man who clearly understood what it was to be a leader, I think you will find the message of *Leaders Eat Last.* When leaders inspire those they lead, people dream of a better future, invest time and effort in learning more, do more for their organizations and along the way become leaders themselves. A leader who takes care of their people and stays focused on the well-being of the organization can never fail. My hope is that after reading this book readers will be inspired to always eat last.

GEORGE J. FLYNN
Lieutenant General, U.S. Marine Corps (Ret.)

THE
FORCE

[OUR NEED TO FEEL SAFE]

CHAPTER 1

Protection from Above

A thick layer of clouds blocked out any light. There were no stars and there was no moon. Just black. The team slowly made its way through the valley, the rocky terrain making it impossible to go any faster than a snail's pace. Worse, they knew they were being watched. Every one of them was on edge.

A year hadn't yet passed since the attacks of September 11. The Taliban government had only recently fallen after taking a pounding from U.S. forces for their refusal to turn over the Al Qaeda leader, Osama bin Laden. There were a lot of Special Operations Forces in the area performing missions that, to this day, are still classified. This was one of those teams and this was one of those missions.

All we know is that the team of twenty-two men was operating deep inside enemy territory and had recently captured what the government calls a "high-value target." They were now working their way through a deep valley in a mountainous part of Afghanistan, escorting their high-value target to a safe house.

Flying over the thick clouds that night was Captain Mike Drowley, or Johnny Bravo, as he is known by his call sign or nickname. Except for the whir of his engines, it was perfectly peaceful up there. Thousands of stars speckled the sky, and the moon lit up the top of the clouds so brightly it looked like a fresh layer of snow had fallen. It was beautiful.

Johnny Bravo and his wingman were circling above in their A-10 aircraft, waiting should they be needed below. Affectionately known as the Warthog, the A-10 is not technically a fighter jet; it's an attack aircraft. A relatively slow-flying, single-seat armored plane designed to provide close air support for troops on the ground. Unlike other fighter jets, it is not fast or sexy (hence the nickname), but it gets the job done.

Ideally, both the A-10 pilots in the air and the troops on the ground would prefer to see each other with their eyes. Seeing the plane above, knowing someone is looking out for them, gives the troops below a greater sense of confidence. And seeing the troops below gives the pilots a greater sense of assurance that they will be able to help if needed. But given the thick cloud cover and the mountainous terrain that night in Afghanistan, the only way either knew the other was there was through the occasional radio contact they kept. Without a line of sight, Johnny Bravo couldn't see what the troops saw, but he could sense how the troops felt from what he heard over the radio. And this was enough to spur him to act.

Following his gut, Johnny Bravo decided he needed to execute a weather letdown, to drop down below the clouds so he could take a look at what was happening on the ground. It was a daring move. With the thick, low-hanging clouds, scattered storms in the area and the fact that Johnny Bravo would have to fly into a valley with his field of vision reduced by the night-vision goggles, performing the weather letdown under these conditions was extremely treacherous for even the most experienced of pilots.

Johnny Bravo was not told to perform the risky maneuver. If anything, he probably would have been told to hang tight and wait until he got the call to help. But Johnny Bravo is not like most pilots. Even though he was thousands of feet above in the safe cocoon of his cockpit, he could sense the anxiety of the men below. Regardless of the dangers, he knew that performing the weather letdown was the right thing to do. And for Johnny Bravo, that meant there was no other choice.

Then, just as he was preparing to head down through the clouds into the valley, his instincts were confirmed. Three words came across the radio. Three little words that can send shivers down a pilot's neck: "Troops in contact."

"Troops in contact" means someone on the ground is in trouble. It is the call that ground forces use to let others know they are under attack. Though Johnny Bravo had heard those words many times before during training, it was on this night, August 16, 2002, that he heard the words "troops in contact" for the first time in a combat situation.

Johnny Bravo had developed a way to help him relate to the men on the ground. To feel what they feel. During every training exercise, while flying above the battlefield, he would always replay in his mind the scene from the movie *Saving Private Ryan* when the Allies stormed the beaches of Normandy. He would picture the ramp of a Higgins boat dropping down, the men running onto the beach into a wall of German gunfire. The bullets whizzing past them. The pings of stray shots hitting the steel hulls of the boats. The cries of men hit. Johnny Bravo had trained himself to imagine that that was the scene playing out below every time he heard "Troops in contact." With those images vividly embossed in his mind, Johnny Bravo reacted to the call for assistance.

He told his wingman to hang tight above the clouds, announced his intentions to the flight controllers and the troops below and pointed his aircraft down into the darkness. As he passed through the clouds, the turbulence thrashed him and his aircraft about. A hard push to the left. A sudden drop. A jolt to the right. Unlike the commercial jets in which we fly, the A-10 is not designed for passenger comfort, and his plane bounced and shook hard as he passed through the layer of cloud.

Flying into the unknown with no idea what to expect, Johnny Bravo focused his attention on his instruments, trying to take in as much information as he could. His eyes moved from one dial to the next followed by a quick glance out the front window. Altitude, speed, heading, window. Altitude, speed, heading, window. "Please. Let. This. Work. Please. Let. This. Work," he said to himself under his breath.

When he finally broke through the clouds, he was less than a thousand feet off the ground, flying in a valley. The sight that greeted him was nothing like he had ever seen before, not in training or in the movies. There was enemy fire coming from both sides of the valley. Massive amounts of it. There was so much that the tracer fire—the streaks of light that follow the bullets—lit up the whole area. Bullets and rockets all aimed at the middle, all aimed squarely at the Special Operations Forces pinned down below.

In 2002 the avionics in the aircraft were not as sophisticated as they are today. The instruments Johnny Bravo had couldn't prevent him from hitting the mountain walls. Worse, he was flying with old Soviet maps left over from the invasion of Afghanistan in the 1980s. But there was no way he was going to let down those troops. "There are fates worse than death," he will tell you. "One fate worse than death is accidentally killing your own men. Another fate worse than death is going home alive when twenty-two others don't."

And so, on that dark night in August, Johnny Bravo started counting. He knew his speed and he knew his distance from the mountains. He did some quick calculations in his head and counted out loud the seconds he had before he would hit the valley walls. "One one thousand, two one thousand, three one thousand . . ." He locked his guns onto a position from which he could see a lot of enemy fire originating and held down the trigger of his Gatling gun. "Four one thousand, five one thousand, six one thousand . . ." At the point he ran out of room, he pulled back on the stick and pulled a sharp turn. His plane roared as he pulled back into the cloud above, his only option to avoid smacking into the mountain. His body pressed hard into his seat from the pressure of the G-forces as he set to go around again.

But there was no sound on the radio. The silence was deafening. Did the radio silence mean his shots were useless? Did it mean the guy on the radio was down? Or worse, did it mean the whole team was down?

Then the call came. "Good hits! Good hits! Keep it coming!" And keep it coming he did. He took another pass, counting again to avoid hitting the mountains. "One one thousand, two one thousand, three one thousand . . ." And another sharp turn and another run. And another. And another. He was making good hits and he had plenty of fuel; the problem now was, he was out of ammo.

He pointed his plane up to the clouds to fly and meet his wingman, who was still circling above. Johnny Bravo quickly briefed his partner on the situation and told him to do one thing, "Follow me." The two A-10s, flying three feet apart from each other, wing to wing, disappeared together into the clouds.

When they popped out, both less than a thousand feet above the ground, they began their runs together. Johnny Bravo did the counting and his wingman followed his lead and laid down the fire. "One one thousand. Two one thousand. Three one thousand. Four one thousand . . ." On cue, the two planes pulled high-G turns together and went around again and again and again. "One one thousand. Two one thousand. Three one thousand. Four one thousand."

That night, twenty-two men went home alive. There were no American casualties.

The Value of Empathy

THAT AUGUST NIGHT over Afghanistan, Johnny Bravo risked his life so that others might survive. He received no performance bonus. He didn't get a promotion or an award at the company off-site. He wasn't looking for any undue attention or reality TV show for his efforts. For Johnny Bravo, it was just part of the "J.O.B." as he puts it. And the greatest reward he received for his service was meeting the forces for whom he provided top cover that night. Though they had never met before, when they finally did meet, they hugged like old friends.

In the linear hierarchies in which we work, we want the folks at the top to see what we did. We raise our hands for recognition and reward. For most of us, the more recognition we get for our efforts from those in charge, the more successful we think we are. It is a system that works so long as that one person who supervises us stays at the company and feels no undue pressure from above— a nearly impossible standard to maintain. For Johnny Bravo and those like him, the will to succeed and the desire to do things that advance the interests of the organization aren't just motivated by recognition from above; they are integral to a culture of sacrifice and service, in which protection comes from all levels of the organization.

There is one thing that Johnny Bravo credits for giving him the courage to cross into the darkness of the unknown, sometimes with the knowledge that he might not come back. And it's not necessarily what you would expect. As valuable as it was, it isn't his training. And for all the advanced schooling he has received, it isn't his education. And as remarkable as the tools are that he has been given, it isn't his aircraft or any of its sophisticated systems. For all the technology he has at his disposal, empathy, Johnny Bravo says, is the single greatest asset he has to do his job. Ask any of the remarkable men and women in uniform who risk themselves for the benefit of others why they do it and they will tell you the same thing: "Because they would have done it for me."

Where do people like Johnny Bravo come from? Are they just born that way? Some perhaps are. But if the conditions in which we work meet a particular standard, every single one of us is capable of the courage and sacrifice of a Johnny Bravo. Though we may not be asked to risk our lives or to save anybody else's, we would gladly share our glory and help those with whom we work succeed. More important, in the right conditions, the people with whom we work would choose to do those things for us. And when that happens, when those kinds of bonds are formed, a strong foundation is laid for the kind of success and fulfillment that no amount of money, fame or awards can buy. This is what it means to work in a place in which the leaders prioritize the well-being of their people and, in return, their people give everything they've got to protect and advance the well-being of one another and the organization.

I use the military to illustrate the example because the lessons are so much more exaggerated when it is a matter of life and death. There is a pattern that exists in the organizations that achieve the greatest success, the ones that outmaneuver and outinnovate their competitors, the ones that command the greatest respect from inside and outside their organizations, the ones with the highest loyalty and lowest churn and the ability to weather nearly every storm or challenge. These exceptional organizations all have cultures in which the leaders provide cover from above and the people on the ground look out for each other. This is the reason they are willing to push hard and take the kinds of risks they do. And the way any organization can achieve this is with empathy.

CHAPTER 2

Employees Are People Too

Before there was empathy at the company, going to work felt like, well, work. On any given morning, the factory employees would stand at their machines waiting to start at the sound of the bell. And when it rang, on cue they would flip the switches and power up the machines in front of them. Within a few seconds, the whir of the machinery drowned out the sound of their voices. The workday had begun.

About two hours into the day, another bell would ring, announcing the time the workers could take a break. The machines would stop and nearly every worker would leave their post. Some went to the bathroom. Some went to grab another cup of coffee. And some just sat by their machines, resting until the bell told them to start work again. A few hours later, the bell would sound again, this time to let them know they were now allowed to leave the building for lunch. This was the way it had always been done.

"I didn't know any better," said Mike Merck, an assembly team leader with a thick Southern drawl who had been with HayssenSandiacre for fourteen years. "I think anyone in the building would have told you the same thing."

But things would change after Bob Chapman took over the

South Carolina company. Chapman is CEO of the equally cumbersomely named Barry-Wehmiller, a collection of predominantly manufacturing companies that Chapman had been steadily buying over the years. Most of the companies that Chapman bought were in distress. Their financials were weak and, in some cases, their cultures were worse. HayssenSandiacre was his latest acquisition. Other CEOs may have brought with them a team of consultants and a new strategy, ready to tell everyone what they had to do to "return the company to profitability." What Chapman brought, in stark contrast, was a willingness to listen. As he did with every company he acquired, he started by sitting down to hear what employees had to say.

Ron Campbell, a twenty-seven-year veteran of the company, had just returned from three months in Puerto Rico, where he had been responsible for installing HayssenSandiacre's manufacturing equipment in a customer's plant. Sitting in the room with Chapman, Campbell was hesitant to talk about what life was like at the company. "First of all," Campbell asked, "if I tell the truth, will I still have a job tomorrow?" Chapman smiled. "If you have any trouble tomorrow about what you say today," he assured him, "you give me a call."

And with that, Campbell started to open up. "Well, Mr. Chapman," he started, "it seems like you trust me a lot more when you can't see me than when I'm right here. I had more freedom while I was away at a customer site than I do here," he said, referring to his time away in Puerto Rico. "As soon as I stepped in the plant, it's like all my freedom just slipped away. It feels like someone has their thumb on me. I had to punch a time clock when I walked in and again when I left for lunch, came back and when I was done for the day. I didn't have to do that in Puerto Rico." This was nothing Chapman hadn't heard before at other factories.

"I walk in the same door with engineers, accountants and other people who work in the office," Campbell went on. "They turn left to go to the office and I go straight into the plant and we are treated completely differently. You trust them to decide when to get a soda or a cup of coffee or take a break; you make me wait for a bell."

Others felt the same. It was like there were two different companies. No matter how much effort they put in, those who stood by the machines didn't feel like the company trusted them simply because they stood on a factory floor instead of sitting at desks. If an office employee needed to call home to let their kids know they would be late, they would simply pick up the phone and call them. On the factory floor, however, if a worker needed to do the same thing, they had to ask permission to use the pay phone.

When Campbell finished, Chapman turned to the personnel leader and told him they needed to take down the time clocks. The bells were to go too. Without making any grand proclamations and without asking for anything in return from the employees, Chapman decided that things were going to be different from now on. And that was just the start.

Empathy would be injected into the company and trust would be the new standard. Preferring to see everyone as human instead of as a factory worker or office employee, Chapman made other changes so that everyone would be treated the same way.

Spare machine parts had always been kept inside a locked cage. If a worker needed a part, they would have to stand in line outside the cage and ask a parts employee to get what they needed. Workers were not allowed to go into the cage themselves. This was management's way of protecting against theft. It may have prevented theft, but it was also a powerful reminder that management didn't trust people. Chapman ordered all the locks removed and all the fences taken down and allowed any employee to go into the area to check out any part or tool they felt they needed.

Chapman took out all the pay phones and made company phones available that any employee could use at any time. No coins needed, no permission required. Any employee would be allowed to go through any door and visit any part of the company whenever they wanted. Every employee would be treated the same way regardless of whether they worked in the administrative offices or on the factory floor. This was going to be the new normal.

Chapman understood that to earn the trust of people, the leaders of an organization must first treat them like people. To earn trust, he must extend trust. He didn't believe that simply because someone went to college or was good at accounting they were more trustworthy than someone who had a GED and was good with their hands. Chapman believed in the fundamental goodness of people and he was going to treat them as such.

In a short period of time, the company started to feel more like a family. Simply by changing the environment in which people worked, the same people started acting differently toward each other. They felt like they belonged and that enabled them to relax and feel valued. People started to care for others as they felt cared for. This caring environment allowed people to fully engage "their heads and hearts," as Chapman likes to say, and the organization began to thrive.

An employee in the paint department faced a personal crisis. His wife, a diabetic, was going to lose her leg. He needed time to help her, but as an hourly worker, he could not afford to lose any pay. He couldn't afford not to work. But this was a different company now. Without being asked, his fellow employees quickly came up with a plan: to transfer their own paid vacation days so he could have more days off. Nothing like this had ever been done before at the company. What's more, it was in clear violation of official company policy. But that didn't matter. "We're thinking about other people more," Merck said. And so with the help of those in the administrative office, that is exactly what they did.

"I never thought you could enjoy a job," said Campbell. "When you have people who trust you, they're going to do a better job for you to earn or keep that trust." In the more than ten years since the chain-link fence came down, there has been almost no theft. And if an employee has a personal problem, they know the leaders of the company—and their fellow employees—will be there for them.

Employees didn't just become more willing to help each other solve problems, however. They also looked after their machines better. This meant fewer breakdowns and fewer work stoppages (which also meant expenses were kept in check). The changes were not only good for the people, they were good for the company too. In the period since Chapman took over, Hayssen-Sandiacre saw revenue increase from $55 million to $95 million, which reflected organic and acquisition growth. They grew without any debt and without the help of a management consultant–driven reorganization. The company grew because of the people who already worked there. They had a renewed commitment to the organization, and it didn't come as a result of any promises of bonuses or threats. They were more committed because they wanted to be. A new culture of caring allowed the people and strategies to flourish.

This is what happens when the leaders of an organization listen to the people who work there. Without coercion, pressure or force, the people naturally work together to help each other and advance the company. Working with a sense of obligation is replaced by working with a sense of pride. And coming to work for the company is replaced by coming to work for each other. Work is no longer a place to dread. It is a place to feel valued.

We See What We Want to See

CHAPMAN LIKES TO tell the story about the first time he visited HayssenSandiacre, which was five years before the transition that Mike Merck and Ron Campbell talk about. It was shortly after Chapman had acquired the company. As the new CEO, no one knew who he was or paid any attention to him as he sipped a cup of coffee before his first meeting. They just went about their business as usual, waiting for the day to start. And it was what Chapman saw while sitting in the cafeteria that March morning in 1997 that started his experiment with the company. He saw something he had never seen before in all of his years in business. It was a scene powerful enough to force him to reexamine nearly every lesson he had ever learned about how to run a company. What he did at HayssenSandiacre would become the basis for how Chapman would run his entire operation. More important, it would transform how he managed the people who worked for him.

As he sat there, Chapman watched a group of employees having their morning coffee together before work . . . and they were having fun. Joking, laughing like they were old friends. They were placing bets for the NCAA March Madness basketball tournament airing that night. They were getting along and seemed to really enjoy each other's company. But as soon as they stood up to start their day, Chapman noticed a dramatic change in their demeanor. As if on cue, their smiles were replaced with sullenness. The laughing stopped. The camaraderie evaporated. "The energy seemed to drain from them," said Chapman.

Chapman was overcome with a feeling of despair. He had bought distressed companies like this before. He had been around their employees before. But, for some reason, he had never been able to see what he saw that day. He couldn't help but feel touched by what he just witnessed, which spurred a thought: Why can't we enjoy ourselves at work like we do when we're not at work?

Up until that day, Chapman had been exactly the kind of executive we teach our MBAs to be. He was good with numbers and he loved the game of business. He made decisions based on data, market conditions and financial opportunities. He was tough when he needed to be and could charm the pants off someone, if that's what was required. He thought business was something that was measured on spreadsheets, and he saw people as one of the many assets he had to manage to help him achieve his financial goals. And as that kind of executive, he was very effective.

Before that moment in the cafeteria, Chapman was able to make hard decisions far too easily. The St. Louis–based company with the hard-to-spell name was saddled with debt and close to bankruptcy when Chapman took over after his father died in 1975. And given the dire situation, he did what any responsible CEO would do in his position. He laid off employees when he felt it was needed to achieve the desired financial goal, renegotiated his debt obligations, was dependent on banks to support growth and took big risks that would create growth that any high-flying executive would have understood. And as a result the company slowly built back up to profitability.

Chapman left the cafeteria and headed to his first meeting. It was supposed to be a meet-and-greet, a simple formality. He, the new CEO, was to introduce himself to the customer service team, and they were to bring the new CEO up to speed. But based on what Chapman saw that morning, he realized that he and his team had the power to make the company a place people wanted to go every day. So he set out to create an environment in which people felt they could express themselves honestly and be recognized and celebrated for their progress. This is the basis of what Chapman calls truly human leadership.

. . . .

When the people have to manage dangers from inside the organization, the organization itself becomes less able to face the dangers from outside.

. . . .

Truly human leadership protects an organization from the internal rivalries that can shatter a culture. When we have to protect ourselves from each other, the whole organization suffers. But when trust and cooperation thrive internally, we pull together and the organization grows stronger as a result.

Nearly every system in the human body exists to help us survive and thrive. Thousands of years ago, other hominid species died off while we lived on . . . and on and on. And even though we have been on the planet for a relatively short period of time compared to other species, we have fast become the most successful and the only unrivaled animal on earth. So successful, in fact, that the decisions we make affect the ability of other animals—even other human beings—to survive or thrive.

The systems inside us that protect us from danger and encourage us to repeat behavior in our best interest respond to the environments in which we live and work. If we sense danger our defenses go up. If we feel safe among our own people, in our own tribes or organizations, we relax and are more open to trust and cooperation.

A close study of high-performing organizations, the ones in which the people feel safe when they come to work, reveals something astounding. Their cultures have an eerie resemblance to the conditions under which the human animal was designed to operate. Operating in a hostile, competitive world in which each group was in pursuit of finite resources, the systems that helped us survive and thrive as a species also work to help organizations achieve the same. There are no fancy management theories and it is not about hiring dream teams. It is just a matter of biology and anthropology. If certain conditions are met and the people inside an organization feel safe among each other, they will work together to achieve things none of them could have ever achieved alone. The result is that their organization towers over their competitors.

This is what Chapman did at Barry-Wehmiller. Quite by accident, he created a work environment and company culture that, biologically, gets the best out of people. Chapman and others like him didn't set out to change their employees—they set out to change the conditions in which their employees operate. To create cultures that inspire people to give all they have to give simply because they love where they work.

This book attempts to help us understand why we do what we do. Almost all of the systems in our bodies have evolved to help us find food, stay alive and advance the species. However, for a lot of the world, and certainly throughout the developed world, finding food and avoiding danger no longer preoccupy our days. We no longer hunt and gather, at least not in the caveman sense. In our modern world, advancing our careers and trying to find happiness and fulfillment are the definition of success. But the systems inside us that guide our behavior and decisions still function as they did tens of thousands of years ago. Our primitive minds still perceive the world around us in terms of threats to our well-being or opportunities to find safety. If we understand how these systems work, we are better equipped to reach our goals. At the same time, the groups in which we work are better able to succeed and thrive as well.

Yet sadly in our modern world, given the systems we've developed to manage our companies, the number of organizations that inspire employees to truly commit themselves is a slim minority. The cultural norms of the majority of companies and organizations today actually work against our natural biological inclinations. This means that happy, inspired and fulfilled employees are the exception rather than the rule. According to the Deloitte Shift Index, 80 percent of people are dissatisfied with their jobs. When people don't even want to be at work, progress comes at much greater cost and effort . . . and often doesn't last. We don't even bother measuring a company's success in decades, instead we focus on successive quarters.

A business environment with an unbalanced focus on short-term results and money before people affects society at large. When we struggle to find happiness or a sense of belonging at work, we take that struggle home. Those who have an opportunity to work in organizations that treat them like human beings to be protected rather than a resource to be exploited come home at the end of the day with an intense feeling of fulfillment and gratitude. This should be the rule for all of us, not the exception.

Returning from work feeling inspired, safe, fulfilled and grateful is a natural human right to which we are all entitled and not a modern luxury that only a few lucky ones are able to find.

There was no "one thing" that Chapman did to transform his organization. It was a series of little things that, over time, dramatically affected how his company operates. Lots and lots of little things, some successful, some less so, but all focused on what he understood in his gut needed to happen. It wasn't until years later, while attending a wedding, that Chapman was able to articulate in much clearer and more human terms what was driving his decisions. Given his love and tenacity for business, how Bob Chapman explains why he made the course change he did may surprise you.

The Awesome Responsibility

SITTING IN THE pews of a church, Chapman and his wife watched a wedding ceremony unfold. The groom stood, staring at his approaching bride. The feeling of love the two had for each other was palpable. Everyone there could feel it. And then, as tradition dictated, the father handed his daughter, his baby girl, to her future husband.

"That's it!" Chapman realized. A father who would do anything to protect his daughter now ceremonially hands the responsibility of that care to another. After he gives her hand away, he will take his place in the pews and trust that her new husband will protect her as he did. "It's exactly the same for a company," Chapman realized.

. . . .

Every single employee is someone's son or someone's daughter. Like a parent, a leader of a company is responsible for their precious lives.

. . . .

Every single employee is someone's son or someone's daughter. Parents work to offer their children a good life and a good education and to teach them the lessons that will help them grow up to be happy, confident and able to use all the talents they were blessed with. Those parents then hand their children over to a company with the hope the leaders of that company will exercise the same love and care as they have. "It is we, the companies, who are now responsible for these precious lives," says Chapman, as he balls his hands into fists with the conviction of a devoted preacher.

This is what it means to be a leader. This is what it means to build a strong company. Being a leader is like being a parent, and the company is like a new family to join. One that will care for us like we are their own . . . in sickness and in health. And if we are successful, our people will take on our company's name as a sign of the family to which they are loyal. Those who work at Barry-Wehmiller talk of their "love" for the company and each other. They proudly wear the logo or the company's name as if it were their own name. They will defend the company and their colleagues like they were their own flesh and blood. And in the case of nearly every one of these kinds of organizations, the people use the company's name as a very symbol of their own identity.

The great irony of all this is that capitalism actually does better when we work as we were designed—when we have a chance to fulfill our very human obligations. To ask our employees not simply for their hands to do our labor, but to inspire their cooperation, their trust and their loyalty so that they will commit to our cause. To treat people like family and not as mere employees. To sacrifice the numbers to save the people and not sacrifice the people to save the numbers.

Leaders of organizations who create a working environment better suited for how we are designed do not sacrifice excellence or performance simply because they put people first. Quite the contrary. These organizations are among the most stable, innovative and high-performing companies in their industries. Sadly, it is more common for leaders of companies to see the people as the means to drive the numbers. The leaders of great organizations do not see people as a commodity to be managed to help grow the money. They see the money as the commodity to be managed to help grow their people. This is why performance really matters. The better the organization performs, the more fuel there is to build an even bigger, more robust organization that feeds the hearts and souls of those who work there. In return, their people give everything they've got to see the organization grow . . . and grow . . . and grow.

To see money as subordinate to people and not the other way around is fundamental to creating a culture in which the people naturally pull together to advance the business. And it is the ability to grow one's people to do what needs to be done that creates stable, lasting success. It is not the genius at the top giving directions that makes people great. It is great people that make the guy at the top look like a genius.

I cannot be accused of being a crazy idealist, of imagining a world in which people love going to work. I can't be accused of being out of touch with reality to believe in the possibility of a world in which the majority of company leaders trust their people and the majority of people trust their leaders. I can't be an idealist if these organizations exist in reality.

From manufacturing to high tech, from the United States Marine Corps to the halls of government, there are shining examples of the positive results an organization will enjoy when the people inside are willing to treat each other not as adversaries, competitors or opposition but rather as trusted allies. We face enough danger from the outside. There is no value in building organizations that compound that danger by adding more threats from the inside.

Only 20 percent of Americans "love" their jobs. Chapman and those like him have called upon us to join them to make that metric grow. The question is, do we have the courage?

We need to build more organizations that prioritize the care of human beings. As leaders, it is our sole responsibility to protect our people and, in turn, our people will protect each other and advance the organization together. As employees or members of the group, we need the courage to take care of each other when our leaders don't. And in doing so, we become the leaders we wish we had.

CHAPTER 3

Belonging

From "Me" to "We"

"FROM THIS DAY on," he shouted, "words like 'I,' 'me,' 'my' will no longer be in your vocabulary. They will be replaced with words like 'we,' 'together' and 'us.'"

This is how it begins.

George's mind raced. He was completely confident when he decided to go, but now that he was actually there, he felt he had made the biggest mistake of his life. But it didn't matter now. Any thoughts he had about what he could have done or should have done would be interrupted by someone yelling inches from his face. Any feelings of excitement he may have felt before were instantly replaced by feelings of stress, isolation and helplessness.

George was part of a process that has happened thousands of times before him and will continue countless times after him. A process honed by years of trial and error. The process of transforming someone into a United States Marine.

It starts in the wee hours of the morning when a new group of recruits, tired and disoriented, arrive at one of two boot camps, one on the East Coast and one on the West Coast. The recruits are greeted by red-faced drill instructors, their voices permanently hoarse from years of straining their vocal cords, who quickly make it abundantly clear who's in charge. Here's a hint: it's not the recruits.

Thirteen grueling weeks later, each Marine will be given their Eagle, Globe and Anchor pin, the symbol that they have completed the process and earned their place inside the organization. Many will grasp the pin tightly in their fist and feel a pride so intense it will bring them to tears. When they arrived at boot camp, each recruit felt insecure and responsible only for themselves. Upon leaving, they feel confident in their own ability, a commitment to and responsibility for their fellow Marines, and a certainty that their fellow Marines feel the same for them.

This feeling of belonging, of shared values and a deep sense of empathy, dramatically enhances trust, cooperation and problem solving. United States Marines are better equipped to confront external dangers because they fear no danger from each other. They operate in a strong Circle of Safety.

The Circle of Safety

A lion used to prowl about a field in which Four Oxen used to dwell. Many a time he tried to attack them; but whenever he came near they turned their tails to one another, so that whichever way he approached them he was met by the horns of one of them. At last, however, they fell a-quarrelling among themselves, and each went off to pasture alone in a separate corner of the field. Then the Lion attacked them one by one and soon made an end of all four.

—Aesop, sixth century B.C.

MARINE BOOT CAMP is not just about running, jumping, shooting and warfare. Like the skills on our résumés, those skills may be part of the job description, but they are not what make Marines so effective. And though Marines will need to learn those skills, just as we are taught skills to help us in our jobs, those things do not build the trust required for the kind of teamwork and cooperation that gets the job done better than everyone else. Those things are not what make high-performing groups perform so remarkably. The ability of a group of people to do remarkable things hinges on how well those people pull together as a team. And that doesn't happen in a vacuum.

The world around us is filled with danger. Filled with things trying to make our lives miserable. It's nothing personal; it's just the way it is. At any time and from anywhere, there are any number of forces that, without conscience, are working to hinder our success or even kill us. In caveman times, this was literally the case. The lives of early humans were threatened by all sorts of things that could end their time on earth. Things including a lack of resources, a saber-toothed tiger or the weather. Nothing personal, it's just life. The same is true today—the threats to our survival are constant.

For our modern-day businesses and organizations, the dangers we confront are both real and perceived. Saber-toothed tigers have been replaced by the ups and downs of the stock market that can affect a company's performance. A new technology could render an older technology or an entire business model obsolete overnight. Our competitors, even if they are not trying to put us out of business, even if they aren't trying to kill us, are still trying to frustrate our success or steal our customers. And if that's not enough, the urgency to meet expectations, the strain of capacity and other outside pressures all contribute to the constant threats that a business faces. At all times, these forces work to hinder growth and profitability. These dangers are a constant. We have no control over them, they are never going to go away and that will never change. That's just the way it is.

There are dangerous forces inside our organizations as well. Unlike the forces outside, the ones inside are variable and are well within our control. Some of the dangers we face are real and can have immediate impact, like layoffs that may follow a bad quarter or an underperforming year. Some of us face the very real threat of losing our livelihoods if we try something new and lose the company some money. Politics also present a constant threat—the fear that others are trying to keep us down so that they may advance their own careers.

Intimidation, humiliation, isolation, feeling dumb, feeling useless and rejection are all stresses we try to avoid inside the organization. But the danger inside is controllable and it should be the goal of leadership to set a culture free of danger from each other. And the way to do that is by giving people a sense of belonging. By offering them a strong culture based on a clear set of human values and beliefs. By giving them the power to make decisions. By offering trust and empathy. By creating a Circle of Safety.

By creating a Circle of Safety around the people in the organization, leadership reduces the threats people feel inside the group, which frees them up to focus more time and energy to protect the organization from the constant dangers outside and seize the big opportunities. Without a Circle of Safety, people are forced to spend too much time and energy protecting themselves from each other.

It is the company we keep, the people around us, who will determine where we invest our energy. The more we trust that the people to the left of us and the people to the right of us have our backs, the better equipped we are to face the constant threats from the outside together. Only when we feel we are in a Circle of Safety will we pull together as a unified team, better able to survive and thrive regardless of the conditions outside.

The Spartans, a warrior society in ancient Greece, were feared and revered for their strength, courage and endurance. The power of the Spartan army did not come from the sharpness of their spears, however; it came from the strength of their shields. Losing one's shield in battle was considered the single greatest crime a Spartan could commit. "Spartans excuse without penalty the warrior who loses his helmet or breastplate in battle," writes Steven Pressfield in his account of the Battle of Thermopylae (the battle upon which the movie *300* is based), "but punish the loss of all citizenship rights the man who discards his shield." And the reason was simple. "A warrior carries helmet and breastplate for his own protection, but his shield for the safety of the whole line."

Likewise, the strength and endurance of a company does not come from products or services but from how well their people pull together. Every member of the group plays a role in maintaining the Circle of Safety and it is the leader's role to ensure that they do. This is the primary role of leadership, to look out for those inside their Circle.

. . . .

Letting someone into an organization is like adopting a child.

. . . .

As gatekeepers, leaders establish the standards of entry—who should be allowed into the Circle and who should be kept out, who belongs and who doesn't. Are they letting people in because of their grades in college or where they worked before or because of their character and whether they fit the culture? Letting someone into an organization is like adopting a child and welcoming them into your home. These people will, like everyone else who lives there, have to share in the responsibility of looking after the household and the others who live in it. The standards a leader sets for entry, if based on a clear set of human values, significantly impact people's sense of belonging and their willingness to pull together and contribute to the team.

Leaders are also responsible for how wide the Circle of Safety extends. When an organization is small, by the nature of its size it is more susceptible to the dangers outside. It is also much simpler to manage the Circle. A small business is often a collection of friends who already know and trust each other. There is little need for bureaucracy to keep those in the Circle safe from internal dangers. As an organization grows, however, the leaders at the top must trust the layers of management to look out for those in their charge. However, when those inside the bureaucracy work primarily to protect themselves, progress slows and the entire organization becomes more susceptible to external threats and pressures. Only when the Circle of Safety surrounds everyone in the organization, and not just a few people or a department or two, are the benefits fully realized.

Weak leaders are the ones who extend the benefits of the Circle of Safety only to their fellow senior executives and a chosen few others. They look out for each other, but they do not offer the same considerations to those outside their "inner circle." Without the protection of our leaders, everyone outside the inner circle is forced to work alone or in small tribes to protect and advance their own interests. And in so doing, silos form, politics entrench, mistakes are covered up instead of exposed, the spread of information slows and unease soon replaces any sense of cooperation and security.

Strong leaders, in contrast, extend the Circle of Safety to include every single person who works for the organization. Self-preservation is unnecessary and fiefdoms are less able to survive. With clear standards for entry into the Circle and competent layers of leadership that are able to extend the Circle's perimeter, the stronger and better equipped the organization becomes.

It is easy to know when we are in the Circle of Safety because we can feel it. We feel valued by our colleagues and we feel cared for by our superiors. We become absolutely confident that the leaders of the organization and all those with whom we work are there for us and will do what they can to help us succeed. We become members of the group. We feel like we belong. When we believe that those inside our group, those inside the Circle, will look out for us, it creates an environment for the free exchange of information and effective communication. This is fundamental to driving innovation, preventing problems from escalating and making organizations better equipped to defend themselves from the outside dangers and to seize the opportunities.

Absent a Circle of Safety, paranoia, cynicism and self-interest prevail. The whole purpose of maintaining the Circle of Safety is so that we can invest all our time and energy to guard against the dangers outside. It's the same reason we lock our doors at night. Not only does feeling safe inside give us peace of mind, but the positive impact on the organization itself is remarkable. When the Circle is strong and that feeling of belonging is ubiquitous, collaboration, trust and innovation result.

This is an important point. We cannot tell people to trust us. We cannot instruct people to come up with big ideas. And we certainly can't demand that people cooperate. These are always results—the results of feeling safe and trusted among the people with whom we work. When the Circle of Safety is strong, we naturally share ideas, share intelligence and share the burdens of stress. Every single skill and strength we have is amplified to better compete and face the dangers in the world outside and advance the organization's interests vastly more effectively.

But there's a twist.

Leaders want to feel safe too. No matter what place we occupy in the pecking order, every single one of us wants to feel like we are valued by the others in the group. If we are having a bad day at work and our performance is suffering, instead of yelling at us, we wish our bosses would ask us, "Are you okay?" And likewise, we as members of the Circle have a responsibility to our leaders—that's what makes us valuable to them, not our numbers. So when our boss comes down hard on us and we don't know the reason, it is equally our responsibility to express concern for their well-being. That's how the Circle of Safety stays strong.

Whether you're in a leadership role or not, the question is, how safe do you feel where you work?

CHAPTER 4

Yeah, but . . .

Ken is a midranking executive who works in operations for a large multinational bank. He makes a good living, though he is not as rich as some of the analysts and traders at the company. He lives in a lovely home in the suburbs with his wife and two kids. From the outside looking in, he should be happy. And, for the most part, he's fine. He wouldn't say he loves his job; "It's fine" is how he generally thinks about it. Ken likes the idea of quitting to do something else, but with kids and a mortgage to pay, that day may have passed. Right now, he needs to be a responsible husband and father. And if that means not loving his work, that's the price he's willing to pay.

What an amazing thought to love our jobs. To feel safe at work. To work for a company that actually cares how we feel about ourselves and the work we do. The number of leaders of companies who work hard to make their employees feel safe when they come in is, sadly, fewer than most of us would like to admit. Work is, well, work.

The kind of idealism I speak about is fine for books that wax on about what our jobs could be like, but the reality is most of us, even if inspired by stories of companies like Barry-Wehmiller, aren't in a position to change anything. We have bills to pay. We have kids to feed. College educations to fund. There is just too much on our plates. And the world out there, the great unknown, is a dangerous place. So we stay put.

Equally so, the idea of running a company in which nearly everyone feels safe and works to take care of each other sounds great. Most leaders intellectually understand the importance and value of putting the well-being of people first. It is the subject of books and many articles in the *Harvard Business Review.* We all write about this stuff like no one knows it. But the reality of running a business, big or small, private or public, makes it nearly impossible to do the things folks like me write about. The pressures from Wall Street, corporate boards and the threats from our competition are intense. And for a small business, just finding enough clients to help keep the doors open is hard enough. What's more, this stuff is expensive, hard to measure and often seems "soft" or "fluffy." And the ability to prove ROI can be near impossible . . . at least in the short term. For any organization that is looking to hit annual goals or simply stay alive, the choice to put people first just can't be a priority. And understandably so. The threats from the outside are just too great to worry about how people feel inside.

As nice as it sounds to build a company like Barry-Wehmiller, the reality is it's just not happening. And without those companies it is going to be harder for us to find a job in a company that truly does care about our well-being. So, we tell ourselves, what we have will have to do. What would be the point of rocking the boat or taking unnecessary risk? The risk is just too high that we may land somewhere worse or get more of the same. So why change? But there is always a cost for the decisions we make.

Our ability to provide for our kids, make ends meet or live a certain lifestyle sometimes comes at the cost of our own joy, happiness and fulfillment at work. That's just reality. And for many of us, that's okay. We convince ourselves that the outside, the unknown, is always dangerous (which it is). At least inside there is a hope of feeling secure. A hope . . .

But there is more to that reality than most of us know about. The price we pay for a perception of stability comes at its own cost. And that cost is far greater than happiness. It's actually a matter of health. Of life and death.

First, that sense of safety we may have now is, for many of us, a lie we tell ourselves. The ease with which many companies use layoffs to help manage expenses to meet annual projections means that we're a lot less safe than we used to be—and certainly less safe than we think we are. If it were a true meritocracy, we could tell ourselves that if we work hard and do well, our jobs will be safe. But this is hardly the case. Although that may be true some of the time, it is not something we can bank on. For the most part, especially for larger organizations, it's a matter of arithmetic. And sometimes the cost to keep us employed simply falls on the wrong side of the equation. And at many companies, that equation is reevaluated annually, which means every year we are at risk.

But the myth of job stability may be the least of our concerns. A 2011 study conducted by a team of social scientists at the University of Canberra in Australia concluded that having a job we hate is as bad for our health and sometimes worse than not having a job at all. Levels of depression and anxiety among people who are unhappy at work were the same or greater than those who were unemployed.

Stress and anxiety at work have less to do with the work we do and more to do with weak management and leadership. When we know that there are people at work who care about how we feel, our stress levels decrease. But when we feel like someone is looking out for themselves or that the leaders of the company care more about the numbers than they do us, our stress and anxiety go up. This is why we are willing to change jobs in the first place; we feel no loyalty to a company whose leaders offer us no sense of belonging or reason to stay beyond money and benefits.

Another study, conducted by researchers at University College London that same year, found that people who didn't feel recognized for their effort at work were more likely to suffer from heart disease. The reason, they surmised, "is largely due to feelings of control [or lack thereof]," said Daryl O'Connor, professor of health psychology at the University of Leeds. "If you feel you've put in a lot of effort and it has not been rewarded," he explained, "this increases stress and, in turn, the risk of heart disease." And . . . it's also bad for business.

....

Misery may love company, but it is the companies that love misery that suffer the most.

....

According to a Gallup poll conducted in 2013 called "State of the American Workplace," when our bosses completely ignore us, 40 percent of us actively disengage from our work. If our bosses criticize us on a regular basis, 22 percent of us actively disengage. Meaning, even if we're getting criticized, we are actually more engaged simply because we feel that at least someone is acknowledging that we exist! And if our bosses recognize just one of our strengths and reward us for doing what we're good at, only 1 percent of us actively disengage from the work we're expected to do. Added to the fact that people who go to work unhappy actually do things, actively or passively, to make those around them unhappy too and it's amazing that anyone gets anything done these days. I would like to say that misery loves company, but in this case, it is the companies that love misery that suffer the most.

The Whitehall Studies

OUR INSTINCTS TELL us the higher we climb up the ladder, the more stress we feel and the weaker our feeling of safety. Consider the stereotype of the high-strung executive facing relentless pressure from shareholders, employees and the firm's largest customers. We are hardly surprised when one of them suddenly drops dead of a heart attack before hitting fifty. It even has a name: "executive stress syndrome." So maybe it's not so bad toiling away in middle management, or even the mailroom. At least our health won't suffer . . . we think.

Decades ago, scientists in Britain set out to study this link between an employee's place on the corporate ladder and stress, presumably in order to help executives deal with the toll stress was taking on their health and their lives. Known collectively as the Whitehall Studies, the studies' findings were both astounding and profound. Researchers found that workers' stress was not caused by a higher degree of responsibility and pressure usually associated with rank. It is not the demands of the job that cause the most stress, but the degree of control workers feel they have throughout their day. The studies also found that the effort required by a job is not in itself stressful, but rather the imbalance between the effort we give and the reward we feel. Put simply: less control, more stress.

The Whitehall Studies are seminal because the scientists studied government employees who have equal health benefits. This meant they were able to control for variances in healthcare standards, which may not be the case if they were to have studied a large public company in the U.S. Though even U.S.-based studies show similar results.

In 2012, a similar study conducted by researchers at Harvard and Stanford examined the stress levels of participants in Harvard's executive MBA program. In this study, researchers looked at participants' levels of cortisol, the hormone the body releases during times of stress, and compared those to levels found in employees who hadn't made it to the top. Leaders, the study showed, have overall lower stress levels than those who work for them.

"It's possible, in other words, that the feeling of being in charge of one's own life more than makes up for the greater amount of responsibility that accompanies higher rungs on the social lad-der," wrote Max McClure, of the Stanford News Service, in an-nouncing the findings.

The findings of the Whitehall Studies are even more dra-matic when you consider the connection between job stress and health. The lower someone's rank in the organizational hierar-chy, the greater their risk of stress-related health problems, not the other way around. In other words, those seemingly strung-out top executives were, in fact, living longer, healthier lives than the clerks and managers working for them. "The more se-nior you are in the employment hierarchy, the longer you might expect to live compared to people in lower employment grades," said a report based on the studies that was conducted in 2004 by public health researchers at University College London. And the discrepancy is not a small one. Workers lowest in the hierar-chy had an early death rate four times that of those at the top. Jobs that gave workers less control were linked to higher rates of mental illness as well.

It's not just in humans that we find this—non-human pri-mates that live in social groups display higher rates of disease and illness, and greater levels of stress-related hormones, when they're lower in the hierarchy. But this is not about our place in the hierarchy per se. For one, we're evolutionarily programmed for hierarchies and we can't get rid of them. More important, the hierarchy is not the solution. Simply earning more money or working our way up the ladder is not a prescription for stress reduction. The study was about our sense of control over our work and, indeed, our lives.

What this means is that the converse is also true. A supportive and well-managed work environment is good for one's health. Those who feel they have more control, who feel empowered to make decisions instead of waiting for approval, suffer less stress. Those only doing as they are told, always forced to follow the rules, are the ones who suffer the most. Our feelings of control, stress, and our ability to perform at our best are all directly tied to how safe we feel in our organizations. Feeling unsafe around those we expect to feel safe—those in our tribes (work is the modern version of the tribe)—fundamentally violates the laws of nature and how we were designed to live.

The Whitehall Studies are not new, and their findings have been confirmed over and over. Yet even with the preponderance of data we still do nothing. Even when we know that feeling insecure at work hurts our performance and our health, sometimes even killing us, we stay in jobs we hate. For some reason, we are able to convince ourselves that unknown dangers outside are more perilous than the dangers inside. And so we adapt and put up with uncomfortable work environments that do not make us feel good or inspire our best work. We have all, at some time, rationalized our position or our place and continued doing exactly what we were doing.

Human resources consultancy Mercer LLC reported that between fourth quarter 2010 and first quarter 2011, one in three employees seriously considered leaving their jobs, up 23 percent from five years prior. The problem was that less than 1.5 percent of employees actually voluntarily left. This is one of the issues with a bad working environment. Like a bad relationship, even if we don't like it, we don't leave. Maybe it's the feeling of the devil-you-know-is-better-than-the-devil-you-don't or maybe it's something else, but people seem to feel stuck in unhealthy work environments.

That a third of all employees want to leave their jobs but don't tells us two things. One, it says that an uncomfortably high number of people would rather be working somewhere else, and two, that they see no other option to improve how they feel about their jobs beyond quitting. There is an alternative route, however. One much simpler and potentially more effective, and it doesn't require us to quit our jobs. Quite the contrary. It requires that we stay.

But that doesn't mean we can get away with doing nothing. We will still need to change the way we do things when we show up at work. It will require us to turn some of our focus away from ourselves to give more attention to those to the left of us and those to the right of us. Like the Spartans, we will have to learn that our strength will come not from the sharpness of our spears but from our willingness to offer others the protection of our shields.

Some say a weak job market or bad economy is the reason to stick it out, in which case leaders of companies should want to treat their people better during hard times to prevent a mass exodus as soon as things improve. And in a good economy, leaders of companies should also want to treat their people well so that their people will stop at nothing to help the company manage when the hard times return (which, inevitably, they will). The best companies almost always make it through hard times because the people rally to make sure they do. In other words, from a strictly business standpoint, treating people well in any economy is more cost effective than not.

Too many leaders are managing organizations in a way that is costing them money, hurting performance and damaging people's health. And if that's not enough to convince us that something has to change, then perhaps our love for our children will.

A study by two researchers at the Graduate School of Social Work at Boston College found that a child's sense of well-being is affected less by the long hours their parents put in at work and more by the mood their parents are in when they come home. Children are better off having a parent who works into the night in a job they love than a parent who works shorter hours but comes home unhappy. This is the influence our jobs have on our families. Working late does not negatively affect our children, but rather, how we feel at work does. Parents may feel guilty, and their children may miss them, but late nights at the office or frequent business trips are not likely the problem. Net-net, if you don't like your work, for your kids' sake, don't go home.

So what is the price we pay for not demanding that our leaders concern themselves with our well-being? We are not, as we think, putting up with miserable so that we may provide for our children. By putting up with miserable, we may be doing them harm.

As for the leaders of companies who think that it's OK to save a number before saving a person, consider the chain of events that ensues as a result.

There is only one way we can solve this problem. By building and maintaining Circles of Safety where we work. Pointing fingers is not the solution, pulling together and doing something is. And the good news is, there are powerful forces that can help us. If we can learn to harness these seemingly supernatural forces, we can put right what is so wrong. This is no soapbox rambling. It is just biology.

[POWERFUL FORCES]

CHAPTER 5

When Enough Was Enough

To say it was a rough neighborhood is an understatement. It was about the worst place anyone would want to live. It was incredibly dangerous. There was no such thing as heating in the winter and there certainly wasn't any air-conditioning in the summer. There were no supermarkets of any sort; the residents were left to forage or hunt for any food they could find. Survival, under these conditions, was something people really had to think about. Every moment of every day, there could always be something out there that could do them harm. Worrying about an education or getting a job wasn't even on the radar. There were no classrooms, and there were no hospitals. As things stood, there were no jobs to be had. None. And for good reason, there were no companies. There weren't even any countries yet. That stuff was so far off in the future, they didn't need to think about it. This is not some post-apocalyptic *Mad Max* scenario. The time is fifty thousand years ago and modern man, *Homo sapiens,* is taking his first steps out in the world. This is where we come from.

Our ancestors were born dirt poor. Opportunities didn't come their way because of the schools they went to or who their parents knew. Any opportunities came from their will and hard work to create them. And create them they did. Our species was built to manage in conditions of great danger and insufficient resources.

Life in Paleolithic times was not like the aftermath of a hurricane. That's not scarcity, that's destruction. Our ancestors were not the stereotypical cavemen we like to imagine. They didn't have oversized brows or walk around hunched over carrying a club. They looked like we do today and were just as smart and capable as we are today. The only things they didn't have yet were all the advancements and advantages of our modern world. Other than that, they were just like you and me.

Nearly everything about humans is designed to help us survive and perpetuate the species through tough times—very tough times. Our physiology and our need to cooperate both exist with our survival in mind. We are at our best when we face danger together. Unfortunately, there are too many leaders of companies who believe, in the face of external challenges, that the best way to motivate their people is by creating a sense of internal urgency or pressure. Based on our biology and anthropology, however, nothing could be further from the truth.

When we feel like we belong to the group and trust the people with whom we work, we naturally cooperate to face outside challenges and threats. When we do not have a sense of belonging, however, then we are forced to invest time and energy to protect ourselves from each other. And in so doing, we inadvertently make ourselves more vulnerable to the outside threats and challenges. Plus, with our attention facing inward, we will also miss outside opportunities. When we feel safe among the people with whom we work, the more likely we are to survive and thrive. That's just the way it is.

In the Beginning . . .

THERE IS SOMETHING about *Homo sapiens* that makes us much better adapted to survive and prosper in the austere conditions into which we were born, even better than some of the other hominid species that were bigger and stronger than we were. Part of our advantage is thanks to the neocortex—our complex, problem-solving brain. It also gives us the ability for sophisticated communication. Unlike other animals able to communicate, we're capable of syntax and grammar. But another critical reason we survived was thanks to our remarkable ability to cooperate. We are a highly social species whose survival and ability to prosper depend on the help of others.

Our ability to work together, to help and protect each other, worked so well, in fact, that our populations did more than survive, they thrived. Elephants survived also, but the life of an elephant today is largely the same as it was millions of years ago. But not us. Our lives are completely different than they were fifty thousand years ago. Though our species was molded to suit our environment, we were so good at working together and solving problems that we found ways to mold our environments to suit us. The better we did, the better we got at changing our conditions to suit our needs instead of being changed to suit the conditions. The problem is, our basic genetic coding remains the same. We are an old-fashioned bunch living in a modern, resource-rich world. This has its obvious advantages but, like everything, comes at a cost.

It's All About the Group

LIVING IN COMMUNITIES that maxed out at about 150 people, we knew everyone and trusted that the people in our group understood it was in their own interest to help the group. The men went out and hunted together and the whole community worked together to raise the young, care for the sick and the elderly and look out for each other.

There was conflict, of course, just like there is conflict in any group. But when push came to shove, they put all their differences aside and worked together. Just as we may have serious issues with one of our siblings, if someone else threatens them, we will rise up to defend them. We always protect our own. Not to do so goes against what it means to be human and ultimately does damage to a group's ability to survive and thrive. This is one of the reasons that treason is punishable in the same way as murder. Given its importance to our ability to survive, we humans take this trust thing really seriously. Our success proves it. Cooperation and mutual aid work better than competition and rugged individualism. Why add another degree of difficulty by fighting against each other when we were already forced to struggle against the hardships of nature, limited resources or other outside threats?

This cooperative village life existed from the Amazonian rain forests to the open plains of Africa. In other words, it was not the physical environment that determined our best chance for survival and success—it was the very biology of our species, the design of the human being itself. The manner in which we evolved—to help each other—worked regardless of where we came from or the unique hardships we may have encountered. Every single human on the planet, regardless of culture, is naturally inclined to cooperate.

As we'd expect, it wasn't all hard work. We are social animals, and being social was as important to us thousands of years ago as it is today. It was a significant way we built and maintained trust and the way we got to know each other. The time we spend getting to know people when we're not working is part of what it takes to form bonds of trust. It's the exact same reason why eating together and doing things as a family really matters. Equally as important are conferences, company picnics and the time we spend around the watercooler. The more familiar we are with each other, the stronger our bonds. Social interaction is also important for the leaders of an organization. Roaming the halls of the office and engaging with people beyond meetings really matters.

Perhaps the closest example of a modern system that mimics our ancestral kinship societies is the college dorm. Though students may have their own rooms (which are usually shared), doors are often left open as students socialize between the rooms. The hallway becomes the center of social life and rooms are for homework and sleeping (and sometimes not even that). The bonds of friendship that form in those dorms are vital. That's where college students tend to develop their closest friendships—not in classrooms.

Our success as a species was not luck—it was earned. We worked hard to get to where we are today and we did it together. We're built to work together. We are, at a deeply ingrained and biological level, social machines. And when we work to help each other, our bodies reward us for our effort so that we will continue to do it.

Our Chemical Dependency

THANKS TO THE trial and error of evolution, almost every detail about our physiology is there for a reason. Mother Nature did not provide us with highly tuned taste buds simply so we could enjoy a fine glass of wine from the Staglin Family Vineyard or savor every bite of a pork bun from Momofuku Ssäm Bar. Our taste buds tell our digestive systems which enzymes to release to best deal with the food that is on its way down, just like our sense of smell helps us detect if food is spoiled or not. Similarly our eyebrows were designed to help channel sweat away from our eyes when we were running toward prey—or running away to avoid becoming prey. Everything about our bodies was designed with one goal—to help us survive. This includes the feelings of happiness.

Just as any parent, teacher or manager knows, if they offer the promise of bounty, like candy, gold stars or performance bonuses—or the threat of punishment—they can get the behavior they want. They know we will focus our attention on tasks that produce the results that earn us rewards. Kids aren't aware that their behavior is being conditioned, but as adults, we're completely aware of what our companies are doing when they offer us incentives. We know that we earn our bonuses only when we get the results *they* want. And for the most part, it works. It works really well, in fact.

Mother Nature figured out a lot earlier than our bosses, however, to use an incentive system to condition us to do certain things to achieve desired results. In the case of our biology, our bodies employ a system of positive and negative feelings—happiness, pride, joy or anxiety, for example—to promote behaviors that will enhance our ability to get things done and to cooperate. Whereas our bosses might reward us with an end-of-year bonus, our bodies reward us for working to keep ourselves and those around us alive and looked after with chemicals that make us feel good. And now, after thousands of years, we are all completely and utterly chemical-dependent.

There are four primary chemicals in our body that contribute to all our positive feelings that I will generically call "happy": endorphins, dopamine, serotonin and oxytocin. Whether acting alone or in concert, in small doses or large, anytime we feel any sense of happiness or joy, odds are it is because one or more of these chemicals is coursing through our veins. They do not exist simply to make us feel good. They each serve a very real and practical purpose: our survival.

The Paradox of Being Human

HUMAN BEINGS EXIST as individuals and as members of groups at all times. I am one and I am one of many . . . always. This also creates some inherent conflicts of interest. When we make decisions, we must weigh the benefits to us personally against the benefits to our tribe or collective. Quite often, what's good for one is not necessarily good for the other. Working exclusively to advance ourselves may hurt the group, while working exclusively to advance the group may come at a cost to us as individuals.

This tension often weighs on our consciences when we make decisions. I appreciate the irony that we even debate, as individuals and as groups, which one is primary. Some believe we should always put others first—that if we don't look out for the group, the group won't look out for us. Others believe we should always put ourselves first and that if we don't take care of ourselves first, then we would be of no use to anyone else. The fact is, both are true.

Even in our own biology, there exists this seeming conflict of interest. Of the four primary chemical incentives in our bodies, two evolved primarily to help us find food and get things done while the other two are there to help us socialize and cooperate. The first two chemicals, endorphins and dopamine, work to get us where we need to go as individuals—to persevere, find food, build shelters, invent tools, drive forward and get things done. I like to call these the "selfish" chemicals. The other two, serotonin and oxytocin, are there to incentivize us to work together and develop feelings of trust and loyalty. I like to call these the "selfless" chemicals. They work to help strengthen our social bonds so that we are more likely to work together and to cooperate, so that we can ultimately survive and ensure our progeny will live on beyond us.

CHAPTER 6

E.D.S.O.

Without Selfish Chemicals,
We Would Starve to Death

IT'S COMMON KNOWLEDGE that we shouldn't go to the supermarket when we're hungry. We always end up buying too much and buying things we don't really need. We buy too much because everything we see we want to eat now . . . because we're hungry, that's obvious. But the more interesting question is, why do we go to the supermarket when we're *not* hungry?

Our ancestors of the Paleolithic era lived in times when resources were either scarce or hard to come by. Imagine if every time we felt hungry, we had to go hunting for a few hours . . . with no guarantee that we'd catch anything. Odds are our species would not have survived very well with a system like that. And so our bodies, in an effort to get us to repeat behaviors that are in our best interest, came up with a way to encourage us to go hunting and gathering on a regular basis instead of waiting until we were starving.

Two chemicals—endorphins and dopamine—are the reason that we are driven to hunt, gather and achieve. They make us feel good when we find something we're looking for, build something we need or accomplish our goals. These are the chemicals of progress.

E Is for Endorphins: The Runner's High

ENDORPHINS SERVE ONE purpose and one purpose only: to mask physical pain. That's it. Think of endorphins as our own personal opiate. Often released in response to stress or fear, they mask physical pain with pleasure. The experience of a "runner's high," the feeling of euphoria many athletes experience during or after a hard workout, is in fact the endorphin chemical surging through their veins. This is one of the reasons runners and other endurance athletes continue to push their bodies harder and harder. It is not simply because they have the discipline to do so; they do it because it actually feels good. They love and sometimes crave the amazing high they can achieve from a hard workout. The biological reason for endorphins, however, has nothing to do with exercise. It has to do with survival.

The caveman application of the chemical feel-good is far more practical. Because of endorphins, humans have a remarkable capacity for physical endurance. Save for all the marathoners out there, most of us can't imagine running for miles and miles on a regular basis. But that's exactly what gave our ancestors an edge while hunting during the Paleolithic era. They were able to track an animal over great distances and then still have the stamina to make it home again. If the trusty hunters gave up at any time simply because they were exhausted, then they, and those in their tribe, would not eat very often and would eventually die off. And so Mother Nature designed a clever incentive to encourage us to keep going—a little endorphin rush.

We can actually develop a craving for endorphins. That's why people who are in the habit of regular exercise sometimes crave going for a run or getting to the gym to help them relax, especially after a stressful day at work. Our ancestors probably wanted to go hunting and gathering not simply because they knew they had to, but because it often felt good to go. Again, the human body wants us to feel good when we go looking for food or when we are doing the hard work of building shelter so that we will more likely do it. Thanks to cars and supermarkets, however, we live in a world with readily available and abundant resources. The body no longer rewards the search for food, at least not with endorphins. In this day and age, we basically get our endorphin hits from exercise or manual labor. With at least one notable exception.

Stephen Colbert, political satirist and host of *The Colbert Report*, commented during an interview on the importance of laughter in tense times. "You can't laugh and be afraid at the same time," he said. And he'd be right. Laughing actually releases endorphins. They are released to mask the pain we're causing to ourselves as our organs are being convulsed. We like laughing for the same reason runners like running—it feels good. But we've all had the experience of laughing so much we want it to stop because it starts to hurt. Like the runner, the hurt actually began earlier, but thanks to the endorphins, we didn't feel it until later. It is the high we get, which continues after the laughing has ceased, that makes it hard to be, as Colbert says, afraid at the same time. During tense times, a little lightheartedness may go a long way to help relax those around us and reduce tensions so that we can focus on getting our jobs done. As President Ronald Reagan famously joked with the chief surgeon on March 30, 1981, as he was wheeled into the operating room at George Washington University Hospital, after being shot by John Hinckley Jr., "I hope you're all Republicans." (To which the surgeon, a self-described liberal Democrat, replied, "We're all Republicans today, Mr. President.")

D Is for Dopamine: An Incentive for Progress

DOPAMINE IS THE reason for the good feeling we get when we find something we're looking for or do something that needs to get done. It is responsible for the feeling of satisfaction after we've finished an important task, completed a project, reached a goal or even reached one of the markers on our way to a bigger goal. We all know how good it feels to cross something off our to-do list. That feeling of progress or accomplishment is primarily because of dopamine.

Long before agriculture or supermarkets, humans spent a good portion of their time in search of the next meal. If we couldn't stay focused on completing basic tasks, like hunting and gathering, we wouldn't last very long. So Mother Nature designed a clever way to help us stay focused on the task at hand. One way we get dopamine is from eating, which is one of the reasons we enjoy it. And so we try to repeat the behaviors that get us food.

It is dopamine that makes us a goal-oriented species with a bias for progress. When we are given a task to complete, a metric to reach, as long as we can see it or clearly imagine it in our mind's eye, we will get a little burst of dopamine to get us on our way. Back in the Paleolithic era, if someone saw a tree filled with fruit, for example, dopamine was released to incentivize them to stay focused on the task and go get the food. As they made progress toward that fruit tree, they would see it getting slightly bigger, an indication they were getting closer. And with each sign of progress, they would get another little hit of dopamine to keep them on their way. And another, and another until they got a big hit when they finally reached their goal. Eureka!

It's the same for us. As we get closer to our goals, the metrics tell us we're making progress and we get another little hit to keep us going. Then finally, when we reach our goal, that intense feeling of "got it" is a big hit of dopamine, our biological reward for all that hard work. Each milestone we pass is a metric, a way to see that the fruit tree is getting closer and closer. Like a marathon runner who passes each mile marker toward the finish line, our bodies reward us with dopamine so that we will keep going, working even harder to reach that huge pot of dopamine, that intense feeling of accomplishment at the end. Obviously the bigger the goal, the more effort it requires, the more dopamine we get. This is why it feels *really* good to work hard to accomplish something difficult, while doing something quick and easy may only give us a little hit if anything at all. In other words, it feels good to put in a lot of effort to accomplish something. There is no biological incentive to do nothing.

Our Goals Must Be Tangible

WE ARE VERY visually oriented animals. We seem to trust our eyes more than any of our other senses. When we hear a bump in the night we want to see that nothing is there before we can relax and go back to bed. When someone we are getting to know makes a promise or claims they have accomplished something, we want to "see it to believe it."

This is the reason we're often told to write down our goals. "If you don't write down your goals," so the saying goes, "you won't accomplish them." There is some truth to this. Like seeing that fruit-filled tree in the distance, if we are able to physically see what we are setting out to accomplish or clearly imagine it, then we are indeed, thanks to the powers of dopamine, more likely to accomplish that goal.

This is the reason we like to be given a clear goal to achieve to receive a bonus instead of being given some amorphous instructions. It's not very motivating or helpful to be told that we will receive a performance bonus if we achieve "more." How much more? Give us something specific to set our sights on, something we can measure our progress toward, and we are more likely to achieve it. This is why people who balance their checkbooks or maintain a budget are more likely to save or not overspend. Saving is not a state of mind; it is a goal to be achieved.

It is also the reason why a corporate vision statement must be something we can see in our mind's eye. That's why it's called a "vision," because we need to be able to "see" it. Like the amorphous instructions, having a vision of "being the most respected company in our category" is useless. Respected by whom? The customers? The shareholders? The employees? The CEO's parents? If we are unable to adequately measure progress toward that vision, then how will we know if we're making worthwhile progress? Visions of being the "biggest" or "the best" or any other words that so often show up in vision statements are, on a biological level, pretty useless if we want to inspire people to work hard to achieve those visions.

A good vision statement, in contrast, explains, in specific terms, what the world would look like if everything we did was wildly successful. Dr. Martin Luther King Jr. told us that he had a dream. That one day, "little black boys and black girls will be able to join hands with little white boys and white girls as sisters and brothers." We can imagine that; we can see what that looks like. And if we find that vision inspiring and worthy of our time and energy, then we can more easily plan the steps we need to take to achieve that vision. Short or long term, the clearer we can see what we are setting out to achieve, the more likely we are to achieve it. It's exciting, thanks to dopamine. This is why the best visions offer us something that, for all practical purposes, we will never actually reach, but for which we would gladly die trying. Each point in our journey is an opportunity to feel like we're making progress toward something bigger than ourselves.

When the system works as designed, we stay well fed, get our work done and make progress. What's more, we are better able to support and provide for those in our family and tribe. Dopamine can help us get through college, become a doctor or work tirelessly to realize an imagined vision of the future.

But there is some fine print at the bottom of the bottle that is often missed. Dopamine is also highly, highly addictive. As helpful as it is, we can also form neural connections that do not help us survive—in fact, they may do the complete opposite. The behaviors we reinforce can actually do us harm. Cocaine, nicotine, alcohol and gambling all release dopamine. And the feeling can be intoxicating. The chemical effects notwithstanding, the addictions we have to these things (and lots of other things that feel good) are all basically dopamine addictions. The only variation is the behavior that is reinforced that gives us the next hit of dopamine.

There is another thing to add to that list of things that can hijack our dopamine reward system: social media. Texting, e-mail, the number of likes we collect, the ding, the buzz or the flash of our phones that tells us "You've got mail," feels amazing. As it should. We have associated the dopamine-releasing feeling of "ooh, something for me" with getting a text or e-mail or the like. Yes, it's true, we hate all that e-mail, but we live for the ding, the buzz or the flash that tells us something's there. Some of us have formed neural connections that drive us to carry our phones in our hands at all times, often looking down and hitting refresh a few times, even though nothing has come in. Gimme dopamine!

It is said that if you wake up in the morning and the first thing you crave is a drink, you might be an alcoholic. If you wake up in the morning and the first thing you do is check your phone to read e-mail or scan through your social media before you even get out of bed, you might be an addict. Craving a hit of chemical feel-good, we repeat the behaviors that we know can produce that hit. In the case of alcohol or gambling, we are aware of it. In the case of our love of our devices and social media, we are less aware of the addictive qualities.

In a performance-driven organization in which dopamine is the primary means of reward—hit the goal, get the money—like gambling, we can become addicted to "making the numbers." The only question is: are our modern addictions innocent or are there unintended side effects that are causing us harm? But I will save that discussion for later.

It is because of dopamine that, in our modern day, we like shopping or collecting things—though there is no rational benefit to most of our hobbies, we enjoy them because they satisfy our prehistoric foraging desires. If we get addicted and can't stop, like any dopamine addiction, as good as it may feel, it often comes at a high cost. We spend more time and money than is wise and sometimes sacrifice our relationships just so we can get another hit.

Accomplishment may be fueled by dopamine. But that feeling of fulfillment, those lasting feelings of happiness and loyalty, all require engagement with others. Though we may not reminisce about that goal we hit a decade ago, we will talk about the friends we made as we struggled to make it.

The good news is we also have chemical incentives that reward us with positive feelings when we act in ways that would earn us the trust, love and loyalty of others. All we have to do to get those feelings is give a little. Which is pretty handy, because, as we all know, we can get even more done together, working with people we trust, than we can alone.

Endorphins and dopamine work together to ensure our survival as it relates to food and shelter. They help us get things done so that we will be housed and fed. It's not an accident that we say we need our jobs to "survive." We really do feel that way. Without endorphins to give us the edge we need to keep going, we would not keep striving even when we were tired and exhausted. Dopamine rewards us with a chemical rush when we've accomplished something, making us want to do it again and again, which is exactly what it takes to find things, build things and get things done. But it's harder to do all things alone, especially the big things. Together is better.

The Selfless Chemicals

FINDING, BUILDING AND achieving are only part of our story. It is the manner in which we make progress that is core to our ability to do well in a dangerous world. It is the selfless chemicals that make us feel valued when we are in the company of those we trust, give us the feeling of belonging and inspire us to want to work for the good of the group. It is the selfless chemicals that keep the Circle of Safety strong.

Without Social Chemicals We'd Be Cold-Blooded

A CARCASS OF a wildebeest floats down a tributary of the Zambezi River in Botswana. The soon-to-be meal passes two hungry crocodiles that both call this part of the river home. Seeing the food, they both lunge at it . . . but only one will win. The faster, stronger of the two will be the one to eat that day. Acting completely out of instinct, it will consume the carcass and swim away with a full stomach and absolutely no care in the world about the other crocodile. And though the other crocodile may swim away hungry, it will harbor no ill will toward its adversary. There is no part of the crocodile's reptilian brain that rewards any cooperative behavior. The animals have no positive feelings when cooperation is offered and thus no incentive to cooperate. They are, by design, cold-hearted loners. That's just how they were designed to work. Nothing personal. All instinct. And, for a crocodile, it works.

We, however, are not like crocodiles. Though we may share the primitive, reptilian portion of our brain with them, our brain continued to grow beyond its reptile roots. We are anything but loners. The addition of the mammalian layer of our brain helped us to become highly functioning social animals. And for good reason. If we weren't adapted to live in tribes and cooperate, we would have died off ages ago. We don't have thick, scaly skin to make us less vulnerable to attack. We don't have rows of sharp teeth like a great white shark, able to keep chomping even after we lose a few. We're just not strong enough to survive alone, let alone thrive. Whether we like to admit it or not, we need each other. That's where serotonin and oxytocin come in. They are the backbone of the Circle of Safety.

There to encourage pro-social behavior, serotonin and oxytocin help us form bonds of trust and friendship so that we will look out for each other. It is because of these two chemicals that we have societies and cultures. And it is because of these chemicals that we pull together to accomplish much bigger things than if we were to face the world alone.

When we cooperate or look out for others, serotonin and oxytocin reward us with the feelings of security, fulfillment, belonging, trust and camaraderie. When firing at the right times and for the right reasons, they can help turn any one of us into an inspiring leader, a loyal follower, a close friend, a trusted partner, a believer . . . a Johnny Bravo. And when that happens, when we find ourselves inside a Circle of Safety, stress declines, fulfillment rises, our want to serve others increases and our willingness to trust others to watch our backs skyrockets. When these social incentives are inhibited, however, we become more selfish and more aggressive. Leadership falters. Cooperation declines. Stress increases as do paranoia and mistrust.

If we work in environments that make it harder to earn these incentives, then our desire to help our colleagues or the organization diminishes. And, absent the presence of commitment, any desire our colleagues may have to help us also declines. A vicious cycle is set in motion. The less our colleagues and leaders look out for us, the less we look out for them. The less we look out for them, the more selfish they become and, as a result, the more selfish we become. And when that happens, eventually everyone loses.

Oxytocin and serotonin grease the social machine. And when they are missing, friction results. When the leaders of an organization create a culture that inhibits the release of these chemicals, it is tantamount to sabotage—sabotage of our careers and our happiness and sabotage of the success of the organization itself.

The strength of the culture, and not its size or resources, determines an organization's ability to adapt to the times, overcome adversity and pioneer new innovations. When the conditions are right, when a strong Circle of Safety is present and felt by all, we do what we do best. We act in the manner for which we are designed. We pull together.

S Is for Serotonin: The Leadership Chemical

"I HAVEN'T HAD an orthodox career and I've wanted more than anything to have your respect," said Sally Field as she stood on the stage gripping the Oscar she'd just won for her role in the film *Places in the Heart.* The year was 1985. "The first time I didn't feel it," she admitted, "but this time I feel it, and I can't deny the fact that you like me, right now, you like me!"

What Sally Field was feeling was the chemical serotonin seeping through her veins. Serotonin is the feeling of pride. It is the feeling we get when we perceive that others like or respect us. It makes us feel strong and confident, like we can take on anything. And more than confidence boosting, it raises our status. The respect Sally Field received from the community significantly impacted her career. An Oscar winner is able to make more money to appear in a film, will have more opportunities to pick and choose the films they would prefer to work on and will command greater clout.

As social animals, we more than want the approval of those in our tribe, we need it. It really matters. We all want to feel valuable for the effort we put forth for the good of others in the group or the group itself. If we could get that feeling alone, then we wouldn't have awards ceremonies, company recognition programs or graduation ceremonies. And there certainly would be no need for any counters to display all the "likes" we get on Facebook, how many views we get on YouTube or how many followers we have on Twitter. We want to feel that we and the work we do are valued by others, especially those in our group.

It is because of serotonin that a college graduate feels a sense of pride and feels their confidence and status rise as they walk across the stage to receive their diploma. Technically, all a student needs to graduate is to pay their bills, fulfill their requirements and collect enough credits. But graduation probably wouldn't feel the same if we received only an e-mail with a generic letter of congratulations and a downloadable attachment of the diploma.

And here's the best part. At the moment that college graduate feels the serotonin course through their veins as they receive their diploma, their parents, sitting in the audience, also get bursts of serotonin and feel equally as proud. And that's the point. Serotonin is attempting to reinforce the bond between parent and child, teacher and student, coach and player, boss and employee, leader and follower.

That's why when someone receives an award, the first people they thank are their parents, or their coach, their boss or God—whoever they felt offered them the support and protection they needed to accomplish what they accomplished. And when others offer us that protection and support, because of serotonin, we feel a sense of accountability to them.

Remember, these chemicals control our feelings. That's why we can actually feel the weight of responsibility when others commit time and energy to support us. We want them to feel that the sacrifices they made for us were worth it. We don't want to let them down. We want to make them proud. And if we are the ones giving the support, we feel an equal sense of responsibility. We want to do right by them so that they can accomplish all that they set out to do. It is because of serotonin that we can't feel a sense of accountability to numbers; we can only feel accountable to people.

This helps explain why it feels different to cross a finish line alone, without spectators, compared to when a crowd cheers as we break the tape. In both cases, the accomplishment is the same, the time is the same, even the effort is the same. The only difference is that in one case, there are others there to witness and cheer for us.

I felt this when I ran the New York City Marathon a few years ago. One of the things that kept me going was knowing that my friends and family had come out to support me. They spent their valuable time and energy to brave the traffic and crowds simply to get a quick glimpse of me as I ran past. We even planned when and where I would be because it made them proud to see me out there doing something hard. And it inspired me to keep pushing myself, simply knowing they were there. I wasn't just running for me anymore; I wasn't just running for the rush of endorphins and dopamine. Because of serotonin, I was now running for them too. And it helped.

If all I wanted to accomplish was to run 26.2 miles, if all I wanted was the dopamine thrill of accomplishment, I could train and do that on any given weekend. But I didn't. I ran on the day my family came out to support me. The day the organizers offered me a crowd to cheer me on. Better still, I got to wear a medal, a symbol of the accomplishment, which made me feel proud when I wore it around my neck. Serotonin feels good.

The more we give of ourselves to see others succeed, the greater our value to the group and the more respect they offer us. The more respect and recognition we receive, the higher our status in the group and the more incentive we have to continue to give to the group. At least that's how it's supposed to work. Whether we are a boss, coach or parent, serotonin is working to encourage us to serve those for whom we are directly responsible. And if we are the employee, player or the one being looked after, the serotonin encourages us to work hard to make them proud.

Those who work hardest to help others succeed will be seen by the group as the leader or the "alpha" of the group. And being the alpha—the strong, supportive one of the group, the one willing to sacrifice time and energy so that others may gain—is a prerequisite for leadership.

O Is for Oxytocin: Chemical Love

OXYTOCIN IS MOST people's favorite chemical. It's the feeling of friendship, love or deep trust. It is the feeling we get when we're in the company of our closest friends or trusted colleagues. It is the feeling we get when we do something nice for someone or someone does something nice for us. It is responsible for all the warm and fuzzies. This is the feeling we get when we all hold hands and sing "Kumbaya" together. But oxytocin is not there just to make us feel good. It is vital to our survival instincts.

Without oxytocin, we wouldn't want to perform acts of generosity. Without oxytocin there would be no empathy. Without oxytocin, we wouldn't be able to develop strong bonds of trust and friendship. And without that, we wouldn't have anyone we could rely on to watch our backs. Without oxytocin, we would have no partner to raise our children; in fact, we wouldn't even love our children. It is because of oxytocin that we trust others to help us build our businesses, do difficult things or help us out when we're in a bind. It is because of oxytocin that we feel human connections and like being in the company of people we like. Oxytocin makes us social.

As a species that can accomplish more in groups than as individuals, we need to have the instinct to know whom to trust. In a group, no one person has to maintain a constant state of vigilance to make sure they are safe. If we are among people we trust and who trust us, that responsibility can now be shared among the entire group. In other words, we can fall asleep at night confident that someone else will watch for danger. Oxytocin is the chemical that helps direct how vulnerable we can afford to make ourselves. It is a social compass that determines when it's safe to open up and trust or when we should hold back.

Unlike dopamine, which is about instant gratification, oxytocin is long-lasting. The more time we spend with someone, the more we are willing to make ourselves vulnerable around them. As we learn to trust them and earn their trust in return, the more oxytocin flows. In time, as if by magic, we will realize that we have developed a deep bond with this person. The madness and excitement and spontaneity of the dopamine hit is replaced by a more relaxed, more stable, more long-term oxytocin-driven relationship. A vastly more valuable state if we have to rely on someone to help us do things and protect us when we're weak. My favorite definition of love is giving someone the power to destroy us and trusting they won't use it.

It's the same in any new relationship. When we first show up to a new job, we're excited, they're excited, everything is perfect. But the trust we need to feel that our colleagues would watch our backs and help us grow, to really feel like we belong, takes time and energy. Personally or professionally, all the same rules of relationship building apply.

. . . .

Inside a Circle of Safety, we feel like we belong.

. . . .

As much as we want to stand out and consider ourselves individuals, at our core, we are herd animals that are biologically designed to find comfort when we feel like we belong to a group. Our brains are wired to release oxytocin when in the presence of our tribe and cortisol, the chemical that produces the feeling of anxiety, when we feel vulnerable and alone. For our prehistoric ancestors, as well as all social mammals, our sense of belonging and confidence that we can face the dangers around us literally depend on feeling safe in our group. Being on the periphery is dangerous. The loner on the edge of the group is far more susceptible to predators than one who is safely surrounded and valued by others.

Someone who feels like a bit of a social misfit because of an unusually high love of *Star Wars* or superheroes finds great camaraderie when attending Comic Con or some other fan convention. To be around others like us makes us feel like we belong and gives us a sense of safety. We feel accepted as part of the group and no longer suffer the anxiety of feeling like we are on the edges. There are few feelings that human beings crave more than a sense of belonging . . . the feeling of being inside a Circle of Safety.

Generosity and Other Ways to Build Trust

I WAS WALKING down the street with a friend of mine when the backpack of a man walking in front of us opened up, spilling papers onto the sidewalk. Without a thought, we bent down and helped him gather up his papers, and I pointed out to him that his bag was open. That tiny favor, that little expense of time and energy, with no expectation of anything in return, gave me a small shot of oxytocin. It feels good to help people. The man we helped also got a small shot of oxytocin, because it feels good when someone does something nice for us too. We stood up and continued walking.

When my friend and I reached the end of the block, we stood and waited for the light to change so we could cross the street. As we stood there, another man standing in front of us turned around and said, "I saw what you did back there. That was really cool." And that's the best thing about oxytocin. Not only does the person performing even the tiniest act of courtesy get a shot of oxytocin, not only does the person on the receiving end of an act also get a shot, but someone who witnesses the act of generosity also gets some chemical feel-good. Simply seeing or hearing about acts of human generosity actually inspires us to want to do the same. I can almost promise you that that guy who turned around to tell us he had seen what we had done very likely did something nice for someone that day. This is one of the reasons we find movies or news stories of incredible selfless acts so inspiring. This is the power of oxytocin. It actually makes us good people. The more good things we do, the more good we want to do. This is the science behind "paying it forward."

Oxytocin is also released with physical contact. That warm feeling we get when we hug someone we like for a few seconds longer—that's oxytocin. It is also the reason it feels nice to hold hands with someone and the reason young children seem to always want to touch and hug their mothers. In fact, there's lots of evidence that children who are deprived of human contact, deprived of sufficient doses of oxytocin, have trouble building trusting relationships later in life. It is also part of the reinforcing bond between athletes, for example, when they high-five, fist-bump or smack each other. It reinforces the bond they share and the commitment they have to work together for their common goal.

Suppose you are about to seal a deal with someone. They have agreed to all the terms laid out in the contract. Just before you sign the contract you stick out your arm to shake your soon-to-be partner's hand. "No, no," they say, "I don't need to shake your hand. I agree to all the terms laid out and I'm excited to do business with you."

"Great," you reply, "so let's shake on it."

"We don't need to," they say again, "I agree to everything and am ready to sign and start doing business." Rationally speaking, you just got everything you wanted in the contract, but their simple refusal to make physical contact, to shake your hand, to reinforce the social bond with a little chemical trust, means one of two things will happen. You will either call the whole deal off or you will go into the deal a little more nervous. That's the power of oxytocin. That's the reason it is a big deal when world leaders shake hands—it is a sign to each other and all who witness that they can do business together. If our president were ever seen shaking hands at a UN event with some horrible dictator, it would cause a massive scandal. A simple handshake. But it's not just a simple handshake; physical contact demonstrates a sign of our willingness to trust . . . even more than the terms of the deal.

Oxytocin really is magical stuff. Not only is it behind the

feelings of trust and loyalty, it also makes us feel good and inspires us to do nice things for others. Mother Nature wants the ones who give to others to keep their genes in the gene pool. That may be one of the reasons oxytocin actually helps us live longer. A person who is good to others in the group is good for the species.

According to a study published in *Proceedings of the National Academy of Sciences* in 2011, people who claim to be happy live 35 percent longer than less happy people. The study of 3,800 men and women aged fifty-two to seventy-nine found that those who rated their happiness the highest were far less likely to die in the following five years than those who were the least happy, even after accounting for demographic factors such as wealth, occupation and health-related behavior such as smoking and obesity.

Oxytocin boosts our immune systems, makes us better problem solvers and makes us more resistant to the addictive qualities of dopamine. Unlike dopamine, which is largely responsible for instant gratification, oxytocin gives us lasting feelings of calm and safety. We don't need to check in to see how many likes or followers we have on Facebook to feel good. Because of oxytocin, just knowing our friends and family are there, just looking at a picture of the people whom we love and who love us, makes us feel good and not feel alone. And when that happens, we want more than anything else to do what we can to help them feel the same way.

CHAPTER 7

The Big C

I t was warm and sunny out. A day just like one would expect for that time of year. There was a calm, gentle breeze that broke the intensity of the sun. It was, by all accounts, a perfect day.

All of a sudden, out of the corner of an eye, the calm was shattered. Perhaps it was a rustle of the grass or maybe he thought he saw something. He couldn't be sure, but, frankly, it didn't matter. All that mattered was that there might have been something out there. Something dangerous. Something deadly.

The anxiety alone was quite enough for the gazelle to stop grazing and immediately lift its head to try to see what it hoped was not a lion. Another gazelle noticed that one of the members of its group was alerted to a possible threat and it too immediately stopped eating to look up—two sets of eyes are better than one. Before long, the whole group had joined in. None of them knew what specifically they were looking for—they only knew that if one of the members of the group felt threatened, they should all feel threatened.

Then, in an instant, one of the gazelles, one that wasn't originally alerted to the potential threat, saw the lion about to pounce and instinctively made a mad dash in the opposite direction. Whether they also saw the lion or not, all the gazelles in the herd followed in the same direction, all running at full speed. The lion attempted to give chase, but couldn't run for long before it ran out of energy. The surprise attack was foiled and all the gazelles got to live another day. This is one of the primary benefits of group living—every member of the group can help look out for danger. If one individual in the group senses danger, the whole group can help spot it before it's too late.

It is a familiar scene played out in many a nature documentary. Sometimes the lion makes the kill and sometimes it doesn't. But the response from the gazelles is always the same. First, one or a few of them sense something is amiss. Then they try to get a bead on the threat, and if there is a threat, they run for their lives. It is that initial feeling, that sense that something might be out there that would do them harm, that sets the whole scene in motion, and at the end of the day, gives the herd a greater opportunity for survival.

That feeling that something is wrong is a natural early warning system all social mammals have, including us. It is designed to alert us to threats and heighten our senses to prepare for possible danger. Absent that feeling, we would only be alerted to danger when we actually saw something or when the attack had already begun. And from a survival standpoint, that would probably be too late.

Those twenty-two Special Operations Forces in Afghanistan that Johnny Bravo risked his life to protect are a perfect example. They could feel something wasn't right that night. That "gut feeling" that they, the gazelle and the rest of us get that something dangerous is lurking is caused by a chemical called cortisol. Cortisol is responsible for the stress and anxiety we experience when something goes bump in the night. It is the first level of our fight-or-flight response. Like a high-security alarm system that automatically calls the police, cortisol is designed to alert us to possible danger and prepare us to take extra measures to protect ourselves to raise our chances of survival.

Apply the same scene of the gazelles to an office scenario.

One person hears a rumor that there are going to be layoffs. He tells a friend at work. And before too long, just like the herd of gazelles, one by one, the word spreads and the whole office starts chatting and worrying, anxious about the impending layoffs. All the employees have a heightened sense of alertness thanks to the cortisol flowing through their veins. The stress they feel will distract them from getting anything else done until they feel that the threat has passed.

In the event of an actual threat, like police responding to an alarm, adrenaline is released into our bloodstream, giving us energy to get away or boosting our strength to face our foe. (If you've ever heard of stories of mothers who suddenly gain superhuman strength to save their children—that comes from adrenaline.) But if there is no threat, we take a deep breath, wait for the cortisol to leave our bloodstream, allow our heart rate to return to normal and relax again.

Cortisol is not supposed to stay in our systems; it is supposed to fire off when we sense a threat and then leave when the threat has passed. And for good reason. The stress on our bodies is serious. The manner in which it reconfigures our internal systems can cause lasting damage if we have to live in a perpetual state of fear or anxiety.

We all know what cortisol feels like when we fear for our well-being. But it is also behind the feelings of anxiety, discomfort or stress we have at work. Unlike gazelles, humans have sophisticated neocortices, the part of our brain responsible for language as well as rational, analytical and abstract thought. Whereas a gazelle reacts to the cortisol in their bodies, we as humans want to know the cause of our stress, to understand or make sense of our feelings. We often try to find the source of what we think is threatening us, real or perceived, to explain our unease. We may blame a boss who lies to us. We may blame a colleague who we fear would stab us in the back to advance their own career. We may beat ourselves up for speaking out of turn at a meeting. We cycle through any number of things we did or did not do to help us understand why we feel anxious. The paranoia cortisol creates is just doing its job. It is trying to get us to find the threat and prepare for it. Fight, run or hide.

Whether the danger is real or imagined, the stress we feel is real. Unlike our rational minds, our bodies do not try to assess what the danger is. We simply react to the chemicals flowing through our bloodstreams to prepare us for what might be lurking. Our Paleolithic brain doesn't care about understanding the threat. It just wants us to increase our chance of survival. What's more, our bodies don't understand that we work in offices and not in the open savannahs. Our ancient early warning system doesn't understand that the "danger" we face is hardly life threatening. Which is why, in an effort to help us protect our interests, that system prompts us to react as if it were.

A friend of mine who works at Columbia University went to an office to fill out some administrative paperwork. He was polite and friendly to the young woman sitting at the desk, but she wasn't that polite or friendly back. Though she didn't say anything rude or wrong, he could sense that she wasn't that concerned about him or his needs. She answered his questions with a word or two and didn't give him any extra help or directions beyond what was minimally required, even when he asked. When he engaged with the next person, again, he felt like he had somehow bothered or upset him simply by asking him to do what was his job. Although, as employees of the same organization, it was in their mutual interest to assist him, the clerical staff seemed ambivalent about, even resistant to, cooperating.

In an office like the one my friend stepped into, people would prefer to keep to themselves, engage only when necessary, do their work and then go home at the end of the day. There is no sense that anyone would risk themselves or go out of their way to offer protection to another. And because of this, though there is no threat of layoffs and the work stress is low, there is a constant low-grade anxiety. As social animals, we feel stress when we feel unsupported. That subconscious unease, the feeling that we are responsible for ourselves and no one else is there to help, the feeling we get that most of the people with whom we work care primarily about themselves, is, to our primitive brain, quite scary. And the problem is not with the people, it is with the environment.

When a gazelle senses trouble, it alerts the rest of its herd, increasing the chances of the survival of all. Unfortunately, many of us work in environments where members of the group don't care much about one another's fate. Which means that valuable information, like impending danger, is often kept secret. As a result, bonds of trust among employees or between leaders and workers are weak, if they exist at all. We are left almost without an option but to put ourselves first. If we fear our boss doesn't like us; if we are constantly worried that if we make a mistake, we will get in trouble; if we think that someone we work with will try to take credit for something we did or stab us in the back to get ahead; if we pay attention to too much media hype; if we fear the company isn't going to make its numbers this year and layoffs may be around the corner; if people are generally disengaged; if we do not feel the Circle of Safety, cortisol starts to seep through our veins. Drip. Drip. Drip.

This is a serious problem. For one thing, cortisol actually inhibits the release of oxytocin, the chemical responsible for empathy. This means that when there is only a weak Circle of Safety and people must invest time and energy to guard against politics and other dangers inside the company, it actually makes us even more selfish and less concerned about one another or the organization.

Working in an unhealthy, unbalanced culture is a lot like climbing Mount Everest—we adapt to our surroundings. Even though the conditions are dangerous, climbers know to spend time at base camp to adapt. In time, their bodies will get accustomed to the conditions so that they can persevere. We do the same thing in an unhealthy culture. If the conditions were violent or shocking, with a threat of layoffs every single day, we would never stay. But when the conditions are more subtle, things like office politics, opportunism, occasional rounds of layoffs and a general lack of trust among colleagues, we adapt.

Like being at base camp on Everest, we believe that we are fine and can cope. However, the fact remains that the human animal is not built for these conditions. Even though we may think we're comfortable, the effects of the environment still take their toll. Just because we become accustomed, just because it becomes normal, doesn't mean it's acceptable. On Everest, even after we've adapted, if we spend too long on the mountain, our internal organs start to break down. In an unhealthy culture, it's the same. Even though we can get used to living with stress and low, regular levels of cortisol in our bodies, that doesn't mean we should.

A constant flow of cortisol isn't just bad for organizations. It can also do serious damage to our health. Like the other selfish chemicals, cortisol can help us survive, but it isn't supposed to be in our system all the time. It wreaks havoc with our glucose metabolism. It also increases blood pressure and inflammatory responses and impairs cognitive ability. (It's harder to concentrate on things outside the organization if we are stressed about what's going on inside.) Cortisol increases aggression, suppresses our sex drive and generally leaves us feeling stressed out. And here's the killer—literally. Cortisol prepares our bodies to react suddenly—to fight or run as circumstances demand. Because this takes a lot of energy, when we feel threatened, our bodies turn off nonessential functions, such as digestion and growth. Once the stress has passed, these systems are turned on again. Unfortunately, the immune system is one of the functions that the body deems nonessential, so it shuts down during cortisol bursts. In other words, if we work in environments in which trust is low, relationships are weak or transactional and stress and anxiety are normal, we become much more vulnerable to illness.

Whereas oxytocin boosts our immune system, cortisol compromises it. That our modern world has seen high rates of cancer, diabetes, heart disease and other preventable illnesses may not be a coincidence. Today these conditions are far more likely to kill us than threats like violent crime or terrorism. The National Counterterrorism Center estimates that more than 12,500 people were killed worldwide by terrorists in 2011. According to FBI statistics, about 165,000 people were murdered in the United States between 2000 and 2010, more than two thirds of them with a firearm (FBI statistics do not include Florida). Compare those numbers to the 600,000 people who die *every year* in the United States from heart disease and the additional nearly 600,000 people who died of cancer in 2012, and the evidence becomes stark. Think about that, seven times more people die each year from heart disease and cancer than all the people murdered in a decade!

Of course, stress alone is not causing all these deaths, but the numbers are so huge and growing, it seems only responsible for the leaders of organizations to take some accountability for how they may be contributing. That something as simple as a corporate incentive system or a corporate culture is actually contributing to those statistics is horrifying. Our jobs are literally killing us.

In contrast, a strong organizational culture is good for our health. The environment in which we work, and the way we interact with one another, *really* matters. A good working environment helps ensure that we can build the bonds of trust required for effective cooperation. Because our ancient legacy systems can't distinguish between the threats we may have faced in the wilds of the Paleolithic Era and the perceived threats we face in a modern work environment, the response is the same. Our bodies release cortisol to help us stay alive. If we work in an environment in which leadership tells the truth, in which layoffs are not the default in hard times and in which incentive structures do not pit us against one another, the result, thanks to the increased levels of oxytocin and serotonin, is trust and cooperation.

This is what work-life balance means. It has nothing to do with the hours we work or the stress we suffer. It has to do with where we feel safe. If we feel safe at home, but we don't feel safe at work, then we will suffer what we perceive to be a work-life imbalance. If we have strong relationships at home and at work, if we feel like we belong, if we feel protected in both, then the powerful forces of a magical chemical like oxytocin can diminish the effect of stress and cortisol. With trust, we do things for each other, look out for each other and sacrifice for each other. All of which adds up to our sense of security inside a Circle of Safety. We have a feeling of comfort and confidence at work that reduces the overall stress we feel because we do not feel our well-being is threatened.

Fire Your Children

CHARLIE KIM COULD sense the tension. Like clockwork, as the end of each fiscal year approached, the feeling around the office would change. It was fear. Fear that if the company didn't make its numbers, some of the people might not make it to the next year. Kim, who founded Next Jump nearly twenty years ago, has been through many ups and downs with the company and knows full well the stunting effects that fear or paranoia can wreak on a business. And so he made a bold decision that would dramatically enhance the Circle of Safety at Next Jump.

"We want Next Jump to be a company that our mothers and fathers would be proud of us for building," says Kim. And a large part of making our parents proud comes in the form of being a good person and doing the right thing. And so he implemented a policy of Lifetime Employment. Next Jump might be the only tech company in the country to do such a thing. No one will get fired to balance the books. And even costly mistakes or poor individual performance are not grounds for dismissal. If anything, the company will spend the time to help figure out what the problem is and help its people overcome it. Like an athlete who goes through a slump, a Next Jumper doesn't get fired, they get coached. About the only situation in which an employee would be asked to leave is if someone worked outside the company's high moral values or if someone actively worked to undermine their colleagues.

It's not as crazy as it sounds. Because it is nearly impossible to get fired once you're in, Next Jump takes much more time and is a lot more discerning about who they hire than a lot of other companies in their industry. They don't just consider skills and experience; they spend a lot of time evaluating the character of the candidates who want to work there. For every one hundred candidates, only one will get a job. "If a leader was told from here on you cannot fire anyone," Kim explains, "but you must still meet consistent growth in revenue and profits, despite market conditions, they would have no choice but to turn to other variables within their control like hiring, training and development." Once someone gets in, the leaders of Next Jump make it their priority to help that person grow.

If they are offering an opportunity for lifetime employment for those who want it, then the leaders of the company have to work hard to bring in the right people. "Firing is an easy option," Kim says. "Tough love, coaching, even a program to help people find a job somewhere else if they decide our company is not for them are all much more effective, but require much more time and attention from the company."

To Kim, raising children has many lessons for running a company. Both require a balancing of short-term needs and long-term goals. "First and foremost, your commitment to them is for life," Kim says. "Ultimately, you want them to become better people." Kim thinks of his employees exactly the same way. He knows most people would never get rid of their children during hard times, so "how can we lay off our people under the same conditions?" he asks. "Despite how much we may fight with our siblings, we can't get rid of family. We have to make it work." Though he may not be the perfect boss or the perfect parent—none of us are—few can dispute how much Kim cares and how hard he works to do the right thing. Even if that sometimes means admitting when he gets it wrong.

One engineer at the company said that he initially thought the Lifetime Employment policy was a nice idea for some of the lower-performing people, but not of much consequence for him, one of the top performers; he wasn't afraid that he would lose his job. What he didn't expect, however, was how much the policy would help him as a group leader. After the policy was implemented, his team started communicating much more openly. Mistakes and problems were pointed out more quickly, long before they escalated. Information sharing and cooperation increased too. Simply because his team no longer feared for their jobs, this group leader saw the performance of his team skyrocket. In fact, the performance of the whole company skyrocketed.

In the years before the new policy, average revenue growth at Next Jump was 25 percent per year. With no other major changes since Lifetime Employment was offered, revenue growth has jumped to 60 percent per year and shows no signs of slowing. Even though many of the engineers at Next Jump get job offers from Google or Facebook or other big tech companies, they don't leave. Next Jump used to see a 40 percent turnover among their engineers, a number on par with the industry. With a greater focus on building their people, Next Jump now has a turnover rate of just 1 percent. It turns out, even when offered big titles and bigger salaries, people would rather work at a place in which they feel like they belong. People would rather feel safe among their colleagues, have the opportunity to grow and feel a part of something bigger than themselves than work in a place that simply makes them rich.

This is what happens when human beings, even engineers, are put in an environment for which we were designed. We stay. We remain loyal. We help each other and we do our work with pride and passion.

When the time is taken to build proper relationships and when leaders choose to put their people before their numbers, when we can actually feel a sense of trust for each other, the oxytocin released in our bodies can reverse many of the negative effects of operating in a high-stress, cortisol-soaked environment. In other words, it's not the nature of the work we do or the number of hours we work that will help us reduce stress and achieve work-life balance; it's increased amounts of oxytocin and serotonin. Serotonin boosts our self-confidence and inspires us to help those who work for us and make proud those for whom we work. Oxytocin relieves stress, increases our interest in our work and improves our cognitive abilities, making us better able to solve complex problems. It boosts our immune systems, lowers blood pressure, increases our libido and actually lessens our cravings and addictions. And best of all, it inspires us to work together.

This is the reason people who "love their jobs" (a very oxytocin thing to say) can easily turn down a job that pays more to stay at the job they love. Compared to a culture in which the leaders incentivize reactionary decisions or activities that focus on immediate gratification, a culture in which the selfless chemicals can flow more freely results in greater organizational stability and better long-term performance. And when that happens, our bonds grow stronger, our loyalties grow deeper and the organization gains longevity. Best of all, we go home happier and live longer and healthier as a result.

This kind of culture is possible in any industry of any size. As long as there are human beings brought together for a common cause, leaders can choose to set any kind of culture they want. There is no upheaval or layoffs required for this. The talent pool does not need to be replaced. Those who don't embrace the values that define the culture may feel the cortisol in their bodies telling them that they don't belong. Feeling the anxiety of being an outsider in the group, they may decide to leave to find a place in which they are a better fit. The others, in contrast, will feel safe among their colleagues. They will feel like they have found a home.

All that is required to accomplish this is for the leaders of a company to make the decision to do it. They have the power to create an environment in which people will naturally thrive and advance the good of the organization itself. Once the culture and values are clearly defined, it becomes the responsibility of all those who belong, whether in a formal position of leadership or not, to act like leaders, work to uphold the values and keep the Circle of Safety strong.

CHAPTER 8

Why We Have Leaders

The hunters returned victorious. After a long day of tracking, a journey that took them miles from home, they were able to kill a deer big enough to feed everyone. Upon their return, many of their tribe rushed in to congratulate them and take the carcass to be prepared for the feast that would soon come. But there was a problem. Everyone was hungry and anxious to eat. When living in populations of about 100 to 150 people, as our ancestors did, clearly the whole tribe couldn't just rush in and grab food; chaos would ensue. So who gets to eat first? Fortunately, the social chemicals inside our bodies direct our behavior to help solve this problem, too.

Companies and organizations are our modern tribes. Like any tribe, they have traditions and symbols and language. The culture of a company is like the culture of any tribe. Some have strong cultures and some have weak cultures. We feel like we belong to some more than others, that we more easily "click" with the people in one culture over another. And, like all tribes, some have strong leaders and some have weak leaders. But they all have leaders.

Almost everything about us is purpose-built to help increase our opportunities for survival and success, and our need for leaders is no exception. An anthropological look at the history of leadership—why we have leaders in the first place—reveals some objective standards as to what makes a good leader . . . and what makes a bad one. And, like some of the other systems inside our bodies that influence our behavior, our need for hierarchies is linked to food and protection.

As much as we all like the idea of being equal, the fact is we are not and never will be . . . and for good reason. Without some rules of order, when the hunters brought back the fresh kill to the tribe, everyone would rush in to eat. There would be a lot of pushing and shoving. Invariably, the ones who were lucky enough to be built like linebackers would get to eat first, whereas "the artist of the family" would consistently get shoved aside or hurt. This is not a very good system if Mother Nature is trying to keep the species alive. The ones who were shoved aside would likely be less willing to trust or work closely with someone who had punched them earlier that afternoon. So to solve the problem, we evolved into hierarchical animals.

When we perceived someone as dominant to us, instead of fighting them for food we voluntarily stepped back and allowed them to eat first. And thanks to serotonin, those to whom we showed deference could feel their status rise in the group, letting them know that they were the alphas. That's how hierarchy works.

Among other advantages, like getting first choice of mate, the alphas were also offered first choice of meat. After they were done eating, the rest of the tribe would get to eat. And though the others would not get the best cuts of meat, they would get to eat eventually and they wouldn't have to get an elbow in the face when they did. This is a system much more conducive to cooperation.

To this day, we are perfectly comfortable with the alphas in our society (assessed in terms relative to our modern community and not just physical strength) getting certain advantages. We have no problem with someone who outranks us at work making more money than us, getting a bigger office or a better parking space. We have no issue with celebrities getting a table in the hard-to-get-into restaurants. We have no problem with the rich and famous getting the best-looking guy or girl on their arm. In fact, we are so comfortable with alphas getting preferential treatment, on some occasions some of us may even get upset or offended if they didn't.

Many of us would find it strange, or even disrespectful, if the president of the United States had to carry his own luggage. Regardless of party, we would be uncomfortable with the notion simply because he is a leader in our political hierarchy. He's the president, after all; he shouldn't have to do that. Some of us would even volunteer to carry the luggage. It is an honor in society to do things to help our leaders. And perhaps at a later date, if they remember or recognize us, they may even throw us a bone while everyone else is watching. And if they did, we would feel a burst of serotonin and feel our status and confidence rise as a result.

It is because of the advantages an alpha gets in a society that we are always trying to improve our own place in the pecking order. We primp and puff ourselves up when we go to bars, with the hope that others will see us as healthy and attractive. Worthy of keeping our genes in the gene pool. We like to talk about our accomplishments, hang our diplomas on our walls and put our trophies on a shelf for all to see what we've achieved. Our goal is to be seen as smart and strong and worthy of the advantages of an alpha. Worthy of the respect of others. All to raise our status in our community.

This is the whole idea behind status symbols (which, because of serotonin, actually do boost our sense of status). There is a reason the logos are on the outside of most expensive items. We want people to see the red stripe down the side of our Prada sunglasses, the double Cs on our Chanel bags or the shiny Mercedes emblem stuck on the front of our cars. In our capitalist society, conspicuous displays of wealth may indicate to others that we are doing well. As symbols of our strength and capacity, they can earn us respect and boost our position in the hierarchy. It's no wonder some of us try to fake our status. Unfortunately, it doesn't work. Though a good fake may trick others into thinking we are more successful than we are, this is biology and we can't fool ourselves.

A 2010 study by three psychology scientists—Francesca Gino of Chapel Hill, Michael Norton of Harvard Business School and Dan Ariely of Duke—showed that people who wear phony couture clothing actually don't feel the same burst of pride or status as those who wear the real thing. Faking it, it turns out, makes us feel phony, as if we are cheating. Status is biological, we have to earn it to feel it. The same study also concluded that those who attempted to cheat their biology were actually more inclined to cheat in other aspects of their lives as well.

Even though we can indeed raise our status with material goods, the feeling doesn't last. There is no social relationship associated with that burst of serotonin. Again, the selfless chemicals are trying to help us strengthen our communities and social bonds. To find a lasting sense of pride, there must be a mentor/parent/boss/coach/leader relationship to back it up.

Leadership status is not just reserved for people; we also offer it to the tribes themselves. Just as we work to raise our individual status within our tribes, companies are constantly trying to raise their status in their respective industries. They tell us how many J.D. Power awards they have won; they report their ranking on the Fortune 1000 list. Smaller companies are quick to share if they are an Inc. 5000 company, a ranking of the fastest-growing small businesses. The reason we love rankings is because we're hierarchical animals and there are perks to being higher in the pecking order.

However, all the advantages of leadership do not come for free. In fact, they come at quite a steep price. And it is this part of the equation that is too often forgotten in many of our organizations today. It is true that the alpha may really be "stronger" than the rest of us. We know that all our respect and adoration really does boost their self-confidence. That's good. Because when the group faces a threat from the outside, we expect the leader, who really is stronger, better fed and oozing with confidence from all the serotonin in their body, to be the first one to rush toward the danger to protect the rest of us. "The cost of leadership," explains Lieutenant General George Flynn of the United States Marine Corps, "is self-interest." That's also the reason we give our alphas first choice of mate. If they die early while trying to defend us, we want to make sure all those strong genes stay in our gene pool. The group isn't stupid. We wouldn't give them all those perks for nothing. That wouldn't be fair.

This is the reason we are so offended by the exorbitant and disproportionate compensations of some of the leaders of investment banks. It has nothing to do with the numbers. It has to do with this social contract deeply ingrained in what it means to be human. If our leaders are to enjoy the trappings of their position in the hierarchy, then we expect them to offer us protection. The problem is, for many of the overpaid leaders, we know that they took the money and perks and didn't offer protection to their people. In some cases, they even sacrificed their people to protect or boost their own interests. This is what so viscerally offends us. We accuse them of greed and excess only when we feel they have violated the very definition of what it means to be a leader.

Few would be offended if it were decided to give Nelson Mandela a $150 million bonus. If it were announced that Mother Teresa was awarded $250 million at the end of the fiscal year, few if anyone would make a stink about it. We know that they upheld their side of the social contract. They were willing to make sacrifices for the good of those who chose to follow them. They considered the well-being of others before themselves and sometimes suffered as a result. And in those cases, we are perfectly happy with our leaders' receiving all the perks we feel they have earned. The same goes for companies. They earn their reputations by being willing to do the right thing for their people and their customers or clients. That reputation suffers when they break the social contract of leadership.

If we consider how we treat celebrities or the wealthy in our materialistic, reality-TV-saturated society, all this science seems to make sense. Some people who inherit money, coerce the system or gain celebrity thanks to the modern media system are afforded certain perks simply because they would appear to have a status higher than ours. But fame is supposed to be a by-product of alpha status, not a way to achieve it. The same is true for financial wealth. It is supposed to be the by-product of accomplishment, not a standard for leadership status alone.

Unless someone is willing to make personal sacrifices for the good of others to earn their place in the hierarchy, they aren't really "alpha material." Simply acting the part is not enough. Just like the phony couture wearer, they may feel insecure about their position, or work extra hard to compensate or try to prove to the public (and themselves) that they are deserving of all the advantages they get.

This is one of the reasons a publicist may recommend to a celebrity client that they get involved in charitable work. In our modern world, that's the game. It is important to uphold the appearance of maintaining that deeply seeded social contract— that our alphas are supposed to serve us. And though there are definite benefits to a celebrity using their bully pulpit to bring attention to a cause or plight, if they really cared, they wouldn't need to publicize every time they did something. Perhaps one of the sacrifices they could make is the spotlight.

The same is true for politicians during election cycles. It is fun to watch the politicians who announce that if elected they will do all these good things because they care about us. And if they lose their election, many go on to do none of those things. The rank of office is not what makes someone a leader. Leadership is the choice to serve others with or without any formal rank. There are people with authority who are not leaders and there are people at the bottom rungs of an organization who most certainly are leaders. It's okay for leaders to enjoy all the perks afforded to them. However, they must be willing to give up those perks when it matters.

Leaders are the ones willing to look out for those to the left of them and those to the right of them. They are often willing to sacrifice their own comfort for ours, even when they disagree with us. Trust is not simply a matter of shared opinions. Trust is a biological reaction to the belief that someone has our well-being at heart. Leaders are the ones who are willing to give up something of their own for us. Their time, their energy, their money, maybe even the food off their plate. When it matters, leaders choose to eat last.

By the objective standards of leadership, those who aim to raise their own status simply so they can enjoy the perks themselves without fulfilling their responsibilities as leaders are, plain and simple, weak leaders. Though they may achieve alpha status and rise in the ranks, though they may possess talents and strengths that could earmark them for alpha status, they only become leaders when they accept the responsibility to protect those in their care. If they choose to sacrifice those in their tribe for personal gain, however, they will often struggle to hold on to their position once they've got it. Again, the group is not stupid. The people always have the power.

The leaders of organizations who rise through the ranks not because they want it, but because the tribe keeps offering higher status out of gratitude for their willingness to sacrifice, are the true leaders worthy of our trust and loyalty. All leaders, even the good ones, can sometimes lose their way and become selfish and power hungry, however. Intoxicated by the chemicals, they can sometimes forget that their responsibility as a leader is to their people. Sometimes these leaders are able to regain their footing, but if they don't, we have little choice but to look past them, lament what they have become, wait for them to move on and look to someone else to lead us.

What makes a good leader is that they eschew the spotlight in favor of spending time and energy to do what they need to do to support and protect their people. And when we feel the Circle of Safety around us, we offer our blood and sweat and tears and do everything we can to see our leader's vision come to life. The only thing our leaders ever need to do is remember whom they serve and it will be our honor and pleasure to serve them back.

The Ceramic Cup

I HEARD A story about a former under secretary of defense who gave a speech at a large conference. He took his place on the stage and began talking, sharing his prepared remarks with the audience. He paused to take a sip of coffee from the Styrofoam cup he'd brought on stage with him. He took another sip, looked down at the cup and smiled.

"You know," he said, interrupting his own speech, "I spoke here last year. I presented at this same conference on this same stage. But last year, I was still an under secretary," he said. "I flew here in business class and when I landed, there was someone waiting for me at the airport to take me to my hotel. Upon arriving at my hotel," he continued, "there was someone else waiting for me. They had already checked me into the hotel, so they handed me my key and escorted me up to my room. The next morning, when I came down, again there was someone waiting for me in the lobby to drive me to this same venue that we are in today. I was taken through a back entrance, shown to the greenroom and handed a cup of coffee in a beautiful ceramic cup."

"But this year, as I stand here to speak to you, I am no longer the under secretary," he continued. "I flew here coach class and when I arrived at the airport yesterday there was no one there to meet me. I took a taxi to the hotel, and when I got there, I checked myself in and went by myself to my room. This morning, I came down to the lobby and caught another taxi to come here. I came in the front door and found my way backstage. Once there, I asked one of the techs if there was any coffee. He pointed to a coffee machine on a table against the wall. So I walked over and poured myself a cup of coffee into this here Styrofoam cup," he said as he raised the cup to show the audience.

"It occurs to me," he continued, "the ceramic cup they gave me last year . . . it was never meant for me at all. It was meant for the position I held. I deserve a Styrofoam cup.

"This is the most important lesson I can impart to all of you," he offered. "All the perks, all the benefits and advantages you may get for the rank or position you hold, they aren't meant for you. They are meant for the role you fill. And when you leave your role, which eventually you will, they will give the ceramic cup to the person who replaces you. Because you only ever deserved a Styrofoam cup."

Eating Last Is Repaid with Loyalty and Hard Work

WHEN THE STOCK market crashed in 2008, like so many other companies, Barry-Wehmiller got hit pretty hard. The old-fashioned American manufacturing company that Chapman was transforming saw an almost immediate 30 percent drop in machine orders. The company makes large industrial machinery, the kinds of machines a large packaged goods company would buy to make the cardboard boxes for their products. The machines that Barry-Wehmiller makes are among the first things to get cut when a company slashes its capital expenditures budget in hard times and opts instead to make do with its aging machines.

Chapman and his team were faced with a blunt truth: they were no longer able to afford to keep all their employees. They simply didn't have the work or the revenue to justify keeping everyone on board. And so, for the first time in a long time, the subject of layoffs was raised.

For many companies, the option would seem obvious, even if unsavory. But Chapman refused to sack people simply because the company was having a hard year. More and more he came to see his company as a family, as a group of people to serve and keep safe and not just as a labor force to be used to serve the company. "We would never dream of getting rid of one of our children in hard times," he says. If anything, the whole family would come together, maybe suffer together, but ultimately work through the hard times together.

And so, instead of layoffs, the company implemented a mandatory furlough program. Every employee, from CEO to secretary, would have to take four weeks of unpaid time off. They could take the weeks off whenever they wanted and the weeks did not have to be taken consecutively. But it was how Chapman announced the program that proved his leadership bona fides. "It is better that we all suffer a little," he told his people, "so that none of us has to suffer a lot."

The protection Chapman offered his people had a massive impact. Unlike in a company that announces layoffs, sending everyone into self-preservation mode, at Barry-Wehmiller the people spontaneously, and completely on their own, set out to do more for each other. Those who could afford the time off more traded with those who could afford it less. Though they were under no obligation to do so, they took off more unpaid time than required just to help someone else out. The overwhelming feeling across the company was one of gratitude for the security they had been given. I suspect in other companies that face hard times, most of the people would also rather lose a month's pay than lose their job.

As soon as things started to pick up again, the furlough program was done away with and the 401(k) contributions that the company had stopped paying in the tough times were not only restored, but were back paid to when the tough times began. The result was astounding. The leaders fulfilled the anthropological obligation of an alpha, to protect the tribe, and in return, the people repaid that protection with an intense loyalty, wanting to do whatever they could to help the company. Few from Barry-Wehmiller ever leave just for more money.

To human beings, the safety a strong tribe provides its members makes the tribe stronger and better equipped to deal with the dangers and uncertainty of the outside world. The reason good leaders do well in hard times is obvious. Their people willingly commit their blood, sweat and tears to see the tribe, the company, advance and grow stronger. They do so not because they have to . . . but because they want to. And as a result, the stronger tribe, the stronger company, is able to guarantee a greater sense of safety and protection to even more people for even longer. Fear, in contrast, can hurt the very innovation and progress so many leaders of companies claim they are trying to advance with every re-org.

E.D.S.O. Revisited

EACH OF THE feel-good chemicals is essential for our survival as individuals and as populations. They play a role based on our needs and the environments in which we work. Our ability to work hard and muscle through hard labor is thanks to endorphins. Our ability to set goals, focus and get things done comes from the incentivizing powers of dopamine. It feels good to make progress, and so we do.

Serotonin is responsible for the pride we feel when those we care for achieve great things or when we make proud the people who take care of us. Serotonin helps to ensure we look out for those who follow us and do right by those who lead us. And the mysterious power of oxytocin helps us form bonds of love and trust. It helps us form relationships so strong we can make decisions with complete confidence that those who care about us will stand by our side. We know that if we need help or support the people who care about us will be there for us, no matter what. Oxytocin keeps us healthy. It opens our minds. It biologically makes us better problem solvers. Without oxytocin, we would only ever make short-term progress. Leaps of greatness require the combined problem-solving ability of people who trust each other.

Like all things human, it is not a perfect system. The chemicals do not fire in equal quantities and in strict allotments. They sometimes release together and they are released in varying amounts. What's more, we can short-circuit the system to release the chemicals for the wrong reasons. The selfish chemicals, endorphins and dopamine, give us short-term rewards to which we can, under the right conditions, become addicted. The selfless chemicals, serotonin and oxytocin, take time to build up in our systems before we can enjoy their full benefits. Though we may enjoy the thrill of reaching a goal or winning a race, that feeling won't last. To get more of that feeling we need to win another race and reach a more distant goal. The bonds of love and trust and friendship take time to feel.

We cannot motivate others, per se. Our motivation is determined by the chemical incentives inside every one of us. Any motivation we have is a function of our desire to repeat behaviors that make us feel good or avoid stress or pain. The only thing we can do is create environments in which the right chemicals are released for the right reasons. And if we get the environment right, if we create organizational cultures that work to the natural inclinations of the human animal, the result will be an entire group of self-motivated people.

The goal for any leader of any organization is to find balance. When dopamine is the primary driver, we may achieve a lot but we will feel lonely and unfulfilled no matter how rich or powerful we get. We live lives of quick hits, in search of the next rush. Dopamine simply does not help us create things that are built to last. When we live in a hippie commune, the oxytocin gushing, but without any specific measurable goals or ambition, we can deny ourselves those intense feelings of accomplishment. No matter how loved we may feel, we may still feel like failures. The goal, again, is balance.

When the system is in balance, however, we seem to gain almost supernatural ability. Courage, inspiration, foresight, creativity and empathy, to name a few. When those things all come to bear, the results and the feelings that go with them are simply remarkable.

[REALITY]

CHAPTER 9

The Courage to Do the Right Thing

Know When to Break the Rules

"HOW MANY SOULS on board?" the air traffic controller asked. As if we were still traversing the globe in wooden ships with tall masts, the archaic terminology referring to the number of people aboard the vessel is a standard question asked when an aircraft declares an in-flight emergency.

"One hundred twenty-six souls," replied the pilot.

The Florida-bound flight was somewhere over Maryland, at an altitude of 36,000 feet, traveling at about 560 miles per hour, when smoke started to pour into the cockpit. Smoke on board an aircraft is one of the most terrifying emergencies a pilot will ever face. They don't always know the cause of the smoke. They don't know if there is a fire. They don't know if the emergency is contained or if it is going to spread . . . and spread out of control quickly. The smoke itself can make seeing or breathing difficult and it is sure to cause panic among the passengers. No matter how you look at it, it's bad.

"Center, KH209," the pilot radioed when he realized the problem.

"KH209, go ahead," replied the controller monitoring the air space.

"KH209, I need to descend immediately. I can't maintain altitude," was the abrupt call from the pilot.

But there was a problem. There was another flight, also flying to Florida, 2,000 feet directly below the troubled aircraft. The FAA rules are simple enough: no two aircraft flying en route may pass each other any closer than 1,000 feet, above or below, or five miles around each other. The rules are there for good reason. Traveling at three quarters the speed of sound, it becomes very difficult to maneuver aircraft without creating a serious risk of collision.

To make matters worse, the two planes were flying on a narrow route toward their destination. Because of a military exercise that was going on in the area, the airspace was restricted to a narrow band, much like a lane of a highway. And though there were other lanes on this highway, there was other traffic in them at the time.

The air traffic controller replied to the pilot's request to descend immediately, "KH209, turn fifteen degrees right and descend."

Not only had the air traffic controller ordered the distressed airplane to enter restricted airspace, but telling the pilot to descend would mean he would pass well within the five-mile buffer of the plane flying beneath him.

Modern airplanes are equipped with collision alarms that alert a pilot when another airplane flies within that 1,000-foot, five-mile buffer. When the alarm sounds, knowing the limited time they have, pilots are trained to react to what could be an impending disaster. The proximity by which these two planes would pass each other—two miles, to be exact—would surely set off the collision alarm of the flight traveling at 34,000 feet. And that would create another problem.

But this was a very experienced air traffic controller sitting at the console that day. He was fully aware of all the aircraft in the area. What's more, he was very aware of all the rules and restrictions. He radioed the pilot of the other aircraft and spoke in very clear, plain English. "AG1446, there is an airplane flying above you. He has declared an emergency. He is going to descend through your altitude at approximately two miles off your right front. He needs to descend immediately."

This same message would be repeated again as the troubled vessel passed through the airspace of another three aircraft as it made its way down.

On that clear day over Maryland, 126 souls were saved because one very experienced air traffic controller decided to break the rules. Keeping people alive was more important than maintaining boundaries.

There were over 9.8 million scheduled domestic and passenger flights on U.S. airlines in 2012. That's nearly 26,800 flights per day. The numbers are staggering. These numbers don't even include the unscheduled, cargo and foreign flights that crisscross America every year.

More than 815 million passengers each year entrust their lives to the pilots who transport us, the mechanics who ensure the aircraft are airworthy and the FAA, which develops the regulations to ensure everything runs as safely as possible.

And then there are the air traffic controllers. We trust these relatively few people to obey the rules to ensure that all those aircraft are kept moving safely across the skies. But in the case of flight KH209, the controller broke the rules. He disobeyed the clear lines set to ensure our safety.

And that's what trust is. We don't just trust people to obey the rules, we also trust that they know when to break them. The rules are there for normal operations. The rules are designed to avoid danger and help ensure that things go smoothly. And though there are guidelines for how to deal with emergencies, at the end of the day, we trust the expertise of a special few people to know when to break the rules.

Organizations that offer people an opportunity to fully commit work tirelessly to train their people. This goes beyond the occasional class on how to write a better PowerPoint or be a more effective presenter; these organizations offer endless opportunities for self-improvement. The more training they offer us, the more we learn. The more experienced and confident we become, the more the organization is willing to give us greater and greater responsibility. And ultimately, the organization—our management and our colleagues—is willing to trust us to know when to break the rules.

We cannot "trust" rules or technology. We can rely on them, for sure, but trust them? No. Trust is a very special human experience, produced by the chemical oxytocin in response to acts performed on our behalf that serve our safety and protection. True trust can only exist among people. And we can only trust others when we know they are actively and consciously concerned about us. A technology, no matter how sophisticated, doesn't care about us at all—it simply reacts to a set of variables. And the rulebook, no matter how comprehensive, cannot consider every eventuality.

Imagine if every time we had a fight with a loved one, they reacted to a set of variables or deferred to the rulebook for advice. How long do you think that relationship would last? This is the reason we find bureaucrats infuriating. They simply default to the rules with no consideration for the people those rules were designed to help or protect. In other words, they don't care. There is no algorithm for a successful relationship—between people or with companies.

The true social benefit of trust must be reciprocal. One-way trust is not beneficial to the individual or the group. What good is a company in which management trusts labor, but labor doesn't trust management? It is hardly a strong marriage in which the wife trusts the husband, but the husband doesn't trust the wife. It's all fine and good for a leader to expect the people to trust them, but if the leader doesn't trust the people, the system will fail. For trust to serve the individuals and the group, it must be shared.

The responsibility of leaders is to teach their people the rules, train them to gain competency and build their confidence. At that point, leadership must step back and trust that their people know what they are doing and will do what needs to be done. In weak organizations, without oversight, too many people will break the rules for personal gain. That's what makes the organizations weak. In strong organizations, people will break the rules because it is the right thing to do for others.

Think about it. Would you feel comfortable watching your family board a plane knowing there is a qualified pilot or controller who will do everything by the book no matter what? Would you let your family get on a plane knowing that the pilot or air traffic controller cared only about what they need to do to get their next bonus? Or would you rather watch your family board a plane knowing there are confident pilots and controllers with lots of experience who will know what rules to break if something should go wrong, possibly putting their bonus at risk as a result? The answer is so plainly obvious. We don't trust rules, we trust people.

The responsibility of a leader is to provide cover from above for their people who are working below. When the people feel that they have the control to do what's right, even if it sometimes means breaking the rules, then they will more likely do the right thing. Courage comes from above. Our confidence to do what's right is determined by how trusted we feel by our leaders.

If good people are asked to work in a bad culture, one in which leaders do not relinquish control, then the odds of something bad happening go up. People will be more concerned about following the rules out of fear of getting in trouble or losing their jobs than about doing what needs to be done. And when that happens, souls will be lost.

CHAPTER 10

Snowmobile in the Desert

Let's face it, we're good. We're really good. I mean, we're the best thing that ever lived. This is not the rambling of an egomaniac, just look at the world around us. Other animals just go about their days, looking for food, procreating and operating on instinct. But not us. We do so much more than operate to survive or grow our population (though we also do that well).

We invent, build and achieve things unachievable by any other species on our planet. Gazelles didn't build the pyramids, we did. Gorillas didn't figure out the combustion engine, we did. And it's all because of our remarkable neocortex—the part of our brain that separates us from all the other mammals. It is our neocortex that gives us the ability to think rationally and critically about our world and solve complex problems. It is because of our neocortex that we can speak and communicate in a way vastly more sophisticated than any other species on the planet. It is this ability that allows us, among many other things, to pass on our lessons to others so they don't need to relearn everything we have learned. Each generation is able to build on the lessons of the previous generations so that we can make real progress in the world. This is what it means to be human. We are achievement machines.

However, as great as our neocortex is at helping us get things done, it is our primitive limbic brain that controls our feelings. Our ability to trust. Our ability to cooperate. Our ability to socialize and build strong communities. It is our limbic brain that feeds the gut reactions and gut decisions that drive our behavior. It gives us the ability to form strong emotional bonds with others. And these strong social bonds allow us to work together to do all the things our *Homo sapiens* neocortices can dream up. If we weren't able to trust each other and work together, no matter how smart we were, we would die young and alone. We would never feel the joy of being in relationships, have the feeling of being in a circle of people with whom we share the same values and beliefs or the intense feeling of goodness that comes from doing something for someone else.

As much as we like to think that it is our smarts that get us ahead, it is not everything. Our intelligence gives us ideas and instructions. But it is our ability to cooperate that actually helps us get those things done. Nothing of real value on this earth was built by one person without the help of others. There are few accomplishments, companies or technologies that were built by one person without the help or support of anyone else. It is clear that the more others want to help us, the more we can achieve.

And it is our ability to get things done together that has produced one of the greatest paradoxes of the modern era. In our pursuit to advance, we have, without intending to, built a world that is making it harder and harder for us to cooperate. The symptoms of this cruel irony are easy to feel in the developed world. Feelings of isolation and high stress have fueled industries that are profiting from our search for happiness. Self-help books, courses and any number of pharmaceuticals make up multibillion-dollar industries designed to help us find that elusive happiness, or at the very least to reduce our stress. In only a few decades, the self-help business alone has grown to $11 billion. The biggest thing the self-help industry seems to have helped is itself.

Our search for happiness and connection has also led us to seek professional advice. In the 1950s, few of us went to weekly sessions with a therapist. Today in the U.S., according to the Hoover Institute, there are 77,000 clinical psychologists, 192,000 clinical social workers, 105,000 mental health counselors, 50,000 marriage and family therapists, 17,000 nurse psychotherapists, and 30,000 life coaches. The only reason the field continues to grow is because of increasing demand. The more we try to make ourselves feel better, the worse we seem to feel.

That only a minority of employees feel fulfilled and truly happy at work is our own doing. We have built systems and con-structed organizations that force the human animal to work in environments in which it does not work best. With an excess of dopamine to drive us and cortisol flowing when we don't need it, we have actually short-circuited our system to do the opposite: to encourage us to look out for ourselves first and be suspicious of others.

If the human being is a snowmobile, this means we were de-signed to operate in very specific conditions. Take that machine designed for one kind of condition—snow—and put it in an-other condition—the desert, for example—and it won't operate as well. Sure, the snowmobile will go. It just won't go as easily or as well as if it were in the right conditions. This is what has hap-pened in many of our modern organizations. And when prog-ress is slow or innovation is lacking, leaders tinker with the machine. They hire and fire in hopes of getting the right mix. They develop new kinds of incentives to encourage the machine to work harder.

Trust is like lubrication. It reduces friction and creates conditions much more conducive to performance.

With an incentivizing cocktail of dopamine, the machines will, indeed, work harder and maybe even go a little faster in the desert. But the friction is great. What too many leaders of organizations fail to appreciate is that it's not the people that are the problem. The people are fine. Rather, it's the environment in which the people operate that is the problem. Get that right and things just go.

To a social animal, trust is like lubrication. It reduces friction and creates conditions much more conducive to performance, just like putting the snowmobile back in the snow. Do that and even an underpowered snowmobile will run circles around the most powerful snowmobile in the wrong conditions. It's not how smart the people in the organization are; it's how well they work together that is the true indicator of future success or the ability to manage through struggle.

Trust and commitment are feelings that we get from the release of chemical incentives deep in our limbic brain. And as such, they are inherently hard to measure. Just as we can't simply tell someone to be happy and expect them to be happy, we can't just tell someone to trust us or to commit to something and expect they will. There are all sorts of things we need to do first before someone will *feel* any sense of loyalty or devotion.

There are some basic tenets that all leaders of organizations must obey to build deep trust and commitment among the people who work for them. And, in a very un-dopamine way, it will take time, energy and the will of people for these things to work.

All this begs the question, how did we get ourselves into the desert in the first place?

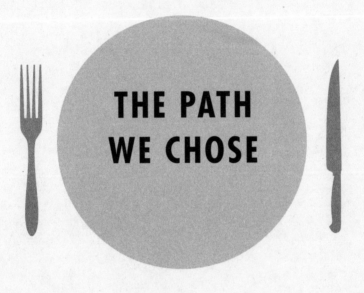

THE PATH
WE CHOSE

[HOW WE GOT HERE]

CHAPTER 11

The Boom Before the Bust

Times were good. Really good. Everyone was making money . . . and everyone was spending it. The result was unprecedented growth. In fact, the total wealth in the country more than doubled in fewer than ten years. There were new technologies and a new kind of media that allowed news and ideas to spread like never before. These were unprecedented times, indeed. This was not the 1980s or the 1990s. This was the 1920s. The Roaring Twenties.

The period after World War I was the time when America first truly became a consumer society. For the first time in years, Americans were relatively wealthy, and with the wealth came good times. With all that disposable income they were able to buy luxuries and new technologies—all the new inventions that could improve the quality of life. Electric refrigerators, telephones, cars and movies all saw their introduction and rise in popularity during the 1920s. And let's not forget about new forms of media that were introduced. In 1920 there was one commercial radio station in the United States—KDKA out of

Pittsburgh. Three years later there were over five hundred stations across the country. And by the end of the decade, there were more than 12 million households with radios.

This new national media allowed for news to be broadcast like never before. It also allowed for national advertising to be broadcast in a way that was previously impossible. Combined with the introduction of chain stores, the popularity of the radio meant that people on one coast could now buy the same things as people on the other coast. And with the arrival of the movies, more and more media focused on the lives of movie stars and sports heroes. We dreamed of living glamorous lives like theirs. With national attention, celebrity was no longer a by-product of success, it became a thing to achieve itself. Fame became a new way to achieve alpha status. It was a time of aspiration.

Thanks to all these new technologies and modern conveniences, the period also gave rise to entirely new industries. Just like the Internet created a need for IT consultants, the automobile created a need for gas stations, for example. It all sounds eerily reminiscent of our modern times—new technologies, new media, new industries, an obsession with the lives of celebrities, the increase of wealth and consumerism and, most significant, thanks to all that excess, a preponderance of waste.

Then something happened. It all suddenly stopped. As much as people try to beat the laws of nature, there is always a correction. Nature abhors imbalance. Nothing can grow forever. And so, despite the expectation of never-ending good times, on October 29, 1929, it all came to a sudden and abrupt halt.

"Black Tuesday," as the crash was called, was a huge "correction" in the stock market. The weight of imbalance and overvaluations had to, at some point, right itself and find balance again. Though corrections are not uncommon, in this case the imbalance was so extreme that the correction was significant enough to start the Great Depression—a period marked by a loss of nearly 90 percent of the stock market's value and unemployment rates that left as many as a quarter of the country jobless.

Unlike their parents, those born during most of the 1920s were too young to actually enjoy the 1920s. They were raised in one of the most austere times in American history. And as our anthropology dictates, with resources scarce, the generation learned to work together and help each other to make ends meet. Waste and excess just weren't an option anymore. The Depression lasted for over a decade and didn't end until nearly 1942. It was the attack on Pearl Harbor on December 7, 1941, that forced America into World War II and pulled it out of the Depression.

The generation that grew up during some of the worst economic times in the country came of age just in time to be drafted and shipped off to do battle with Hitler's armies. The entire country went straight from the Great Depression into a great war.

By the time America entered World War II, the population of the United States was about 133 million, of which about 16 million marched off to war. That's about 12 percent of the population. Today America's population is more than 315 million and less than 1 percent serve in the military. That includes active duty, civilian, guard and reserve forces. (Of course, these are different times and we are not involved in a world war—a war in which we would bear any burden or pay any price to protect what we believed in.) During World War II, given the sheer volume of people who put on a uniform, nearly everyone knew someone who served in the military. Many parents watched their own sons march off to battle. Today, simply because most of us aren't friends with someone in the military, we have trouble understanding how people can maintain such a deep sense of selfless service.

Unlike today's conflicts, World War II wasn't a war that happened at a distance. It wasn't viewed on television or on a computer screen. It was a war that touched the lives of most of the country. The entire nation was involved in the war effort. According to *The War*, the seminal World War II documentary by Ken Burns and Lynn Novick, 24 million people relocated to take defense jobs. And millions of women, African Americans and Latinos found unprecedented opportunities in the workforce. Many others bought war bonds to help finance the war. Buying a war bond gave those who couldn't offer physical support the feeling that they too were a part of the effort. And for those who couldn't afford war bonds, they contributed by planting victory gardens, growing fruit and vegetables to help reduce the burden of rationing. This is one of the reasons we call this generation the Greatest Generation. It was defined not by excess and consumerism, but by hardship and service.

This was not a time when the country sat back and complained, pointed fingers and debated if we should or should not be at war. This was a time when the whole country came together. According to a poll published in the November 1942 issue of *Life* magazine, over 90 percent of the country believed that America should keep fighting in the war. This was a population that overwhelmingly supported the draft before the war and continued to believe that military training should be compulsory after the war. As a nation, we believed in service. And nearly everyone, in some way, shape or form, sacrificed and served for the good of each other. Nearly all Americans felt a part of something bigger than themselves.

When the war was finally won, the men who survived the battles returned home to parades and parties. But the celebration wasn't just for those who had risked their lives on the front lines; rather, it was for all who had participated and sacrificed in their own way. Almost everyone shared the feeling of accomplishment and sense of relief that came with the Allied victory. As well they should have. They had worked hard for that feeling. They earned it.

With the war behind them and the economy booming, the men and women of the Greatest Generation, those raised during the Depression then sent off to war, felt that they had missed out on their youth; many were even bitter. They felt that they had already spent so much of their lives sacrificing that they wanted to try to reclaim some of what they had lost. And so they got to work.

The importance of hard work, the necessity of cooperation and the value of loyalty—everything they knew about getting things done—defined how companies operated when this generation ran them. The 1950s were defined as an era of giving one's entire life to one company and of one company expecting their people to work there for their entire lives. At the end of a long career, an employee would receive their proverbial gold watch, the ultimate symbol of gratitude for a life of service to the company. And it worked . . . for a while.

The Eight-Hundred-Pound Boomer in the Room

EVERY GENERATION SEEMS to confound or rebel against the generation before it. Each new generation embodies a set of values and beliefs molded by the events, experiences and technologies of their youth . . . which tend to be a little different from those of their parents. And when populations grow at a steady pace, the push and pull between the generations, the impulse of a new generation to change everything and the desire of an older generation to keep things the same work like a system of checks and balances. It offers a natural tension that helps to ensure we don't break everything while also allowing us to make progress and change with the times. One point of view or a single, uncontested power is rarely a good thing. Like the visionary and the operator inside a company, Democrats and Republicans in Congress, the Soviets and Uncle Sam in geopolitics, even Mom and Dad at home, the value of two opposing forces, the tension of push and pull actually keeps things more stable. It's all about balance.

But something happened at the end of the Second World War that upset the normal system of checks and balances. A break in the natural order that would quite literally and quite by accident set America on an entirely new course. Returning from war, people celebrated. And celebrated. And celebrated. And nine months later, there began a period of population growth never seen before in the United States: the Baby Boom.

U.S. BIRTHS PER 1,000 POPULATION

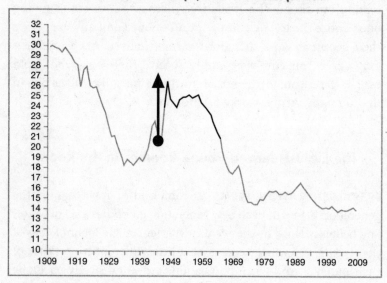

In 1940, there were 2.6 million children born. In 1946, the number of children born was 3.4 million. There was a small boom at the end of World War I, but it was the massive spike in births that began after World War II that tipped the balance. A disparity that was compounded by the relatively slow birth rate during the Depression and the war.

The end of the Boomer generation is typically regarded as 1964, the year the number of births dipped below 4 million for the first time in more than a decade. All told, the Boomers added 76 million people to the population, a growth rate of nearly 40 percent (compared to a less than 25 percent increase between 1964 and 1984).

And the dramatic change doesn't stop there. Unlike their parents, who were raised during a time of economic depression

AVERAGE U.S. INCOME

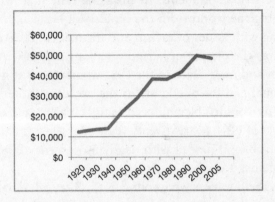

and war rations, the Boomers were raised in times of rising affluence and prosperity. Starting at the end of the war, wealth and GDP in America did nothing but grow at a steady pace. This was a good thing for all those Boomers. The parents who fought or sacrificed were now able to give their children a life completely opposite to their own. Whereas the Greatest Generation was defined by the need to serve others, the Boomer generation started on a path of taking for themselves. As our wealth and attitudes changed, we started to transform from a country that would fight to protect a way of life into a country that would fight to protect the way we prefer to live.

Growing up under the protection of their newly wealthy parents, the first group of Boomers became teenagers in the 1960s. And, like all good teenagers, they rebelled against their parents' push for them to work hard and devote themselves to a job or a company until they got that gold watch. They rejected the quiet suburbs and their parents' focus on material wealth. *Leave It to Beaver* was not their idea of "the good life"; individualism, free love and narcissism were.

In 1960s America, however, the hippies who chose to live a life with less than they needed did so for the simple fact that, as a country, we had more than we needed. Don't get me wrong,

I'm not saying the Greatest Generation was perfect. In fact, they had some serious problems. At the same time that Americans were saving the world from the tyranny of Nazism, they were struggling with issues of racism and inequality. The American Dream was the picture of harmony as long as you were white, Christian and male. Back in the U.S., women were still considered unqualified for public life or the executive suite. African Americans wouldn't be embraced as full citizens until the Civil Rights Act of 1964, nearly twenty years after the war had ended. And even then, it passed with nearly 30 percent of the Senate voting against it.

When the Boomers were young, it was they who forced civil rights on an older generation bent on maintaining an unhealthy and unjust status quo. It was, indeed, the young Boomers who demanded better pay for women and refused to blindly accept the injustices that prevailed in our society. They might have become the second Greatest Generation had they continued on that path. But that's not how it went.

As the disproportionately large generation of Boomers started aging, they changed course. And that's when our modern-era problems started to arise. The maturing Boomers, as a generation, started to operate in different ways . . . in more selfish ways. They now set out to protect the world with which they were most familiar—a world of rising wealth and affluence.

By the 1970s, the older Boomers were now graduating from college and starting to make their way into the workforce. In a decade marked by an unpopular war and the Watergate scandal, Richard Nixon seemed to offer a foreboding look at the generation he served. His own selfish ambitions drove decisions that were at best unethical and at worst illegal.

The Boomers witnessed events that only reinforced their early beliefs that "government can't be trusted," "we have to look out for ourselves" and "we need to change the way things are done." Forget the status quo—the Boomers aspired to self-realization. Having a spiritual guru was like going to the gym today. They learned to disco. They wore polyester. And they sealed their reputation as the generation that defined, as Thomas Wolfe described in a 1976 issue of *New York* magazine, the "Me" decade. They became a group that seemed to be more concerned about their own happiness and well-being than the happiness or well-being of those around them.

As the Boomers grew older and started to enter the workforce, making their own contribution to our economy, they brought all this self-centeredness and cynicism with them. Except, in this case, there were vastly fewer of the previous generation to balance the ideals of this new me-before-we generation.

The late seventies also saw the introduction of new theories about how to conduct business. Shaken by the Vietnam War, a presidential scandal, an oil crisis, the rise of globalization and, near the end of the decade, a revolution in Iran that involved American lives, economic theories became more protectionist in nature. They tended to focus on how to safeguard our rising wealth rather than to share it or use it to support causes of national importance, like the war bonds of earlier generations. Service to others as part of our national identity was slowly being replaced by service to ourselves as a national priority.

U.S. GDP IN REAL DOLLARS, IN BILLIONS

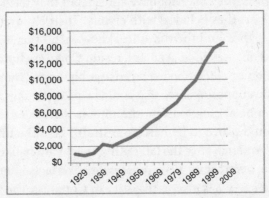

Throughout this time, America's household affluence continued to skyrocket. Gross domestic product grew from $3.87 tril-
lion in 1965 to $4.7 trillion in 1970 to $6.52 trillion in 1980;
that's 68 percent growth in fifteen years. It looked like a steep
slope up with barely a bump in the road. We were getting
wealthier and wealthier, as individuals and as a country. Though
the wealthiest Americans were getting wealthier at a disproportionately higher rate than the rest of the country, even the poor-
est Americans at least stayed the same or even rose by a small
degree. The point is, no segment of the population got significantly poorer.

With the 1970s coming to a close, Americans started to replace their bell-bottom jeans with Members Only jackets and to
rip up their shag carpeting. The Baby Boomers were finally
coming of age. They started to work at more senior levels at
companies and in government. The coddled Boomers, the ones
who didn't have to suffer much, the ones who grew up in a society that could afford for them to put themselves first, were now
starting to take positions in which they could affect political,
business and economic theory en masse. It's worth noting that
it was when the Boomers arrived that relationships in Congress
really started to suffer. Until the early 1990s, members of the
opposing parties, while still prone to the same theatrics they are
today, were able to sit down together with the goal of reaching a
compromise. They may not have agreed, but they tried. And for
the most part they behaved with civility. Their children went to
school together, and their families knew each other. They even
socialized on weekends. And as a result, Congress functioned.

The Boomer generation would emerge bigger and more powerful than any opposing force that could help keep things in check.
Without a balancing tension, the impulses and desires of one
group would prove to be hard to restrain. Like the unchecked
power of America after the fall of the Soviet Union, like the dictator who overthrows his predecessor, like legislation passed
when one party has a supermajority in Congress, the Boomers

would start to impose their will on the world around them, surrounded only by outnumbered voices telling them they couldn't. By the 1980s and 1990s, this "shockwave," this "pig in the python," as the Baby Boom is sometimes described because of its sheer size and force, this demographic bulge able to remodel society as they passed through it, was fully in charge.

CHAPTER 12

The Boomers All Grown Up

The 1980s were now upon us and we were no longer a country trying to figure out how to rally a population and win a war; we were now trying to figure out how to capitalize on the amazing boom years in which we were living—the Roaring Eighties.

During this period, new economic theories were being proposed to protect the wealth the Boomers were accumulating—a classic symptom of excess. Where the radio, automobile and electric refrigerator were the "must have" items of the 1920s, another new technology became all the rage in the 1980s. The IBM PC, MS-DOS, Apple's Macintosh and Microsoft Windows all contributed to the rise and spread of the personal computer. "A PC on every desk," as Bill Gates, the young founder of Microsoft, envisioned. We no longer needed to go to work to have power—we could have power alone at home too. The individual could compete against the corporation. Even the new technologies of the day supported the desire for more individualism.

We were also becoming more and more comfortable with products having shorter lifespans. Other inventions of the 1980s included the disposable camera and disposable contact lenses. Disposability, another symptom of our excess, was now an industry to be pioneered. We were actually looking for more things we could throw out. And there was one other thing we started to view as disposable: people.

The Day We Embraced Layoffs

AUGUST 5, 1981. That's the date it became official.

It's rare that we can point to an exact date when a business theory or idea becomes an accepted practice. But in the case of mass layoffs, we can. August 5, 1981, was the day President Ronald Reagan fired more than 11,000 air traffic controllers.

Demanding more pay and a shorter workweek, PATCO, the air traffic controllers' union at the time, was embroiled in a vicious labor dispute with the Federal Aviation Administration. When the talks broke down, PATCO threatened to go on strike, ostensibly shutting down airports and causing the cancellation of thousands of flights during one of the busiest travel periods of the year.

Such a strike is illegal, according to the sometimes controversial Taft-Hartley Act of 1947. The act essentially prohibits any labor strike to cause unfair harm to those not involved in the dispute or to do any damage to any commerce that would negatively affect the general welfare. This is the reason police and emergency room nurses are forbidden to strike. The damage such a strike would cause is believed to outweigh any grievances over unfair pay or hours.

Without an acceptable deal and, worse, without the ability to find common ground, on August 3, PATCO's members refused to go to work. Given the strike's impact on the country, President Reagan got personally involved, ordering the air traffic controllers back to work. Meanwhile, contingency plans were put into place, with supervisors (who were not members of the union), a small group of controllers who had chosen not to strike and military air traffic controllers enlisted to cover the losses. Though not a perfect solution, these temporary workers were able to keep the majority of flights going. The effect of the strikes was not as severe as expected, and so, on August 5, 1981, President Reagan fired 11,359 air traffic controllers, nearly every controller working for the FAA at the time. And it didn't stop there.

Reagan banned every one of the strikers from ever working for the FAA again for the rest of their lives, a ban that remained in effect until President Clinton lifted it in 1993. Many of the air traffic controllers who were fired that day were war veterans (which is where they learned the trade) or civil servants who had worked hard to earn their middle-class incomes. Because of the ban and the fact that their skills were hardly transferable to other industries (there's not a huge demand for air traffic controllers outside of the FAA), many of them found themselves in poverty.

This is not a story about whether Reagan should or should not have fired the air traffic controllers. This is not a story about labor disputes and the right of unions to stand up to management. This is a story of something quite diabolical. This is a story about the long-term repercussions when a leader sets a new tone about what is acceptable or unacceptable behavior inside an organization.

In an attempt to alleviate one short-term strain on our country, President Reagan inadvertently created a new, longer-lasting one. By firing all the air traffic controllers, he sent a message to business leaders across the nation. He unwittingly blessed the swift and even aggressive decision to use mass layoffs to guard against a short-term economic disruption. Though I am certain Reagan never intended it as such, some eager CEOs interpreted his actions as permission for them to do the same. There was now a precedent for protecting commerce before protecting people. And so, for the first time ever, the social conventions that had restrained many a CEO from doing something that many may have wished they could in the past were instantly gone.

With the tacit approval from on high, the practice of laying off people in mass numbers to balance the books started to happen with greater frequency. Layoffs had existed before the eighties, but usually as a last resort and not an early option. We were now entering a time in which even meritocracy mattered less. How hard someone worked or how much they sacrificed or contributed to the company no longer necessarily translated into job stability. Now anyone could be laid off simply to help balance the books for that year. Careers ended to make the numbers work. Protecting the money, as economic theory, replaced protecting the people. Under such conditions, how can we ever feel safe at work? How can we ever feel committed to the jobs we have if the leaders of our companies aren't committed to us?

The very concept of putting a number or a resource before a person flies directly in the face of the protection our anthropology says leaders are supposed to offer. It's like parents putting the care of their car before the care of their child. It can rip apart the very fabric of the family. Such a redefining of the modern leader wreaks the same havoc on relationships in our companies (or even our society) as it does in our families.

Starting in earnest in the 1980s, public institutions and industries succumbed to this new economic perspective. The consumer products industry, the food industry, the media, banking, Wall Street, even the Congress of the United States have all, to varying degrees, abandoned the people they exist to serve in favor of more selfish priorities. Those in positions of authority and responsibility more readily allow outside constituents—sometimes unengaged constituents—to influence their decisions and actions. By agreeing to offer a supply to meet the demands of outsiders, these leaders who act like followers may make the profit they expect, while harming the people they claim to be serving. Long-term thinking gives way to short-term thinking and selfish replaces selfless, sometimes even in the name of service. But it's service in name only.

This new leadership priority rattles the very foundation upon which trust and cooperation are built. This has nothing to do with restricting a free market economy. This has to do with forgetting that people—living, breathing people, those who will play a greater role in our ability to innovate, make progress and beat our competition—are now no longer viewed as our most valuable asset as we aim to compete with the numbers. If anything, prioritizing performance over people undermines the free market economy.

The better the products, services and experiences a company is able to offer its customers, the more it can drive demand for those products, services and experiences. And there is no better way to compete in a market economy than by creating more demand and having greater control over the supply—which all boils down to the will of those who work for us. Better products, services and experiences are usually the result of the employees who invented, innovated or supplied them. As soon as people are put second on the priority list, differentiation gives way to commoditization. And when that happens, innovation declines and the pressure to compete on things like price, and other short-term strategies, goes up.

In fact, the more financial analysts who cover a company, the less innovative the company. According to a 2013 study that appeared in the *Journal of Financial Economics*, companies covered by a larger number of analysts file fewer patents than companies covered by fewer analysts. And the patents those companies do generate tend to have lower impact. The evidence supports the idea that "analysts exert too much pressure on managers to meet short-term goals, impeding firms' investment in long-term innovative projects." Put simply, the more pressure the leaders of a public company feel to meet the expectations of an outside constituency, the more likely they are to reduce their capacity for better products and services.

When Leaders Eat First

SINCE THE BOOMERS took over the running of business and government, we have experienced three significant stock market crashes. One in 1987 that corrected for a period of excessive

speculation and, some argue, an overreliance on computer programs to make trades instead of people. One in 2000, after the
burst of the dot-com bubble. And one in 2008 that followed the
collapse of the overvalued housing market. Before 1987, there
hadn't been a stock market crash since the Great Depression,
which itself followed the excess and overvaluations of the 1920s.
If we do not find ways to correct the imbalance ourselves, the
laws of nature will always balance it for us.

. . . .

*Too many of the environments in which we work
today frustrate our natural inclinations to trust and
cooperate.*

. . . .

For a species born in a time when resources were limited and
dangers were great, our natural inclination to share and cooperate is complicated when resources are plenty and outside dangers are few. When we have less, we tend to be more open to
sharing what we have. A Bedouin tribe or nomadic Mongolian
family doesn't have much, yet they are happy to share because it
is in their interest to do so. If you happen upon them in your
travels, they will open up their homes and give you their food
and hospitality. It's not just because they are nice people; it's because their survival depends on sharing, for they know that
they may be the travelers in need of food and shelter another
day. Ironically, the more we have, the bigger our fences, the
more sophisticated our security to keep people away and the
less we want to share. Our desire for more, combined with our
reduced physical interaction with the "common folk," starts to
create a disconnection or blindness to reality.
Unfortunately, too many of the environments in which we

work today do more to frustrate than to foster our natural inclinations to trust and cooperate. A new set of values and norms has been established for our businesses and our society—a system of dopamine-driven performance that rewards us for individual achievement at the expense of the balancing effects of serotonin and oxytocin that reward us for working together and building bonds of trust and loyalty. It is this imbalance that causes stock markets to crash. It is this imbalance in corporate cultures that affects the stability of large organizations. (Enron, Tyco, WorldCom and Lehman Brothers are just a few examples of large, "stable" organizations that collapsed because of imbalances in their cultures.) The seeming lack of effort to want to change this system only creates greater imbalance of the chemicals. And so the vicious cycle continues. Our health is at risk. Our economy is at risk. The stability of our companies is at risk. And who knows what else.

The big Boomer generation has, by accident, created a world quite out of balance. And imbalance, as history has proven over and over, will self-correct suddenly and aggressively unless we are smart enough to correct it ourselves slowly and methodically. Given our inclination for instant gratification and the weak Circles of Safety in our organizations, however, our leaders may not have the confidence or patience to do what needs to be done.

Obviously, we can't simply blame an entire generation for the ills we face today. Nor can we blame an industry, any particular CEO or "the corporations." There aren't comic book–style archenemies running companies, trying to take over the world, who we can simply set our sights on overthrowing to right all that is wrong. But there is a lack of empathy and humanity in the way we do business today. There are smart executives running companies and managing systems, but there seems to be a distinct lack of strong leaders to lead the people.

As Bob Chapman, CEO of Barry-Wehmiller, is fond of saying, "No one wakes up in the morning to go to work with the hope that someone will manage us. We wake up in the morning and go to work with the hope that someone will lead us." The problem is, for us to be led, there must be leaders we want to follow.

Dehumanization

OUR INTERNAL WIRING, though complicated and messy in practice, is pretty straightforward in intention. Designed during a time when we lived in small groups with limited resources and great dangers around us, our chemical incentive system was built to help us manage and thrive in what was a very tangible world. We knew all the people with whom we lived and worked. We saw the things we needed and we worked together to get them. We saw the things that threatened us and we worked together to protect each other from them.

The problem now is that we have produced an abundance of nearly everything we need or want. And we don't do well with abundance. It can short-circuit our systems and actually do damage to us and to our organizations. Abundance can be destructive not because it is bad for us, per se. Abundance can be destructive because it abstracts the value of things. The more we have, the less we seem to value what we've got. And if the abstraction of stuff makes us value it less, imagine what it does to our relationships.

The scale at which we are able to operate today is sometimes too big for us to wrap our heads around. By its very nature, scale creates distance, and at distance, human concepts start losing their meaning. A consumer is just that: an abstraction of a person who we hope will consume whatever we have to offer. We try to guess what this "consumer" wants so that they will consume more of what we have. And if they do, we will keep track of lots of metrics so that we may better manage the process. And as our processes, metrics and scale continue to grow, we employ technology to help us operate at greater speed and scale. In other words, the human beings, the end users of all this, become so far removed from the people who mean to serve them that they simply become just another metric to be managed. The more distance there is between or the more things we do that amplify the abstraction, the harder it becomes to see each other as human. It is not the abundance we need to manage or restrict, it is the abstraction.

We no longer see each other as people; we are now customers, shareholders, employees, avatars, online profiles, screen names, e-mail addresses and expenses to be tracked. The human being really has gone virtual. Now more than ever, we are trying to work and live, be productive and happy, in a world in which we are strangers to those around us. The problem is, abstraction can be more than bad for our economy . . . it can be quite deadly.

[THE ABSTRACT CHALLENGE]

CHAPTER 13

Abstraction Kills

"Let me out of here!" he shouted. "Let me out! Let me out!" Kept in a small room with no windows, he started banging on the wall to get the attention of the others. "You have no right to hold me here!" he screamed.

The man enlisted to help that day sat at the control console. He started to get nervous. He could hear the muffled pleas from the other room. He looked up at the man in charge, and, as if stating something not already terribly obvious, said, "He's in pain."

But the man in charge showed no emotion. Nothing. He said only one thing: "The experiment requires that you continue." And so the man enlisted to help that day turned back to the control panel, muttering to himself, "It's got to go on. It's got to go on." He flipped the switch and administered another electric shock to the stranger in the other room.

"You have no right to hold me here!" shouted the man in the other room again. But no one answered him and the experiment continued. "Let me out!" he continued to scream hysterically. "My heart's bothering me! Let me out!" Then suddenly, the screaming stopped and the experiment was over.

As World War II was moving toward its conclusion, the main architects of the Nazi movement—Adolf Hitler, Heinrich Himmler and Joseph Goebbels—managed to escape capture by committing suicide. Others were not able to avoid justice. They were rounded up and put on trial for their roles in the systematic genocide committed during the war. Crimes against humanity was one of the charges levied against the twenty-four most senior Nazis captured, most of whom were found guilty for their respective roles. But there was one man who was conspicuously absent during the Nuremberg Trials.

Nazi SS-Obersturmbannführer, or lieutenant colonel, Adolf Eichmann played a significant role in the organizing of the Holocaust. He was responsible for managing the logistics of rounding up and deporting mass numbers of Jews and other unwanted groups to the ghettos and concentration camps across Eastern Europe. He was the one who oversaw the process that sent innocent men, women and children, young and old, to the death camps. But after the war, using falsified papers, he was able to escape Germany and make his way to Argentina. For fifteen years Eichmann lived a relatively normal, suburban life under the name Ricardo Klement until he was captured by Israeli agents in 1960 and brought back to face trial in Jerusalem.

Eichmann's capture reignited debate over how the Holocaust could have happened in the first place. It wasn't possible for just a few warped minds to have effectively committed genocide on such a remarkable scale. That amount of planning and organization and logistics required the help of thousands if not millions of people. It required the involvement of all levels of soldiers perpetrating the actual crimes and millions of ordinary Germans willfully turning a blind eye.

Some believed that there was a collective intent, that an entire population had abandoned all humanity and morality. Others saw it differently. The common defense that many Nazis and Germans offered after the war was less dramatic. "We had no choice," they said, "we were just following orders." That was the mantra. Whether they were senior officials held accountable for their roles, or ordinary soldiers and civilians who tried to rebuild a sense of normalcy after the upheaval of the war, they were able to rationalize their actions, avoiding personal responsibility by holding their superiors accountable. This is what they would tell their grandchildren. "We were just following orders."

Stanley Milgram, a Yale psychologist, wanted to understand more. Were we humans such lemmings that if someone who outranked us, someone in a position of authority, ordered us to do something entirely counter to our moral code, our sense of right and wrong, we would simply obey? Sure it's possible on a small scale, but on such a mass scale?

So in 1961, just a few months after Adolf Eichmann's trial began in Israel, Milgram designed an experiment to understand our obedience to authority. The experiment was relatively simple. In each enactment, there were two volunteers. One would play the role of the teacher and the other would play the role of the student. The person who played the student was actually another scientist involved in the experiment. (To assign the roles, the real volunteer was asked to pick a piece of paper out of a hat that indicated if they would be the teacher or the student. In fact, both folded pieces of paper said "teacher" on them, giving the illusion to the volunteer that their role was picked by chance.)

The volunteers who played the role of the teachers, recruited from a newspaper ad and told they were taking part in an investigation into memory and learning, sat at a console with a series of switches. Each one was told that a series of questions would be asked of the student. If the student got the wrong answer or refused to answer the question, the teacher was to flip a switch on the console to administer an electric shock to the student. In fact, the only electric shocks administered during the entire experiment were mild, 15-volt shocks given to the teachers just so they could have a sense of what it felt like.

There were thirty switches on the console, labeled from 15 volts to 450 volts. With each switch labeled in 15-volt increments, it was made very clear to the teacher that with each switch the shocks would get increasingly more severe. To make sure that the teacher understood the implications of the increasing severity of the shocks, there were also labels placed above certain ranges. The voltage range of 15 to 75, for example, was labeled "Slight Shock." Written above the 75-to-120-volt range of switches was "Moderate Shock." The 135-to-180-volt range was labeled "Strong Shock." "Very Strong Shock," "Intense Shock" and "Extreme Intensity Shock" covered the next few ranges until the voltages reached "Danger: Severe Shock" above the 375-to-420-volt switches. The final range, 435 to 450 volts, was painted red and marked simply "XXX." There was no confusion as to what the switches meant.

The 160 volunteers were put through the experiment with four variations, 40 volunteers for each setup. In one variation, the scientist playing the student sat right next to the teacher and the teacher had to physically place the student's hand onto a shock plate. In another variation, the student was in the room with the teacher. The teacher could see and hear the student's reactions after each shock was administered. There was no uncertainty about the impact of each successive decision to flip a switch.

In another variation, the student was kept in a separate room. Though the teacher was unable to see the effects of the shocks, they could clearly hear the student's protests and screams through the walls. In all of these variations, the teacher could hear the scientist playing the role of the student pretending to express discomfort at first and then shouting and pleading for the experiment to end as it progressed. "Stop!" they would scream. "This hurts!" In yet one more variation, however, the student was kept in another room, and but for thumping on the walls, the teacher could neither see nor hear the student's reactions to the shocks.

As expected, all the volunteers expressed concern. As they realized or believed they were causing pain to the student, they would look up to the scientist, standing next to them in a white lab coat with clipboard in hand, and ask if they should continue despite the pain they were knowingly inflicting. The first time the volunteer expressed a desire to stop the experiment or no longer be a part of it, the scientist would say, "Please continue." If the volunteer expressed a desire to stop a second time, the scientist would always say, "The experiment requires that you continue."

As they went further and further down the line of switches, some of the volunteers started to get nervous. Very nervous. They started sweating and shaking. Although extremely uncomfortable, most went on with the experiment. Upon the third request to halt the experiment, the scientist replied coldly, "It is absolutely essential that you continue." After a fourth protest, the scientist responded simply, "You have no other choice, you must go on." If any other protests were expressed, the experiment would immediately end.

How far do you think you would go? How much pain could you cause someone before you would stop? Most of us would say we would not go very far and that we would have quit long before we believed we had caused any serious harm to someone. And the scientists expected the same thing. Before the experiment, they predicted that 2 percent to 3 percent would go all the way, and those people would exhibit psychopathic tendencies. But the actual results were horrifying.

When the volunteers had to physically place the student's hand on the shock plate, 70 percent quit the experiment without going very far. When the volunteers were in the same room but didn't have to physically touch the student, the number went down slightly, with 60 percent refusing to continue. But when they could neither see the students in pain nor hear their cries, only 35 percent refused to continue. That means 65 percent of the volunteers were able to go through the entire experiment, reach the final switch and, for all intents and purposes, kill someone.

The experiment has been criticized for being unethical, and for good reason. Nearly eighty people who woke up that morning with the belief they were good people went home that day with the knowledge they could kill someone. Though they expressed concern, though they were nervous, though they had a sense that what they were doing could have a negative impact, even a seriously negative impact, the majority still went all the way.

Upon the conclusion of the experiment, despite believing that the student may be hurt or worse, the volunteers expressed concern for their own culpability, insisting that they should not be held responsible. Not a single volunteer showed any concern for the student's well-being. None asked to look in the other room. They were more concerned with their own skins.

Eventually, the volunteers were debriefed and shown that the student, who was played by a scientist, was fine and unhurt. They were assured that no shocks were given and that no pain was caused at any time. Some of those who obeyed, who went all the way, now felt remorse for what they had done. They had a sense of personal responsibility. Others who went all the way, in contrast, justified their actions by blaming the scientists. If there were any repercussions, they reasoned, it would be the guys in charge, not them, who would be held responsible. After all, they were just doing as they were told. Some even went so far as to transfer blame to the student. "He was so stupid and stubborn," said one volunteer trying to come to terms with his actions, "he deserved to be shocked."

Interestingly, nearly all those volunteers who refused to continue to take part in the experiment once they realized they were causing pain to someone else felt accountable to a greater moral imperative. Some were religious but all of them felt they were accountable to a higher authority than the scientists in the room.

The reality is, Milgram's experiment is being carried out every single day in offices across the country and around the world. The cycle of abstraction endemic to our brand of capitalism is easily seen when we take a broader view of Milgram's conclusions. Abstraction is no longer restricted to physical space; it also includes the abstracting nature of numbers. The bigger our companies get, the more physical distance is created between us and the people who work for us or buy our products. At such scale, we can no longer just walk into the aisles and count the cans of soup on the shelf either. Now we rely on documents that report the numbers of what we've sold and how much we've made. When we divorce ourselves from humanity through numerical abstraction, we are, like Milgram's volunteers, capable of inhuman behavior. Just like the conditions Milgram set in his experiment, the physical separation between us and those on the receiving end of our decisions can have a dramatic impact on lives . . . the lives of people who cannot be seen or heard. The more abstract people become, the more capable we are of doing them harm.

CHAPTER 14

Modern Abstraction

Milgram's Findings Come to Life

IN 2009, THE *New York Times* and nearly every other major news outlet carried a story about an outbreak of salmonella that killed nine people and sickened more than seven hundred others. The outbreak triggered the biggest food recall in American history. The contamination was traced to products made by over three hundred companies using peanuts and peanut meal supplied by the Peanut Corporation of America (PCA) of Lynchburg, Virginia. Did the head of PCA do everything in his power to make sure the people who trusted him and his company were safe? Sadly, no.

FDA investigators concluded that PCA knowingly shipped tainted products (charges the company denies). And the extensive evidence that company executives put enormous pressure on employees to meet targets is hard to ignore. Stewart Parnell, the president of the Peanut Corporation of America, sent an e-mail to one of his plant managers complaining the positive salmonella tests were "costing us huge $$$$$, causing obviously a huge lapse in time from the time we pick up peanuts until the time we can invoice," according to court documents. (The company went out of business in 2009. Four years later, as this book was going to press, federal prosecutors filed criminal charges against Mr. Parnell and his team.) When our relationships with customers or employees become abstract concepts, we naturally pursue the most tangible thing we can see—the metrics. Leaders who put a premium on numbers over lives are, more often than not, physically separated from the people they serve.

Putting Mr. Parnell aside, what about all the people who worked in the company who did as they were told? In a weak culture, employees see their employer just as Milgram's subjects saw the scientist—as the final authority figure. A leader who presides over a weak culture does not invest in programs to build the confidence of their people so that they will do the right thing. Instead, command and control perpetuates a system in which people will more likely do the thing that's right for them. Uncertainty, silos and politics—all of which thrive in a command-and-control culture and work counter to the concept of a Circle of Safety—increase our stress and hurt our ability to form relationships to the point where self-preservation becomes our primary focus.

Anything that separates us from the impact our words and actions have on other people has the potential to lead us down a dangerous path. As Milgram showed us, when we cannot see the impact of our decisions, when the lives of people become an abstraction, 65 percent of us have the capacity to kill someone. When we are unable to see or hear the people we are hurting, fears of getting in trouble, losing our jobs, missing the numbers or disturbing our place in the pecking order become primary drivers of decisions. And just like the German soldiers who defended their actions by pleading they were "just following orders" or Milgram's subjects who muttered to themselves "the experiment must continue," we have our own modern mantras to defend ourselves or pass on accountability when our decisions harm others. We work to "provide shareholder value" or "fulfill our fiduciary duty," all the while defending our actions as "within the law" or claiming that the decisions made were above our pay grade.

During the time I was researching this book, I had an argument with an investment banker at a dinner I attended. With my new understanding in hand, I pressed and pressed him on his responsibility to the people who are impacted by his decisions. I was stunned how he parroted Milgram's volunteers. "I don't have the authority to make those kinds of decisions," he said to me. "It's not my job. My job is to find the best value for my clients," he defended. When we do not feel safe from each other in the environments in which we work, our instincts drive us to protect ourselves at all costs instead of sharing accountability for our actions.

In 2008, faced with the reality of what the banking industry did to the economy, some bankers went beyond simply blaming the mortgage companies. Just like Milgram's executioners trying to distance themselves from any role they played in the harm caused, even blaming the student, some bankers went so far as to blame the American homeowner for their troubles. Jamie Dimon, CEO of JPMorgan Chase, told his shareholders in 2010, "We're not evicting people who deserve to stay in their house."

The Responsibility of Business

"THERE IS ONE and only one social responsibility of business," said Milton Friedman in 1970, six years before winning the Nobel Prize in Economics, "to use its resources and engage in activities designed to increase its profits so long as it stays within the rules of the game." By the "rules" I believe Friedman was referring to the law, a well-intentioned yet imperfect set of guidelines filled with accidental or sometimes political loopholes designed by well-intentioned or sometimes political people.

Friedman's words seem to have become the standard for American capitalism today. Over and over, companies demonstrate a preference for adhering to the letter of the law in their aim to drive profit over any moral responsibility they may have to people they serve or the country or economy within which they operate. Translated to Milgram's experiment, too many leaders of companies prefer to obey the scientist instead of a higher moral authority. They can justify their actions as within the law while ignoring the intention of the laws they aim to uphold.

Apple Inc. managed to sidestep paying tens of billions of dollars in taxes by setting up subsidiaries in Ireland, where companies are taxed based on where they are incorporated (Apple is incorporated in the United States). The U.S. tax code, in contrast, calculates a company's tax liability based on where it makes or keeps its money (Apple was keeping all the money it made in Asia and Europe in Ireland). This distinction allowed Apple to fall between the cracks of the two countries' tax laws and, in so doing, between 2009 and 2012, it kept $74 billion out of the reach of the IRS, or any taxing authority for that matter. This is a fact Apple does not deny. As one of the great innovators of our day, the technique Apple pioneered of routing profits through Irish subsidiaries and the Netherlands then to the Caribbean to avoid American taxes has been copied by many other companies since. Yet Apple, according to Friedman's thinking, broke no rules.

We have an absolute need to form bonds of trust. Our survival depends on it. To that end, our primitive brain is constantly evaluating the words and behaviors of companies exactly the same way it evaluates the words and behaviors of individuals. On a biological level, trust is trust, regardless with whom it is formed. If someone says or does something that makes us feel that we couldn't trust them with our lives, then we keep our distance. Simply following the law means we should trust cheating boyfriends or girlfriends because they broke no laws of marriage. As social animals morality also matters. Our (or indeed a company's) sense of right or wrong, despite the letter of the law, matters on a social level. This is the very foundation of civil society.

Timothy Cook, Apple's CEO, raised the question of responsibility at a congressional hearing about the matter. "Unfortunately, the tax code has not kept up with the digital age," he said. Is it the governing authority's responsibility to close all loopholes or do companies bear some responsibility also? Is this an act of civil disobedience by Apple to force the government to do better? Apple is a good company that does good things, like giving to education, but because most people are unaware of those things, when they hear about Apple's tax avoidance, it can affect how we trust the company. But the problem is bigger than Apple. It seems to be the standard for doing business today—to exploit the loopholes until the rules catch up (and sometimes lobby against changing the rules). And if that's the case, then no one should have any problems with the decisions made by the Oceanic Steam Navigation Company.

Within the Law

THE LARGEST SHIPS in the period before the turn of the twentieth century were predominantly ferries. They moved huge numbers of people from one place to another within close proximity to the shore. Logically, the regulations that outlined the responsibilities of the ship owners were based on how ships were used at that time—as ferries. By the time the *Titanic* set sail in 1912, however, the regulations had not yet been updated to reflect this new breed of oceangoing vessel (the equivalent to Timothy Cook's "digital age"). The *Titanic* carried as many lifeboats as was required by the law, which was sixteen. The problem was, the *Titanic* was four times larger than the largest legal classification of ships of the day.

The Oceanic Steam Navigation Company, the *Titanic*'s owner, adhered to the outdated regulation (in fact, they actually added four more inflatable rafts). Unfortunately, as we all know, on

April 14, 1912, just four days after leaving port on its maiden voyage, the *Titanic* struck an iceberg far from any shoreline. There were not enough lifeboats for everyone and more than 1,500 of the 2,224 passengers and crew on board died as a result. A ship four times bigger than the largest classification carried only a quarter of the lifeboats they actually needed. Not surprising, only a few more than a quarter of the passengers and crew survived that day.

The entire shipping industry was fully aware that the outdated regulation would soon be updated. In fact, additional space was added aboard the deck of the *Titanic* in expectation of a "lifeboats for all" requirement. But lifeboats were expensive. They require maintenance and could affect a ship's stability, so executives at the Oceanic Steam Navigation Company decided not to add the lifeboats until the regulation said they had to. Though there were not enough lifeboats for all the passengers on board the *Titanic,* the company was in full compliance with applicable rules.

The disturbing correlation between Apple's arguments against paying taxes and the decision of the *Titanic*'s owners not to add lifeboats doesn't stop there. Just as the shipping industry lobbied against the change in regulations in the early twentieth century, arguing that having so many lifeboats sitting visibly on the decks would hurt business because people would think their vessels were unsafe, Apple and others contend that paying their actual tax liability would hurt their ability to compete. (Incidentally, this is the same argument that car manufacturers used in the 1950s as seat belt requirements were being considered. They feared that the existence of a seat belt would lead people to think their cars were unsafe.)

It may be worth noting that, as reported by the Congressional Budget Office, in 2011 American taxpayers contributed $1.1 trillion to the government whereas corporate taxes totaled just $181 billion. Though lives may not be at stake in this shell game many companies play, on a strictly biological level, such behavior makes it very hard for the rest of us to really trust them. Being a company of high moral standing is the same as being a person of high moral character—a standard not easily determined by the law but easily felt by anyone.

Given the scale at which so many companies now operate, it seems fair that the leaders of many large companies have no choice but to manage their businesses on spreadsheets and screens, often far removed from the people their decisions will ultimately impact. But if Milgram's numbers play out, it would mean that 650 of the leaders of Fortune 1000 companies, the largest companies in America, are able to make decisions without consideration for their impact on the lives of human beings.

This goes straight back to the conditions in which we, the human animal, operate best. If we are to reduce the damaging effects of abstraction on our decision making, based on Milgram's experiment, a sense of a higher authority—God, a noble cause, a compelling vision for the future or some other moral code and not a shareholder, customer or market demand—is essential. When our leaders give us something noble to be a part of, offer us a compelling purpose or reason why we should come to work, something that will outlive us, it seems to give us the power to do the right thing when called upon, even if we have to make sacrifices to our comfort in the short term. And when a leader embraces their responsibility to care for people instead of caring for numbers, then people will follow, solve problems and see to it that that leader's vision comes to life the right way, a stable way and not the expedient way.

It is not about good people or bad people. Like Milgram's volunteers, many of us work out of sight of the people our decisions affect. That means we are working at a significant disadvantage if we have any desire to do the right thing (which is different from doing what's legal). One cannot help but to recall Johnny Bravo who, above the clouds and unable to have a visual contact with the Special Operations Forces below, felt it necessary to fly down just so he could see those he was there to protect. When we opt to stay above the clouds, relying only on information fed to us instead of going down to see for ourselves, not only is it harder to make the right moral decisions, it makes it even harder to take responsibility when we fail to do so. The good news is, there are things we can do to help us manage the abstraction and keep our Circles strong.

CHAPTER 15

Managing the Abstraction

Numbers of People Aren't People,
They're Numbers

"THE DEATH OF one man is a tragedy," Joseph Stalin reportedly said. "The death of a million is a statistic." Stalin was a man who well understood statistics. As General Secretary of the Communist Party of the Soviet Union from 1922 to 1952, he is said to have been responsible for the deaths of millions of people, most of whom were Soviet citizens. Like so many dictator types, he had a cult of personality, operated with extreme brutality, trusted very few people and was very, very paranoid. But he was also absolutely right about how we perceive a tragedy that befalls one person over that of hundreds, thousands or even millions.

Here are two stories to show you what I mean. Both stories are completely true.

STORY 1

When I wrote this book, the country of Syria was being torn apart by what was basically a civil war. Inspired by the Arab Spring that

swept across the region, the Syrian people rose against the dictatorship of Bashar al-Assad, who took control of the country in 2000
when his father, Hafez al-Assad, died after twenty-nine years of
equally brutal rule. In over forty years of Assad rule, two generations of Syrian men and women have known nothing else. This is a
modern media world, however, and as much as the Syrian government tried to suppress news of uprisings in neighboring nations,
word of these rebellions made it through. But in stark contrast to
the peaceful uprising in Tunisia, the Syrian rebellion was met with
extreme and intense brutality by the Assad government.

World opinion did nothing to affect the Assad regime as it
continued to pound a disorganized and ill-equipped rebellion
with the full might of the army. United Nations estimates, at the
time of this book, were that over 100,000 Syrians were killed by
the Syrian military, including nearly 1,500 in a single chemical
attack. A good many of them innocent civilians.

STORY 2

An eighteen-year-old girl was lying in the middle of the street in San
Clemente, California. She had been hit by a car driven by a seventeen-
year-old girl. Unconscious with one of her legs broken and pointing
sideways at an unnatural angle, she was in bad shape. Cami Yoder,
an Army reservist, who happened to be driving past, pulled over to
see if she could help. Kneeling down beside the injured young
woman, Cami took her vitals. The girl wasn't breathing and her
pulse was faint, at best. Immediately, Cami began CPR and mouth-
to-mouth resuscitation to try to keep the young woman alive. Not
much later an ambulance arrived and the paramedics took over.
They stabilized the young woman and took her to the hospital.

A few days after the incident, Cami wondered how the girl was
faring. She was able to find the news story online and learned
what had happened. She had died. This young woman, her whole
life ahead of her, was gone.

Which story evoked a stronger feeling, the first one or the second one? A story about tens of thousands of people struck down by their own military as they stood up for something noble does not have the same emotional impact on us as the story of one person does. We mourn the death of one young woman with an empathy that we are seemingly unable to muster for thousands of young women and children and others struck down as senselessly and even more brutally.

This is one of the shortcomings of using numbers to represent people. At some point, the numbers lose their connection to the people and become just numbers, void of meaning. We are visually oriented animals. We can pursue things we can see. If it is a person in need, we can rush to their aid. If there is a clear vision of a future state brighter than our world today, we can work to build it. And if it is to advance a metric from one number to another, we can do that too. But when numbers are the only thing we can see, our ability to perceive the distant impact our decisions may have is frustrated.

It's one thing for big numbers to represent money or products. But when big numbers start representing human beings, as Stalin told us, our ability to empathize starts to falter. If your sister, the major breadwinner in her family, loses her job, it will have a significant impact on the lives of your niece and nephew. And that loss would be a deep emotional burden on your sister, her family and probably you too. But a decision made using a spreadsheet to lay off four thousand people at some large corporation loses tangibility and becomes something that just needs to be done to meet certain goals. The numbers no longer represent people who support their families but simply abstractions to be calculated.

Be it a politician or someone working in a company, perhaps the most valuable thing we can do if we are to truly serve our constituents is to know them personally. It would be impossible to know all of them, but to know the name and details of the life of someone we are trying to help with our product, service or policy makes a huge difference. The moment we are able to make tangible that which had previously been a study or a chart, the moment a statistic or a poll becomes a real living person, the moment abstract concepts are understood to have human consequences, is the moment our ability to solve problems and innovate becomes remarkable.

Rule 1. Keep It Real—
Bring People Together

AS IF THE abstracting qualities of numbers and scale aren't enough to deal with when trying to run an organization, these days we have the added complication of the virtual world. The Internet is nothing short of awe inspiring. It gives the power to operate at scale or spread ideas to anyone, be it a small business or a social movement. It gives us the ability to find and connect with people more easily. And it is incredible at speeding the pace of commercial transactions. All of these things are good. But, just as money was developed to help expedite and simplify transactions by allowing payment to be rendered without barter, we often use the Internet as a means to expedite and simplify communication and the relationships we build. And just as money can't buy love, the Internet can't buy deep, trusting relationships. What makes a statement like that somewhat tricky or controversial is that the relationships we form online feel real.

We can, indeed, get bursts of serotonin when people "like" our pictures, pages or posts or when we watch ourselves go up in a ranking (you know how much serotonin loves a ranking). The feelings of admiration we get from virtual "likes" or the number of followers we have is not like the feelings of admiration we get from our children, or that a coach gets from their players. It is simply a public display of "like" with no sacrifice required—a new kind of status symbol, if you will. Put simply, though the love may feel real, the relationship is still virtual. Relationships can certainly start online, but they only become real when we meet face-to-face.

Consider the impact that Facebook and other online communication tools have had on teen bullying. One quarter of all teenagers in the U.S. say they have experienced "cyberbullying." What we've learned is that abstractions can lead people to abhorrent behavior, to act like they're not accountable. An online community gives shy people a chance to be heard, but the flip side is it also allows some to act out in ways they probably never would in real life. People say horrible things to each other online, things they probably would never say in person. The ability to maintain distance, even complete anonymity, has made it easier to stop acting as humans should—with humanity. And despite the positive feelings we can have when meeting people online, unlike real friendships based on love and trust, the feelings we get don't last too long after we've logged off and they rarely if ever stand the test of time.

It seems to stir controversy when I talk about the fact that no matter how great social media is, it is not as effective for building strong bonds of trust as real human contact is. Social media fans will tell me about all the close friends they've made online. But if social media is the end-all-be-all, then why do over thirty thousand bloggers and podcasters descend on Las Vegas every year for a huge conference called BlogWorld? Why don't they meet online? Because nothing can replace face-to-face meetings for social animals like us. A live concert is better than the DVD and going to a ball game feels different from watching on TV, even though the view is better on television. We like to actually be around people who are like us. It makes us feel like we belong. It is also the reason a video conference can never replace a business trip. Trust is not formed through a screen, it is formed across a table. It takes a handshake to bind humans . . . and no technology yet can replace that. There is no such thing as virtual trust.

On the Web site for NMX (the official name for the Blog-World event), there's a promotional video in which people talk about what is so great about going to the event. "Sharing ideas" is a frequent advantage discussed. "Getting to meet so many different people," "bringing everyone together" and "meeting people who do what I do, who are on the same journey." These are also frequent themes. And of course, my personal favorite, said by someone who follows many of the bloggers who attend the conference, "I got to shake their hands and that was awesome!" Even bloggers have to appreciate the irony of bringing together the champions of the blogosphere to meet in person to share ideas about the supremacy of the blogosphere.

Real, live human interaction is how we feel a part of something, develop trust and have the capacity to feel for others. It is how we innovate. It is why telecommuters never really feel like they are a part of the team as strongly as the ones who go to work every day. No matter how many e-mails they send or receive, no matter how kept in the loop they are, they are missing all the social time, the gaps, the nuance . . . the humanity of being around other humans. But what do we do in hard times when we need good ideas most? We cut back on conferences and business trips because video conferencing and webinars are cheaper. Perhaps. But only in the short term. Given how relatively new social media is, the long-term impact of all this dehumanizing is still yet to be fully realized. Just as we are feeling the impact today of the policies and practices implemented in the 1980s and 1990s that prioritized profit over people, we will have to wait a generation before we feel the full effects of our modern bias to replace real interaction with virtual ones.

Rule 2. Keep It Manageable— Obey Dunbar's Number

IN 1958, BILL Gore quit his job at DuPont to pursue his belief in the possibilities of the polymer polytetrafluoroethylene, or PTFE, commonly known as Teflon. That same year, he and his wife, Vieve, started W. L. Gore & Associates in their basement. It was a friendly place, and everyone knew everyone else. But the discovery of a new polymer—expanded polytetrafluoroethylene (ePTFE)—by their son Bob changed the course of Bill and Vieve's company forever. ePTFE, or GORE-TEX, as it's more commonly known, had nearly infinite applications in medical, fabric and industrial markets. It was only a matter of time before the humble, family-oriented company outgrew its basement headquarters and moved into a factory. Business was booming and as demand grew, so did the factory and the number of people in its employ.

As the story goes, one day Bill Gore walked out onto the floor of his factory and realized he didn't recognize many of the people. Things had gotten so big that he simply did not know who was working for him anymore. Something told him that this couldn't be good for him, his employees or the company. After doing some counting, Gore concluded that to maintain the sense of camaraderie and teamwork he felt was essential for the factory to run smoothly, it should have only about 150 people. That was the magic number.

Instead of trying to eke out more efficiencies by increasing the size of the existing factory, Gore would simply build an entirely new factory, sometimes right next door to an old one. Each factory was capped at 150 people. It turned out, Bill Gore was onto something. Business continued to boom under this model and, as important, the relationships among the employees stayed strong and cooperative. Today the still privately held company has sales of $3.2 billion per year and employs more than 10,000 people around the world, and it still attempts to organize its plants and offices into working groups of about 150 people.

Though Bill Gore was trusting his gut based on his own observations, it's no coincidence that he arrived at the 150-person limit. Robin Dunbar, British anthropologist and a professor in the Department of Experimental Psychology at Oxford University, arrived at this same conclusion. Professor Dunbar figured out that people simply cannot maintain more than about 150 close relationships. "Putting it another way," he likes to say, "it's the number of people you would not feel embarrassed about joining uninvited for a drink if you happened to bump into them in a bar."

The earliest groups of *Homo sapiens* lived in hunter/gatherer tribes that maxed out between 100 and 150 people. Amish and Hutterite communities are about 150 in size. The Bushmen of South Africa and Native Americans also live in groups that cap out at about 150. Even the size of a company of Marines is about 150 people. That magical number is the number of close relationships we are naturally designed to manage. Any more than that starts to cause a breakdown if rigid social systems, or effective hierarchy and bureaucracy, are not implemented to help manage the scale. This is the reason senior leaders must trust midlevel leaders, because no one person can effectively manage large numbers of people if there is to be a strong sense of trust and cooperation.

The reasons groups function best when they do not get bigger than about 150 people make perfect sense when you look closely. The first reason is time. Time is a constant—there are only twenty-four hours in a day. If we gave only two minutes to everyone we knew, we wouldn't get to know people very well and deep bonds of trust would likely never form. The other is brain capacity. We simply can't remember everyone. Which is why Dunbar's Number is about 150; some can remember more and some remember fewer. In addition, as Dunbar has noticed in his research, when groups get bigger than about 150, the people are less likely to work hard and less likely to help each other out. This is a pretty significant finding as so many businesses work to manage their growth by focusing on cost efficiencies but ignore the efficiencies of human relationships. And ultimately, it is the strength of those human relationships that will help an organization manage at scale.

Many people thought that with the introduction of the Internet Dunbar's Number would be rendered obsolete. The ability to communicate with large numbers of people would become more efficient, giving us the capacity to maintain more relationships. It turns out not to be the case. Our anthropology wins again. Even though you may have eight hundred friends on Facebook, odds are high that you do not personally know them all and they may not all personally know you. If you were to sit down and try to contact all of them directly, as the journalist Rick Lax wrote about on wired.com, you would learn very quickly that Dunbar's Number wins. Lax was surprised how few of his two thousand "friends" he actually knew or who actually knew him.

In small organizations, where we are able to know everyone, it is much easier for us to do the work necessary to look after them. We are, for all the obvious reasons, more likely to look after people we personally know than those we don't. If a person on a factory floor knows who the accountant is and the accountant knows who the machinists are, they are more likely to help each other.

When a leader is able to personally know everyone in the group, the responsibility for their care becomes personal. The leader starts to see those for whom they are responsible as if they were their own family. Likewise, those in the group start to express ownership of their leader. In a Marine platoon of about forty people, for example, they will often refer to the officer as "our" lieutenant. Whereas the more distant and less seen senior officer is simply "the" colonel. When this sense of mutual ownership between leader and those being led starts to break down,

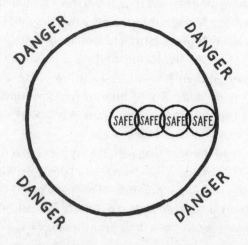

when informality is replaced by formality, it is a sure sign the group may be getting too big to lead effectively.

This means, for larger organizations, the only way to manage the scale and keep the Circle of Safety strong is to rely on hierarchies. A CEO can "care" about their people in the abstract, but not until that abstraction is mitigated can the care be real. The only way to truly manage at scale is to empower the levels of management. They can no longer be seen as managers who handle or control people. Instead, managers must become leaders in their own right, which means they must take responsibility for the care and protection of those in their charge, confident that their leaders will take care of them.

Professor Dunbar learned that in bigger companies, ones with many hundreds or thousands of employees who are not distributed into groups of fewer than 150, employees tend to have more friends outside of their jobs than inside. The larger the group of people we work with, the less likely we are to develop any kind of trusting relationships with them.

I had the opportunity to take a tour of the old offices of a large social media company in Northern California. (I can't say which one it was because the company requires that every visitor sign a restrictive nondisclosure agreement before they let them in the building.) The office was a large, loft-style open space with rows of people working together. The goal of the open space was to encourage open communication and a cross-pollination of ideas. The manager giving the tour made a comment that I found interesting, given Dunbar's own findings.

This company grew in part because of a culture of amazing cooperation, sharing and open communication, he told me. The company believed it was because of the open-plan layout. And so, as the company grew, they kept that same layout—the one that I was being shown. But for reasons they couldn't quite explain, cooperation and open communication did not improve as the company grew. In fact, as my tour guide admitted, it got worse. Dunbar wins again.

Rule 3. Meet the People You Help

IN 2010, ADAM Grant, a management professor at the Wharton School of Business at the University of Pennsylvania and author of *Give and Take: A Revolutionary Approach to Success,* set out to study the effectiveness of his college's fund-raising department and to understand what worked and what didn't. The job was straightforward: employees called on alumni and tried to persuade them to donate money to a scholarship fund for exceptional students whose families couldn't afford to pay for college. The fund-raisers were instructed to describe the university's dire financial position and the impressive accomplishments of the prospective recipients. The alumni would hear about the university's need to increase its investment in computer science, say, or business administration, to help create the next generation of leaders. This was, after all, the future workforce of the new economy, the callers would tell them. By all accounts, the pitch was pretty inspiring.

Yet as hard as they would try, fund-raisers were having only moderate success. Their numbers didn't improve even with an arsenal of research about the sting of the recession on university budgets. Furthermore, the job had all the characteristics of any mundane work—repetitive tasks, long hours sitting still and occasionally rude customers. Needless to say, turnover in the fund-raising department was extraordinarily high, leading to even worse morale. So Grant came up with an idea to improve the effectiveness of the fund-raisers . . . and it took only five minutes.

Professor Grant arranged for students who received the scholarships to come to the office and spend five minutes describing to fund-raisers how the scholarship they received changed their lives. The students told them how much they appreciated the hard work of the fund-raising department. Even though the people impacted by the work of the fund-raisers were only there for a short time, the results were astounding. In the following month, the fund-raisers increased their average weekly revenue by more than 400 percent. In a separate similar study, callers showed an average increase of 142 percent in the amount of time they spent on the phone and a 171 percent increase in the amount of funds they raised.

As social animals, it is imperative for us to see the actual, tangible impact of our time and effort for our work to have meaning and for us to be motivated to do it even better. The logic seems to follow Milgram's findings, except in this case, it's positive. When we are able to physically see the positive impact of the decisions we make or the work we do, not only do we feel that our work was worth it, but it also inspires us to work harder and do more.

A control group that had not received a visit from a student showed no improvement in sales or time spent on the phone. A third group that simply listened to a manager describe how much a scholarship meant to a student also showed no increase in performance. In other words, our bosses telling us how important our work is, is nowhere near as powerful as us getting to see it ourselves.

The loan department of Wells Fargo Bank had a similar experience. When they invited a customer to come into the bank and describe how a loan had changed their life—how it allowed them to buy a house or pay off a debt—it had a dramatic effect on the motivation of bank employees to help more people do the same. They could see for themselves the impact their work was having in someone's life. This is a significant shift in how the employees perceived their jobs and it is foundational to having a sense of purpose in the work we do. Without necessarily being aware of it, many of the employees stopped coming to work to sell loans and started coming to work to help people. Further proof of how much the quality of our work improves when we can attach a human being to the results was seen in a study that found that simply showing radiologists a photograph of a patient led to a dramatic improvement in the accuracy of their diagnostic findings.

Adam Grant conducted another study on lifeguards at a community recreation center. One group of lifeguards was given reading material of testimonies from other lifeguards about how their work helped them advance their personal goals. A second group was given materials to read of firsthand accounts of lifeguards who had actually saved the lives of swimmers. Those who had read about lifeguards saving people's lives were far more motivated at work and devoted more time to helping swimmers than those who read about how the job could help them personally.

Many of us would say we're not surprised by these findings. After all, it seems rather obvious. Or does it? Grant surveyed several thousand executives to find out how important it was to them that they feel their work has value. The results: only 1 percent of the executives said managers should bother showing employees that their work makes a difference. If anything, many companies try to explain the value our work will have in our own lives, the benefits we will reap if we hit a goal, as opposed to the benefit that others will derive. But remember our biology: we are naturally cooperative animals that are biologically more inspired and motivated when we know we are helping others.

This is one of the reasons I love the organization charity: water. If you give them a donation (which you can do at charitywater .org), besides the fact that 100 percent of that donation goes to the cause they are championing, to bring clean drinking water to the 700 million people who don't have it, they will actually send you a photograph and GPS coordinates of the well your money paid for. Though going to Africa and meeting the people yourself is even better, it is quite powerful to see the actual result of the donation you give.

Most of us, unfortunately, never see the people whose lives our work touches. For the vast majority, the closest we come to "seeing" results is evaluating numbers on spreadsheets or reading about what "customers" like in a report. If the line on the graph goes up, we are told we've done well and we should feel proud of what we've accomplished. We are expected to feel something for the numbers and think about the people. Our want to invest more time and energy is, however, biologically tied to the opposite—to feel for the people and think about the numbers. It makes sense for social animals that our sense of purpose is always human.

Rule 4. Give Them Time, Not Just Money

LET'S SAY YOU'RE moving to a new house. To help you out, one of your friends pays for the moving company. A very generous offer worth $5,000. Another friend comes to your house and helps you pack the boxes, load the truck, travel with you to the new house, unload and unpack the boxes. Two weeks later, both friends need a favor from you on the same day. Which would you feel more inclined to help, the one who wrote a check or the one who committed time and energy?

Money is an abstraction of tangible resources or human effort. It is a promissory note for future goods or services. Unlike the time and effort that people spend on something, it is what money represents that gives it its value. And as an abstraction, it has no "real" value to our primitive brains, which judge the real value of food and shelter or the behavior of others against the level of protection or safety they can offer us. Someone who gives us a lot of money, as our brains would interpret their behavior, is not necessarily as valuable to our protection as someone willing to commit their time and energy to us.

Given our obsessive need to feel safe among those in our tribe—our communities and our companies—we inherently put a premium value on those who give us their time and energy. Whereas money has relative value ($100 to a college student is a lot, $100 to a millionaire is a little), time and effort have an absolute value. No matter how rich or poor someone is, or where or when they are born, we all have 24 hours in a day and 365 days in a year. If someone is willing to give us something of which they have a fixed and finite amount, a completely nonredeemable commodity, we perceive greater value. If we waste money, we can make more (especially in our society). But we've all had the experience of sitting in a meeting or watching a movie . . . or maybe even reading this book . . . and thinking to ourselves, "I will never get this time back." You can save time if you stop reading now, but I cannot give back the time you spent to get here. Sorry.

And it's not just time. The energy we give also matters. If a parent goes to watch their kid's soccer game but looks up from their mobile device only when there is cheering, they may have given their time, but they haven't given their energy. The kid will look over to see their parent's head down most of the game, busy texting or e-mailing the office or something. Regardless of the intentions of that parent, without giving their attention, the time is basically wasted for both parent and child. The same is true in our offices when we talk to someone while reading our e-mails or sit in a meeting with one eye on our phone. We may be hearing all that is said, but the person speaking will not feel we are listening, and an opportunity to build trust—or be seen as a leader who cares—is squandered.

Just as a parent can't buy the love of their children with gifts, a company can't buy the loyalty of their employees with salaries and bonuses. What produces loyalty, that irrational willingness to commit to the organization even when offered more money elsewhere, is the feeling that the leaders of the company would be willing, when it matters, to sacrifice their time and energy to help us. We will judge a boss who spends time after hours to help us as more valuable than a boss who simply gives us a bonus when we hit a target.

If a colleague told you that over the weekend they gave $500 to charity, what would you think of them? We'd think they were nice but we would probably wonder why they were telling us. Did they want a medal or something? If another colleague told us that over the weekend they volunteered their time to paint a school in the inner city, what would you think of them? "That's cool," we'd think to ourselves, "I should do more." Simply hearing about the time and energy someone gave to others can inspire us to want to do more for others too (remember your oxytocin).

Though we may get a shot of chemical feel-good from the money we give, it doesn't last long and it isn't likely to affect how others view us. Someone participating in a walk-a-thon finds it personally fulfilling and does more to raise their status than the one who simply donated to their effort. Giving time and energy actually does more to impact the impression others have of us than giving money. This is the reason a CEO with a bad reputation can't redeem themselves by writing checks to charity. That's not behavior that we would view as valuable to the tribe. It is also the reason we are more tolerant of the missteps or occasional bad decisions made by a CEO whom we believe to be genuinely committed to the protection of their people.

A leader of an organization can't simply pay their managers to look out for those in their report. A leader can, however, offer their time and energy to those in their care, and in turn those managers would be more willing to give their time and energy to their subordinates. Then their subordinates would, in turn, be more inclined to give time and energy to their direct reports. And, at the end of the chain, the people with outward-facing jobs are more likely to treat the customer better. It's just biology. The oxytocin and serotonin make us feel good when time and energy are given to us, which inspires us to give more of ourselves to others. Business is a human enterprise. It may even be why we call a business a "company"—because it is a collection of people in the company of other people. It's the company that matters.

Rule 5. Be Patient—
The Rule of Seven Days and Seven Years

I WENT ON a first date with a woman recently. It was an amazing first date. We spent nearly eight hours together. We went for brunch and strolled around the city. We went to a museum, then went for dinner. We talked and talked the whole time. We were both smiling, giggling, we even started holding hands a few hours in. As a result of that amazing first date, we've decided to get married. Needless to say, we are both very excited.

You flinched a bit when you read that last bit, didn't you? It's normal. When we hear stories like that, our immediate reaction is "that's crazy." But you weren't on my date with me. We're in love . . . I swear.

The fact is, we instinctively know that the strong bond of human trust cannot be formed after one date or even after one week. In contrast, if I told you I've been dating the same woman for seven years and we're not married yet, you might think, "What's wrong then?"

The strong positive feeling we may have after a great first date, or even a great job interview, is not love or trust. It's a predominantly dopamine-fueled feeling telling us that we think we've found what we're looking for. Because it feels good, we can sometimes mislabel it as something more stable than it is, even if both parties feel it. This helps us explain how that love-at-first-date may crumble soon after. It also helps us understand why someone we loved in an interview, a few months into the job, doesn't turn out to be a good fit for the organization. It's because we didn't actually spend enough time to get to know if we can, indeed, rely on the person. Jumping straight in, even if it "feels right," is nothing short of gambling. It may work out, but the odds are against you. It is just as bad if we stay too long without ever feeling like we belong. If we've been at a job for seven years and still don't feel it . . . well . . . maybe it's time to move on.

Our internal systems are trying to help us navigate the social world so that we can find people who may be more willing to give of themselves to help us and be a part of our Circle of Safety. It takes time to get to know someone and build the trust required to sustain a relationship, personal or professional.

Our world is one of impatience. A world of instant gratification. A world ruled by dopamine. Google can give us the answer we want now. We can buy online and get what we want now. We can send and receive information instantaneously. We don't have to wait a week to see our favorite show, we can watch it now. We have gotten used to getting what we want when we want it. This is all fine and good for movies or online shopping, but it's not very helpful when we are trying to form the bonds of trust that can withstand storms. That takes time, and there's no app that can speed that up.

I have no data to say exactly how long it takes to feel like we trust someone. I know it takes more than seven days and I know it takes fewer than seven years. I know it is quicker for some and slower for others. No one knows exactly how long it takes, but it takes patience.

CHAPTER 16

Imbalance

For an animal designed to live and work in conditions in which resources were relatively scarce, having too much of anything can create some inherent problems for the forces that influence our behavior. For 40,000 years, we lived in a predominantly subsistence economy. We rarely had significantly more than we needed. It was only about 10,000 years ago, when we first became farmers instead of hunters and gatherers, that we started to move into a surplus economy. Able to produce more than we needed, we could now grow our populations beyond about 150 people. We could trade our surplus with others. We could afford to waste more than was thought prudent in an earlier age. And we could afford to have standing armies and intellectual and ruling classes.

Whenever a group moves from subsistence to surplus, ruling classes, those with the greatest surplus, work hardest to mold society to meet their expectations. The question is, are they using their surplus to effect change that is good for society or for themselves? It should come as no surprise that the richest companies work so hard to lobby legislators to make (or eliminate) regulations to suit their interests. They have more resources to use, protect and further accumulate. And if not properly managed, the cultures of these organizations can fall out of balance.

"Destructive Abundance" is what I call the result of this imbalance. It is what happens when selfish pursuits are out of balance with selfless pursuits. When the levels of dopamine-incentivized behaviors overwhelm the social protections afforded by the other chemicals. When protecting the results is prioritized above protecting those who produce the results. Destructive Abundance happens when the players focus almost exclusively on the score and forget why they set out to play the game in the first place.

For all the organizations that have suffered from Destructive Abundance, there is a clear pattern that provides lessons for the rest of us. In nearly all those organizations, the cultures weren't managed properly. There was almost always a leader who didn't take their responsibility as a leader to heart. Once the Destructive forces of the Abundance really set in, integrity started to falter and cooperation gave way to politics until the people themselves became just another commodity to be managed, like the electricity bill.

Destructive Abundance almost always follows when challenge is replaced by temptation.

CHALLENGES
AND
TEMPTATION

[DESTRUCTIVE ABUNDANCE]

CHAPTER 17

Leadership Lesson 1:
So Goes the Culture,
So Goes the Company

A Culture Sacrificed

"LONG-TERM GREEDY." These were the words Gustave "Gus" Levy, the venerable senior partner at Goldman Sachs, would use to describe the way the company operated. The year was 1970, and Goldman was a "gentleman's" organization, one that believed in partnership and doing what was best for the client and the firm. Given their reputation these days, it sounds funny, but Goldman bankers were known as "billionaire Boy Scouts" for their seeming desire to always try to do the right thing for clients. "Long-term greedy" meant that sometimes it was worth taking a short-term hit to help a client because the loyalty and trust it produced would in time pay back in spades. And pay back it did.

Like so many organizations with a strong culture, Goldman Sachs grew while rivals struggled or failed. Starting in the 1970s and lasting until the early 1990s, it seemed Goldman could do no wrong. "Up until the 1990s, their reputation was very high," writes Suzanne McGee, a journalist and author of the book *Chasing Goldman Sachs.* "If an IPO was underwritten by Goldman Sachs, that was akin to *Good Housekeeping*'s seal of approval."

While we must be careful not to romanticize Goldman's culture (just as we must not romanticize the Greatest Generation), there is no question that it was considered the gold standard on Wall Street. And as with all strong cultures, it was hard to get in. By hard, I don't mean the academic standards—I mean something even more difficult. There was a time when even the most academically qualified candidates could not count on getting a position at Goldman. They had to be a good fit for the culture. They were expected to put the needs of the firm above their own. The partners had to sense that they could trust their people even more than their people could make them rich. The people, in turn, had to believe in long-term greed. It was because their culture was built on these high standards of character that Goldman did well in hard times. While other crews were busy trying to save themselves, sometimes even abandoning ship, Goldman's people came together to see their ship through rough waters.

But something happened. Starting in the 1990s, and certainly accelerating after the company went public in 1999, there's evidence that the partnership culture started to break down. The time was ripe for a new mentality to take hold at Goldman. "The regulations that had kept finance boring had all but disappeared by the time Goldman's IPO was issued," wrote Harvard Law professor Lawrence Lessig in a column for CNN.com. "Bold (and sometimes reckless) experiments ('financial innovations') created incredible opportunities for firms like Goldman to profit."

In this atmosphere, the quickly expanding firm began to embrace a new kind of trader, a decidedly more aggressive personality than the investment bankers who had previously occupied the firm's ranks. The standards by which new people were brought in now put academic pedigree and prior success before cultural fit.

The arrival of the new broker caused resentment among those who were proud of the company they had built and of the culture they devoted their lives to uphold and protect. And the company split into two distinct camps: the old Goldman and the new Goldman. One culture was built on loyalty and long-term greed, the other built on numbers and short-term targets. One was built on a balance of social chemicals, the other built on an imbalance that was tilted decidedly toward dopamine.

The more people Goldman let in who were driven to maximize their own wealth and status, sometimes at the expense of the firm or the client's long-term advantage, the more damage it did to the culture of the company, its overall reputation and ultimately the decisions the firm made.

William Cohan highlights this in his book *Money and Power: How Goldman Sachs Came to Rule the World*. "The first time Goldman had actual layoffs, as in fired people because the firm was having a bad year (as opposed to for individual performance reasons), was in the early 1990s, and it was highly traumatic," Cohan writes. Think about that. Goldman Sachs did not embrace the concept of layoffs until the 1990s. Something had clearly changed.

By 2010, with Goldman Sachs' role in the mortgage-backed securities crisis, coupled with the huge bonuses it gave out just months after receiving a government bailout, the company's tarnished reputation was at its lowest point. It was no longer the most trusted firm on Wall Street but rather a symbol of its excess and greed. Its CEO, Lloyd Blankfein, even issued an apology: "We participated in things that were clearly wrong and we have reasons to regret and apologize for," he said in November 2009. But it was too late (and halfhearted, many felt). No longer called Boy Scouts, the Goldman Sachs leaders were considered something closer to crooks. This story is not unique to Goldman Sachs. I use Goldman to illustrate what is happening in a good too many of our companies across all sorts of industries.

Every culture has its own history, traditions, languages and symbols. When we identify with a culture, we articulate our belonging to that group and align ourselves with a shared set of values and beliefs. We may define ourselves, in part, by the culture of our country of citizenship—for example, I am an American—or by the culture of an organization—such as, I am a Marine. This doesn't mean we think about our cultural identity on a daily basis. But when we are away from the group or if our tribe is threatened from the outside, it becomes more important. It can even become our primary focus. Remember how the country came together as one after the events of September 11?

In strong corporate cultures, employees will form similar attachments. They will identify with the company in a very personal way. The employees of WestJet, Canada's rebellious populist airline akin to America's Southwest Airlines, don't say they work for WestJet—that would make it a job. They call themselves WestJetters. It's an identity. When we don't have a sense of belonging, we wear a T-shirt stamped with the company logo to sleep in or while painting the house. When we have a sense of belonging, however, we wear the company schwag in public and with pride.

. . . .

In a weak culture, we veer away from doing "the right thing" in favor of doing "the thing that's right for me."

. . . .

When cultural standards shift from character, values or beliefs to performance, numbers and other impersonal dopamine-driven measurements, our behavior-driving chemicals fall out of balance and our will to trust and cooperate dilutes. Like adding water to a glass of milk, eventually the culture becomes so watered down it loses all that makes it good and healthy, and by then it only looks like or vaguely tastes like milk. We lose our sense of history, of responsibility to the past and of shared tradition. We care less about belonging. In this kind of weak culture, we veer away from doing "the right thing" in favor of doing "the thing that's right for me."

To work for Goldman Sachs used to mean something more. It wasn't just a description of a place of employment. For those who fit the culture, it said something about what kind of person they were. It told the outside world what they could expect from them. And it was largely positive. A person could take pride in the association. But the leaders of the company didn't protect what took so long to build.

As Goethe, the great nineteenth-century thinker, reportedly summed up, "You can easily judge the character of a man by how he treats those who can do nothing for him." If character describes how an individual thinks and acts, then the culture of an organization describes the character of a group of people and how they think and act as a collective. A company of strong character will have a culture that promotes treating all people well, not just the ones who pay them or earn them money in the moment. In a culture of strong character, the people inside the company will feel protected by their leaders and feel that their colleagues have their backs. In a culture of weak character, the people will feel that any protection they have comes primarily from their own ability to manage the politics, promote their own successes and watch their own backs (though some are lucky enough to have a colleague or two to help). Just as our character defines our value to our friends, so too does the culture of a company define its value to those who know it. Performance can go up and down; the strength of a culture is the only thing we can truly rely on.

It's always fascinating to pay attention to the words people choose when describing their relationship with their jobs. Words like "love" and "pride" are feelings associated with oxytocin and serotonin, respectively. Or in the case of Goldman

Sachs, the lack thereof. "I don't feel safe," a current employee at Goldman Sachs told me. "I could lose my job at any moment. Goldman has no heart," she said. That she would say the company has "no heart" is a recognition of the lack of empathy in the culture. And when empathy is lacking, aggression, fear and other destructive feelings and actions dominate.

A former Goldman employee who worked at the firm in the 2000s, well into the cultural transformation, described an atmosphere of ruthlessness, with managers pitting one team of advisers against another as they fought for a project or client. He described an environment with no trust, no mutual respect and, above all, no accountability when things went wrong. The environment was one of win at all costs, even if it meant squashing a coworker (not to mention a client). Not surprisingly, despite the status one got from working at Goldman (a status probably built from the venerable years before), the former employee and nearly all his colleagues left for other companies within two years. It was just too much for a human to put up with if they wanted to maintain their sanity and be happy, if not successful. But the leaders allowed this culture to continue.

On March 14, 2012, the *New York Times* carried an editorial by Greg Smith, then an executive director of Goldman Sachs, in which he announced his immediate resignation from the firm, where he had worked for twelve years. In it, he wrote about the firm's "toxic" culture:

> The culture was the secret sauce that made this place great and allowed us to earn our clients' trust for 143 years. It wasn't just about making money; this alone will not sustain a firm for so long. It had something to do with pride and belief in the organization. I am sad to say that I look around today and see virtually no trace of the culture that made me love working for this firm for many years. I no longer have the pride, or the belief. Leadership used to be about ideas, setting an example and doing the right thing. Today, if you make enough money for the firm (and

are not currently an ax murderer) you will be promoted into a position of influence. . . . When the history books are written about Goldman Sachs, they may reflect that the current chief executive officer, Lloyd C. Blankfein, and the president, Gary D. Cohn, lost hold of the firm's culture on their watch.

When we assess how we "feel" about our jobs, we are very often responding to the environments in which we work. It is not just about the work we are doing, per se. And when a culture changes from a place where people love to work into a place where they go to work simply to take something for themselves, the finger gets pointed at the people who run the company. People will respond to the environment in which they operate. It is the leaders who decide what kind of environment they want to build. Will they build an inner circle around those closest to them or will they extend the Circle of Safety to the outer edges of the organization?

The vast majority of people who work at Goldman Sachs, despite what some critics would like to believe, are neither bad nor evil. However, the environment their leaders have created for them to work in makes it possible for them to do bad or evil things. As humans, our behavior is significantly influenced by the environments in which we work . . . for better and for worse.

In November 2008, terrorists armed with automatic weapons attacked various sites in Mumbai, India, killing over 160 people. The Taj Mahal Palace Hotel was one of those sites. What makes the story of the Taj extraordinary, however, is that its employees risked their lives to save the guests.

There are stories of telephone operators who, after having made it out safely, ran back into the hotel to call guests to help them get out. There are other stories of kitchen staff who formed a human shield to protect guests as they tried to escape the carnage. Of the 31 people who died at the hotel that day, nearly half of them were staff members.

Rohit Deshpandé, a Harvard business professor who researched the events at the Taj, was told by senior management at the hotel that they couldn't explain why their people acted so bravely. But the reason is not elusive—it was the result of the culture those leaders had cultivated. One of the finest hotels in the world, the Taj insists that its people put the interests of their guests before those of the company; in fact, they are often rewarded for doing so.

Unlike the culture of Goldman Sachs these days, at the Taj grades and pedigree play less of a role in how they select their people. They've learned that graduates from second-tier business schools, for example, often treat others better than those from top-tier business schools . . . and so they prefer to hire from the second tier. Respect and empathy are valued over talent, skill or motivation for personal advancement. Once hired, the staff's inclinations are reinforced and encouraged, which in turn builds a strong culture in which people can be trusted to improvise rather than do things by the book. The Taj knows its people will "do the right thing," not the thing that's right for them. So goes the culture, so go the people.

I am always struck when a CEO of a large investment bank is shocked to learn that there was a "rogue trader" in their midst who, in pursuit of personal gains or glory, made decisions that caused damage to the rest of the company. What else should we expect from a culture that reinforces and rewards self-interested behavior? Under these conditions, a CEO is basically gambling that their people will "do the right thing." But it's not the people who set the course. It's the leadership.

Bad Cultures Breed Bad Leaders

KIM STEWART WAS just one of the many employees who suffered as a result of a toxic environment. She knew on her first day at Citigroup that there was something wrong with the culture. "I remember I came home and told my husband, 'I have to limit the number of smart things I say.'" The problem wasn't that she thought her boss or her colleagues were stupid, but rather that they felt threatened (a perfectly valid feeling to have in an organization with a weak Circle of Safety). There seemed to always be an air of suspicion and mistrust at the office.

Stewart recalls that when she first joined the investment banking division in 2007, she immediately set out to understand the way the company closed certain kinds of deals. She went to her boss and asked him to confirm her understanding of the process, which he did. So why was her first deal an embarrassing disaster? Stewart later found out that her boss, concerned that her success might threaten his own status, intentionally left out a key part of the deal-making process, ensuring she would bomb. It was as if he wanted her to fail in order to make his performance look better.

"At Citi," Stewart says, "the feeling was 'I don't want anybody to know as much as I do because then I am expendable.'" This is a behavior designed for nothing but self-preservation. It is a classic symptom of a cortisol-rich, unsafe culture where valuable information is hidden to advance or protect an individual or a small group of individuals even though sharing would benefit the others in the group and the organization as a whole. Everybody feared being one-upped by a colleague, Stewart recalls. Nobody felt safe. And not because the company needed to make cutbacks; it was simply the culture.

It would be another year before the company would suffer enormous financial losses, leading to its rescue by the federal government, in large part due to an atmosphere of hoarding information rather than sharing it. One cannot but wonder how the financial crisis would have turned out had more of the banks had healthier, chemically balanced cultures in which the people didn't feel threatened by each other.

Of course, cutbacks did come eventually. In November 2008, the company had one of the single largest rounds of layoffs on record in any industry in history. On one day, Citi issued 52,000 pink slips, amounting to about 20 percent of its workforce.

Stewart's department was cut by more than half, down from 190 to 95, and bonuses were slashed. Once the dust settled, you would think the leaders of the organization would have been humbled. But they weren't.

Instead, the atmosphere got worse. Stewart recalls that in late 2011, a few years after the crisis, when the company was back in the black, her new boss at Citi, a managing director, arrived to introduce himself. He told the employees he was interested in only three things: revenue, net income and expenses. Then he added privately to Stewart, "If you think I'm going to be your mentor and give you career advice, you're wrong." So goes the leadership, so goes the culture.

A Culture Protected

MOST PEOPLE ARE familiar with Post-it Notes. But what most people do not know is how they came to be. Unlike so many companies that develop products by imagining and trying to build them, 3M owes the development of Post-it Notes, and so many of its other products, to one simple thing: its culture of sharing.

Spencer Silver, the scientist who is partially credited with the creation of the Post-it, was working in his lab at the Minnesota-based company, actually trying to develop a very strong adhesive. Unfortunately, he wasn't successful. What he accidentally made was a very weak adhesive. Based on the job specs given to him, he had failed. But Silver didn't throw his "failure" in the trash out of embarrassment. He didn't keep his misstep a secret out of fear for his job or guard it closely in the hopes of someday profiting from it. In fact, the unintentional invention was shared with others at the company . . . just in case someone else could figure out a way to use it.

And that's exactly what happened. A few years later, Art Fry, another scientist at 3M, was in church choir practice getting frustrated that he couldn't get his bookmark to stay in place. It kept falling out of the page, off the music stand and onto the floor. He remembered Silver's weak adhesive and realized he could use it to make the perfect bookmark! And that was the birth of what would become one of the best-recognized brands in history, with four thousand varieties sold in over a hundred countries.

Innovation at 3M is not simply the result of educational pedigree or technical expertise. Innovation is the result of a corporate culture of collaboration and sharing. In stark contrast to the mind-set of leaders at some investment banks, 3M knows that people do their best work when they work together, share their ideas and comfortably borrow each other's work for their own projects. There's no notion of "mine."

In another company, Silver's botched formula might never have made its way into Fry's hands. But not at 3M. "At 3M we're a bunch of ideas," Fry is known to have said. "We never throw an idea away because you never know when someone else will need it." The cross-pollination of ideas—combined with an emphasis on sharing across product lines—has led to an atmosphere of collaboration that makes 3M a place where employees feel valued. "Innovation from interaction" is one of the company's favorite mottoes. Employees are encouraged to present new ideas at internal Tech Forums, regular gatherings of peers from other divisions. One sure sign that all this collaborating is working is that more than 80 percent of 3M's patents have more than one inventor.

This kind of culture has nothing to do with the kind of industry 3M is in. Even an industry that is less collaborative by the nature of its product or service can benefit from sharing. Huge improvements can happen just by getting a fresh set of eyes on the work. Hearing one person's solution to a problem can inform someone else how to solve a problem of their own. Isn't this the idea of learning—to pass on our knowledge to others?

Take a look at the products 3M develops and you will be amazed at how their innovation leaps from one division to another. Scientists in a 3M lab developing products for the automotive industry set out to create a substance that would help auto body shops mix the filler they used to fix dents. The technology they used came from a 3M lab for creating dental products, from a substance dentists use to mix the putty for dental impressions. In another example, a 3M technology used to brighten highway signs would later be used to invent "microneedle patches," which allow injections to be delivered painlessly. The cross-pollination of ideas produces innovation to a degree that would make most people's heads spin.

The company has over twenty thousand patents with over five hundred awarded in 2012 alone. In 2009, in the middle of a very tough economy, when other companies were slashing their R&D budgets to save money, 3M still managed to release over a thousand new products. 3M's products are ubiquitous, though typically unnoticed—and almost always taken for granted. If everyday products had a "3M inside" sticker on them like computers had an "Intel inside" sticker, the average consumer would see that sticker sixty to seventy times a day. 3M has succeeded not because they hire the best and the brightest (though I am sure they would argue that they do), but because they have a corporate culture that encourages and rewards people for helping each other and sharing everything they learn. Though 3M surely has its share of problems and bureaucracy, they work very hard to foster collaboration.

Inside a Circle of Safety, when people trust and share their successes and failures, what they know and what they don't know, the result is innovation. It's just natural.

CHAPTER 18

Leadership Lesson 2:

So Goes the Leader,
So Goes the Culture

I Before You. Me Before We.

HE WANTED TO be in charge. He wanted to be the leader. And no one was going to stand in his way . . . not even the current leader. This is how Saddam Hussein came to power in Iraq. Even before he took power, he formed strategic alliances that would bolster his position and help ensure his own rise. And once in power, he showered his allies with wealth and position to keep them "loyal." He claimed to be on the side of the people. But he wasn't. He was in it for himself, for the glory, fame, power and fortune. And all his promises to serve were part of his strategy to take.

The problem with such transitions is that they create a culture of mistrust and paranoia. Though things may be functional while the dictator is in power, once he is ousted, the whole country is left on shaky ground for years to come. These stories are not exclusive to the rise of dictators in unstable nations or plots of HBO series. All too often, similar scenarios play out in modern corporations. Stanley O'Neal's ascent at Merrill Lynch in 2001 is just one example.

Born during the heart of the Baby Boom in the small town of Wedowee, in eastern Alabama, O'Neal, the grandson of a former slave, went to Harvard Business School on a scholarship from General Motors. He later took a job at GM and quickly rose through the ranks of the firm's treasury department. But he had his sights set on other things, bigger things. And so, despite having no real interest or experience in the brokerage business, he moved on to Wall Street. One of only a handful of African Americans to make it to the top rungs in the banking industry, O'Neal had the opportunity to become one of the great leaders of our day, a symbol of what's possible in America. But he chose a different path.

In 1986, he joined Merrill Lynch, and within a few years had become head of the junk bond division (which, ironically enough, would under his leadership become the biggest junk bond operator after Drexel Burnham Lambert's Michael Milken pleaded guilty to securities fraud in 1990). O'Neal later took over Merrill's huge brokerage division, eventually becoming the firm's CFO. When the Internet bubble burst in the late 1990s, he quickly laid off thousands of employees, impressing his boss—then CEO David Komansky—with his boldness, while cementing his growing reputation as a ruthless manager. In mid-2001, with Komansky as his ally, O'Neal elbowed out several other contenders to become president of the company. But he wanted more.

O'Neal wanted to do away with Merrill Lynch's employee-centric culture, something he saw as an obstacle. Affectionately known as "Mother Merrill" (a hint to the days when the culture was more balanced and human), Merrill Lynch was a great place to work. It was no secret, however, that O'Neal despised the culture, viewing it as soft and unfocused, something that got in his way. With no interest in fostering any particular healthy corporate culture, the business was all about competition, and a competitive atmosphere is, indeed, what he created. The culture he engineered was not one in which the people of Merrill simply competed furiously with outsiders. This was a culture in which people competed intensely against each other.

Again, a leader always sets the tone inside an organization and putting oneself before others was the tone O'Neal set. When 9/11 struck, Merrill was deeply affected, with hundreds of employees injured and three killed. Yet during the twelve months of emotional upheaval following that tragic event, like other Wall Street firms, O'Neal laid off thousands of employees and closed offices.

Having marginalized his rivals, by 2002, O'Neal's chess game was complete: The Merrill board forced his old friend Komansky to retire early and made O'Neal chairman and CEO. With the gregarious Komansky gone, the cultural transformation was nearly complete. Though not perfect, Komansky would at least occasionally wander down to the employee cafeteria to eat with the others. O'Neal saw no value in that. He had no interest in fraternizing with his people. Instead, he used a private elevator to reach his office on the thirty-second floor. Employees were also instructed not to speak to him in the halls and to stay out of his way if they passed by him. Never one to let a good perk go to waste, on weekends O'Neal would use the corporate jet to fly to his home on Martha's Vineyard.

We work to advance the vision of a leader who inspires us and we work to undermine a dictator who means to control us. As the trust evaporated, it should come as no surprise that O'Neal's biggest threat, as in any dictatorship, would come from within. In a Circle of Safety, the people work to protect their leader as a natural response to the protection their leader offers them. This was not the case at O'Neal's Merrill, however. O'Neal's direct reports had begun working behind the scenes to put pressure on the Merrill board to undermine him. O'Neal caught wind and quickly squelched his opposition. It wouldn't take long for O'Neal to completely isolate himself at the top, allowing the culture of Merrill to be almost entirely driven by the intoxication of dopamine and the dread and paranoia of cortisol. The days of "Mother Merrill" were long gone.

By this point, the attention of the firm's leadership was focused on creating the high-risk bonds that would help fuel the rise and collapse of the mortgage market. Is it any wonder the company was in no position to ward off the trouble that was about to befall it? In the summer of 2006, the investment chief, Jeff Kronthal, warned O'Neal of dangers ahead. Instead of working with Kronthal or implementing any safeguards for the good of the company, O'Neal fired him. O'Neal believed that if there was trouble ahead, only he could manage it, and so he tightened his grip to keep all the control.

In October 2007, the company announced it had lost over $2.2 billion in the third quarter and written off $8.4 billion in failed investments. Finally, O'Neal's reign had come to an abrupt and inglorious end. He had successfully managed to isolate himself from his employees and his board, topped off by a decision to reach out to Wachovia about a possible merger without first discussing it with his directors. Any support he might have gotten was gone. How much was all that control worth? O'Neal left Merrill Lynch in disgrace with a severance package worth more than $160 million.

I am often amused by the irony of CEOs who believe in a "pay for performance" incentive model inside their companies then expect huge payouts when they leave the company in shambles. Why do shareholders and boards not write into their contracts a prohibition against any severance if a CEO leaves the company in disgrace? Would that not at least be consistent and in the best interest of the company and its shareholders? But I digress.

O'Neal represented an extreme version of the thinking that had taken over Wall Street, and in the end it caused his downfall. He had isolated himself from the people he led and, making matters worse, he had so successfully fostered internal competition that, not surprisingly, those who had once been on his team turned against him. As I have already shown, the problem is not how a company conducts its business per se. The problem lies with the quality of relationships within the organization—starting with the leader.

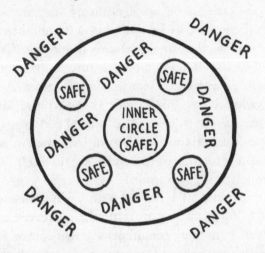

The more attention leaders focus on their own wealth or power, the more they stop acting like leaders and start taking on more of the attributes of tyrants. Mark Bowden wrote a remarkable piece about Saddam Hussein in the *Atlantic Monthly*. In it he describes how the tyrant leader "exists only to preserve his wealth and power." And this is the problem. "Power," as Bowden further explains, "gradually shuts the tyrant off from the world." And, as we already know, when distance is created, abstraction settles in and soon after that comes the paranoia. The tyrant sees the world against them, which only compels them to shut out even more people. They set up more and more rigid controls around their inner circle. And as their isolation increases, the organization suffers.

Absent any care from above, those inside the organization are less likely to cooperate. Instead, competing against each other becomes the best way to advance. And when that happens, the success individuals in the group may enjoy will not be met with congratulations from others, but with jealousy. If a leader were purely evil or if we believed there was no chance to enter their inner Circle, then the seeds of rebellion would form. But when the possibility exists that we might make it in, or if, on the other hand, we are unsure whether we will be thrown to the wolves, we become almost immobilized. It is the rustle in the grass, the fear of what may be lurking, that initiates the flow of cortisol into our bloodstreams. It is the cortisol that makes us as paranoid and focused on self-preservation as the isolated leader above. This is what O'Neal did at Merrill. He changed the culture from one that offered certainty of protection to one of uncertainty. And, as in Iraq, there was no solid foundation left for the company to sustain itself. There just wasn't enough trust to go around.

O'Neal's rise and fall is not just a story of how one man's ambition can bring down a company. In the end, everyone and everything suffers in these conditions. All that control focused at the top can lead to only one outcome: eventual collapse.

True Power

DAVID MARQUET WAS a career submariner. Graduating near the top of his class from the Naval Academy, he's a pretty smart guy. In fact, it is partly because of his smarts that he climbed his way up the ranks of the U.S. Navy. Knowing the right answers, he was able to give good instructions and issue good orders. He was the leader because he was in control (at least that's what he had been taught).

The Navy, like many organizations, rewards smart, goal-oriented people with recognition and promotion. And so Captain Marquet was recognized and promoted. He worked his way up to earn one of the great honors any naval officer could earn: his own command. He was to be the captain of the USS *Olympia*, a nuclear-powered,

Los Angeles–class, fast-attack submarine. The Navy has "Boomers," huge submarines that carry and launch nuclear missiles. The smaller, nimbler fast-attack subs are designed to hunt down the other guys' Boomers and, if it comes to it, destroy them before they have the chance to launch their missiles. An elaborate game of cat and mouse played across the expanse of the globe's oceans. And Captain Marquet was now a key player in the game.

To prepare for the big job, Captain Marquet spent a year studying *Olympia*'s systems and crew. And, in typical Marquet fashion, he worked hard to learn as much as he could. He learned every wire, every pipe and every switch the *Olympia* had. He pored through the personnel files to get to know everything he could about his crew. Like many people in charge, he felt he needed to know as much if not more than his crew to be a credible leader. Given the importance and honor of his new position, this time was not going to be an exception.

Less than two weeks before Captain Marquet was scheduled to take command of the *Olympia*, he got an unexpected call from the powers that be. There was a change in plans. He would not be captaining the *Olympia* after all. Instead, he was assigned to take command of the USS *Santa Fe*, a slightly newer *Los Angeles*–class submarine. But there was one other little detail—the crew of the *Santa Fe* ranked last in nearly every readiness and retention measurement the Navy had. While the *Olympia* was considered the best of the best, the *Santa Fe* was at the bottom, the Bad News Bears of nuclear subs. But Captain Marquet was a smart guy and saw the change as a challenge. Like many a senior executive with a strong ego and a big brain, he saw himself as the one who would take charge and turn this ship around. If he gave good orders, he would have a good ship. And if he gave great orders, he would have a great ship . . . at least that was his plan.

And so, on January 8, 1999, Captain Marquet stepped off the dock at Pearl Harbor and onto the $2 billion, slightly-longer-than-a-football-field vessel that 135 crew members would now call home. As one of the newest ships in the fleet, the *Santa Fe* had a good deal of equipment that was different from what Captain Marquet had trained up on for the *Olympia*. When someone used to being in control is in a situation they don't fully understand, they can often be blind to their own ignorance. Or worse, they may choose to hide what they don't know for fear of having others question their authority. Even though he knew he would have to rely more on his crew to fill the gaps in his knowledge, Captain Marquet kept that fact to himself. His technical knowledge was the basis of his leadership authority and with that gone, he, like many leaders, worried he would lose the respect of his crew.

As it turns out, old habits die hard. Instead of asking questions to help him learn, Captain Marquet defaulted to what he knew best—being in control—and started issuing orders. And it seemed to work. Everything seemed to go smoothly. The crew jumped to his words, an aye-aye here and an aye-aye there. There was no question who was boss. The serotonin flowed through Captain Marquet's veins and it felt good.

The next day while out at sea, Captain Marquet decided to run a drill. He had the nuclear reactor manually shut down to simulate a reactor failure. He wanted to see how his crew would react if faced with the real thing. And for a while, everything seemed to go well. The crew performed all the necessary checks and precautions and switched to running the submarine on a battery-powered motor, or EPM. Though not nearly as powerful as the nuclear reactor, the EPM could keep the submarine running at slow speeds.

But the captain wanted to push his crew further to see how they would do with a little more pressure. He gave the officer of the deck, the ship's navigator and most experienced officer on board, a simple instruction: "Ahead two thirds." This meant that he wanted the crew to run the electric motors at two thirds of their maximum power. It would drive the ship faster but it would also run the batteries down more quickly, which would add a sense of urgency to get the reactor up and running again.

The officer of the deck acknowledged the captain and re-peated the order out loud, instructing the submarine's driver to turn up the speed. "Ahead two thirds," he said to the helmsman. And nothing happened. The submarine's speed remained the same.

Captain Marquet peered out from behind the periscope to look at the junior enlisted crew member who should have exe-cuted the order. The young sailor sitting at the controls was squirming in his seat. "Helmsman," Captain Marquet called out, "what's the problem?" To which the young sailor replied, "Sir, there is no two-thirds setting." Unlike every other subma-rine Captain Marquet had ever been on, the newer *Santa Fe* didn't have a two-thirds setting on the battery-powered motor.

Captain Marquet turned to the navigator, who had been aboard for over two years, and asked him if he knew there was no two-thirds setting. "Yes sir," replied the officer. Dumbfounded, Captain Marquet asked him, "Then why did you issue the order?"

"Because you told me to," said the officer.

It was at that point that Captain Marquet was forced to face the reality of the situation: his crew had been trained to follow instructions and he had been trained for another submarine. And if everyone was going to blindly follow his orders simply because he was in charge, then something very, very bad could happen. "What happens when the leader is wrong in a top-down culture? Everyone goes off a cliff," Captain Marquet would later write. If he was going to succeed, he would have to learn to trust his bottom-ranked crew more than he trusted himself. He had no choice.

A nuclear-powered submarine is not like a company. In a company, we think that when things go wrong we can simply replace our staff or change technology to make it work better. It's an option that a good too many leaders of companies think is an advantage. It also assumes that the right people are being let go and the right people are being hired. What if we were forced to run our companies like Captain Marquet had to run his sub-marine? He couldn't return to shore and ask for a better crew

and a more familiar ship. This is the challenge that Captain Marquet now faced. As much as he knew and as smart as he was,
everything he thought he knew about leadership was wrong. He
couldn't have his crew blindly follow his orders anymore—the
consequences could be devastating. Now he needed everyone to
think, not just to do.

GIVE AUTHORITY TO THOSE CLOSEST TO THE INFORMATION

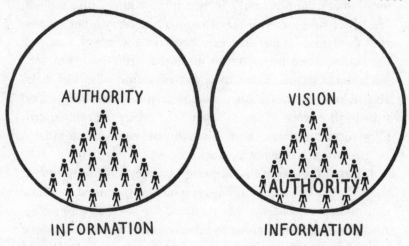

"Those at the top," explains Captain Marquet, "have all the
authority and none of the information. Those at the bottom," he
continues, "have all the information and none of the authority. Not
until those without information relinquish their control can an organization run better, smoother and faster and reach its maximum
potential." The problem, Captain Marquet says, was that he was
"addicted" to being in control. And the crew, as in so many organizations that follow a flawed interpretation of hierarchy, were
trained for compliance. In organizations in which few take responsibility for their own actions, at some point something bad is going
to happen. Something bad that was probably highly preventable.

One can't help but think again about the companies that suffer
thanks to the decisions of a few selfishly minded people within

their organizations. Whether these individuals act unethically, commit a crime or simply work counter to the interests of the organization, neither they nor their leaders seem to take responsibility. Instead they point fingers. Republicans blame Democrats and Democrats blame Republicans when things don't get done. Mortgage companies blamed the banks and banks blamed the mortgage companies for the 2008 financial meltdown. Let us be grateful none of *them* are responsible for the care of nuclear-powered submarines.

Captain Marquet came to understand that the role of the leader is not to bark commands and be completely accountable for the success or failure of the mission. It is a leader's job instead to take responsibility for the success of each member of his crew. It is the leader's job to ensure that they are well trained and feel confident to perform their duties. To give them responsibility and hold them accountable to advance the mission. If the captain provides direction and protection, the crew will do what needs to be done to advance the mission. In his book *Turn the Ship Around!*, Captain Marquet goes through all the specific steps he took—that any organization can take—to develop an environment in which those who know more, the people who are actually doing the work, are empowered to make decisions.

One of the things Captain Marquet did was change the culture of permission to a culture of intent. He literally banned the words "permission to" aboard the *Santa Fe*.

"Sir, request permission to submerge the ship."

"Permission granted."

"Aye-aye, Sir. Submerging the ship."

This standard way of operating was replaced with simply "Sir, I intend to submerge the ship."

The chain of command remained intact. The only difference was a psychological shift. The person performing the action now owned the action instead of carrying out an assigned task. When pushed on just how far he took this "I intend" idea, Captain Marquet is quick to point out that there are only three things that he can't delegate. "I can't delegate my legal responsibilities, I can't delegate my relationships and I can't delegate my knowledge. Everything else, however, I can ask others to take responsibility for," he says.

What is so remarkable about this model and what is so important about these three responsibilities is that though they cannot be handed off, they can all be shared. And that's what the best leaders do. They share what they know, ask knowledgeable people for help performing their duties and make introductions to create new relationships within their networks. Poor leaders hoard these things, falsely believing it is their intelligence, rank or relationships that make them valuable. It is not. In an organization with a strong Circle of Safety, not only is the leader willing to share knowledge, but so too is everyone else. Again, the leader sets the tone.

When our leaders reveal their gaps in knowledge and missteps, not only are we more willing to help, but we too are more willing to share when we make mistakes or when things go wrong. Inside the Circle, mistakes are not something to be feared. In organizations in which there is no safety provided, people are more likely to hide mistakes or problems out of self-preservation. The issue is, those mistakes and problems, if not addressed, often add up and appear later when they become too big to contain.

This is what Captain Marquet was forced to learn. Only when confronted with a failed model, when he reached a point of failure or despair or realized that people acting under these conditions could never be expected to do their best work, did his entire focus and effort change course. Captain Marquet resisted acting on his instinct to take control. Now he took great delight in giving it away and seeing others rise to the responsibility they were given. The relationships aboard the submarine strengthened and the overall culture of trust and cooperation dramatically improved. They improved so much, in fact, that under his leadership, the crew of the *Santa Fe,* once the lowest rated in the entire U.S. submarine fleet, became the best-rated crew in Navy history.

"The goal of a leader is to give no orders," Captain Marquet explains. "Leaders are to provide direction and intent and allow others to figure out what to do and how to get there." And this is the challenge most organizations face. "We train people to comply, not to think," Captain Marquet goes on. If people only comply, we can't expect people to take responsibility for their actions. The chain of command is for orders, not information. Responsibility is not doing as we are told, that's obedience. Responsibility is doing what is right.

Captain Marquet did more than take his ship from worst to first. That in itself was a finite accomplishment and of no significant value to the long-term success of the organization he served. That's like making the quarter or the year but ignoring the decade. Captain Marquet created an environment in which the chemicals that incentivize behavior were more balanced. The systems he put in place aboard the *Santa Fe* rewarded trust and cooperation and not just obedience and achievement. As the crew's oxytocin and serotonin levels increased, so did their pride and their concern for each other and the success of the ship. With the social chemicals flowing, they also became much better at solving problems together.

Unlike the people in Stanley O'Neal's Merrill Lynch, the crew of the *Santa Fe* went from waiting to be told what to do and working to protect their own hides to sacrificing for each other and working for the good of the whole. They didn't try to undermine their captain; they wanted to make him proud. And everyone benefited.

The reenlistment rate went from only three the year before Captain Marquet took command to thirty-three (the Navy's average is fifteen to twenty). On average, about two to three officers per submarine will get selected for their own command. In contrast, nine out of the fourteen officers aboard the *Santa Fe* went on to command their own ships. The *Santa Fe* didn't just make progress, it made leaders.

In physics, the definition of power is the transfer of energy.

We measure the power of a lightbulb in watts. The higher the wattage, the more electricity is transferred into light and heat and the more powerful the bulb. Organizations and their leaders operate exactly the same way. The more energy is transferred from the top of the organization to those who are actually doing the job, those who know more about what's going on on a daily basis, the more powerful the organization and the more powerful the leader.

CHAPTER 19

Leadership Lesson 3:
Integrity Matters

The Foxhole Test

THE COLONEL APOLOGIZED for being a few minutes late for the meeting. He was dealing with an "incident," as he called it. An imposing figure, he was every bit a Marine. Posture as straight as a two-by-four. Broad shoulders. Slim waist. His uniform perfectly pressed and worn with pride. His head held high, he oozed confidence. As the officer in charge of the Marine Corps Officer Candidates School, or OCS, in Quantico, Virginia, he took his responsibility very seriously.

Though technically a school designed to train the officer corps, OCS, the Marines will tell you, is more of an officer selection process. It's hard to get thrown out of boot camp (basic training for enlisted Marines), but if someone doesn't meet the standards to be a leader of Marines at OCS, then they won't become an officer. Simply wanting to be a leader and being willing to work hard is not enough. Unlike in the private sector, where being good at doing is often rewarded with a position of leading, in the Marines, leadership is also a matter of character—not just strength, intelligence or achievement.

On this particular day, something had happened with one of the officer candidates that warranted the attention of the colonel. In fact, it was so serious that they were considering throwing the candidate out of OCS altogether. My curiosity bubbling, I asked what the candidate had done that could potentially end his career as an officer in the Marine Corps. It must have been pretty serious. I wondered what crime he had committed.

"He fell asleep on watch," said the colonel.

"That's it?" I said. "You guys are stricter than I thought." This guy fell asleep. He wasn't in combat; he didn't put any lives at risk. He fell sleep in the woods . . . of Virginia. "And that's enough to end his career?" I thought to myself.

"It has nothing to do with his falling asleep," said the colonel. "When we asked him about it, he denied it. When we asked him about it again, he denied it again. Only when we showed him irrefutable proof did he say, 'I'd like to take responsibility for my actions.' The problem we have," said the colonel, "is that taking responsibility for one's actions must happen at the time you perform your actions, not at the time you get caught."

He went on to explain that in the Marine Corps, trust and integrity are considered matters of life and death. If this would-be leader were put in charge of a platoon of Marines and those Marines could not completely trust that the information their officer was giving them was the truth—good, bad or indifferent— then the Marines might hesitate, question the officer's decisions or fail to pull together as a team. And when that happens, when we cannot trust the very people who are supposed to be responsible for us, bad things occur. In the case of the Marines, this means people could die.

If Marines told to obey their officer suspect for a second that the officer would avoid the truth or not take responsibility for their actions, simply to cover their own tail or make themselves look better, then the Circle of Safety shrinks and the entire fabric and efficacy of the group of Marines decays. The Marines are as good as they are not simply because they are big, strong and fearless. They are also good at what they do because they trust each other and believe, without a doubt, that the Marine to the left of them and the Marine to the right of them, regardless of rank, will do what needs to be done. This is the reason Marines are so effective as a group.

The same is true in every organization, even ones in which the decisions are not a matter of life and death. When we suspect the leaders of a company are saying things to make themselves or the company look better than they are or to avoid humiliation or accountability, our trust in them falters. It is a natural response. Our brain interprets the information we receive with *our* survival in mind. If we suspect our leaders are bending the truth to favor their own interests, then our subconscious mind prefers we don't climb into a foxhole with them.

Another Marine also fell asleep during the same exercise at OCS. He owned up to it immediately and was given an appropriate punishment. From a leadership perspective, the Marines have no problem with him. He made a mistake, and that's fine. He was honest and took responsibility for his actions immediately. Leadership, the Marines understand, is not about being right all the time. Leadership is not a rank worn on a collar. It is a responsibility that hinges almost entirely on character. Leadership is about integrity, honesty and accountability. All components of trust. Leadership comes from telling us not what we want to hear, but rather what we *need* to hear. To be a true leader, to engender deep trust and loyalty, starts with telling the truth.

How Not to Build Trust

"INTEGRITY," SAID THE CEO, "is the bedrock of our foundation."

According to *Merriam-Webster's Collegiate Dictionary*, "integrity" means a "firm adherence to a code of especially moral or artistic values." This means that operating with integrity is sometimes a higher standard than operating within the confines of the law. "Incorruptibility" is the word offered as a synonym. Integrity is more than a word written on the wall with all the other "company values"; it is the reason we trust one another—the "bedrock" of trust, to use the CEO's choice of words.

We need to know that the information we are given by others and especially our leaders, good or bad, is the truth. We need to know that when someone says something, they mean it. If we doubt their integrity, then we cannot trust them with our lives or the lives of those we love. If we doubt someone's integrity, we would hesitate before jumping into a foxhole with them. The integrity of those in our community is, as our brain perceives it, a matter of life and death.

As humans, as social animals, we are hardwired to constantly assess the information people give us and the actions they perform. It is a constant and ongoing process. We do not trust someone after they tell us just one thing, even if it is the truth. Trust evolves once we have enough evidence to satisfy our brain that a person or an organization is, indeed, an honest broker. This is the reason integrity, for it to work, must be a practice and not simply a state of mind. Integrity is when our words and deeds are consistent with our intentions. A lack of integrity is at best hypocrisy and at worst lying. The most common display of a lack of integrity in the business world is when a leader of an organization says what others want to hear and not the truth.

This is the reason we don't trust politicians. Though we may sit down with a list of statements a politician has made and agree with every single one of them, the reason we tend not to trust them is because we suspect they do not believe all the things they are saying. We don't even agree with everything our close friends and family say or believe, so it stands to reason that if a politician is in perfect alignment with us they are not being completely honest.

Politicians spend time on the road shaking hands and learning about us when they are campaigning. But if they really cared about us, then they would spend time shaking hands and meeting us all year-round and not just when it suited their agenda. Ron Paul, a 2012 presidential candidate, held opinions that were not popular with the country. Yet he was much more trustworthy than almost all the other candidates because he was willing to express those opinions knowing full well they would not get him elected. Moreover, those opinions were consistent with things he has said in the past. I do not agree with Ron Paul on many issues and would not vote for him, yet I would be more likely to trust him in a foxhole than I would some of the people I do vote for. All for one reason: he has integrity.

Integrity is not about being honest when we agree with each other; it is also about being honest when we disagree or, even more important, when we make mistakes or missteps. Again, our need to build trusting relationships, as our social brain sees things, is a matter of life and death, or in the case of our modern Western lives, a matter of feeling safe, secure and protected versus feeling isolated and vulnerable. We need people to admit when they falter and not try to hide it or spin the story in an attempt to protect their image. Any attempt at spin is self-serving, and such a selfish motivation can do damage to our group should danger present itself. This is not a complex idea.

For leaders, integrity is particularly important. We need to trust that the direction they choose is in fact a direction that is good for all of us and not just good for them. As members of a tribe who want to feel like we belong and earn the protection and support of the group, we will often follow our leaders blindly with the belief (or hope) that it is in our interest to do so. This is the deal we make with our leaders. We in the group will work hard to see their vision become a reality and they will offer us protection along the way, which includes honest assessments and commentary. We need to feel that they actually care about us. It's just like that CEO said.

"Integrity is the bedrock of our foundation," Michael Duke, the former CEO, president, director and chairman of the Global Compensation Committee and chairman of the Executive Committee of Walmart (yes, that was his full title), told shareholders. "Our culture is who we are. It isn't just words written on a wall at the Home Office or stapled to the bulletin board in the back room of a store. It makes us special. It sets us apart from the competition. And it appeals to people everywhere. So wherever we go and whatever changes we may make, we must keep our culture strong. I truly believe the retailer that respects individuals, that puts customers first, that strives for excellence, that is trusted will win the future."

I admire leaders who believe in the value of culture. I respect leaders who put people first. And I have deep loyalty to those who believe integrity is the bedrock of an organization. These beliefs are the makings of a very strong culture, one in which the people are committed to one another and to the organization. A people-first attitude and a commitment to integrity are at the core of the U.S. Marine Corps culture and they drive decisions at Barry-Wehmiller (even if they don't issue press releases that say so).

How are we to feel, then, when Duke said at the same shareholders' meeting where he talked about integrity that his number one priority was "growth"? I thought it was customers! Does that mean that culture, defined as the aggregate of the common values and beliefs of a group of people, is just a list of things written on the wall?

According to Walmart's 2011 proxy statement, Duke made $18.1 million that year. What the proxy statement doesn't reveal is that the company had changed the manner in which Duke's bonus was calculated. For many years, the CEO's bonus was based on same-store sales, but the board that Duke chairs changed the criterion to overall sales—an easier goal to hit. It turns out that same-store sales had been in decline for two years, which would have hurt Duke's compensation. With the rule change, his "performance" evaluation could take advantage of overall revenues, a number heavily buoyed by Walmart International.

Jackie Goebel, a Walmart employee from Kenosha, Wisconsin, like Duke, is given an annual bonus based on company performance. In 2007, her bonus, which was based on same-store sales, was more than $1,100. But unlike Duke's, her bonus structure was not changed and, as a result, in the same year Duke earned his $18.1 million, Ms. Goebel was given $41.18. The rules were changed not to benefit everyone in the organization—just the guy at the top.

Despite the fact that the priorities Mike Duke and the board expressed to one group do not appear to be the priorities they expressed to another group, and even though they seemed to act in a manner completely the opposite of the definition of integrity, it was not entirely their fault. The problem was that they only learned about the impact their decisions had on others from reading numbers on spreadsheets. This is one of the side effects of Destructive Abundance. When operating at such scale, how can they possibly be expected to extend the Circle of Safety beyond themselves and other senior executives—the people they actually knew?

When our leaders operate under conditions of abstraction, they will naturally work to prioritize their own interests over those of others. Inner circles take precedence over wider Circles of Safety. Not only that, but an example is set for the rest of the company as well. When leaders take steps to protect their own interests, particularly when those steps are taken at the expense of others, they send a message to everyone else that it is okay to do the same. And this was where Duke could and should have been held accountable for the decisions that call his integrity into question.

The leaders of companies set the tone and direction for the people. Hypocrites, liars and self-interested leaders create cultures filled with hypocrites, liars and self-interested employees. The leaders of companies who tell the truth, in contrast, will create a culture of people who tell the truth. It's not rocket science. We follow the leader.

Between 2005 and 2009, the general manager of Ralph Lauren's Argentinian subsidiary, along with some of his employees, had been regularly paying bribes to government officials in exchange for fast-tracking shipments and allowing the company to skirt import regulations. The employees made the bribes through a customs broker, and even went so far as to create fake invoices to cover their tracks. They created fake labels to disguise the payments, describing them as "loading and delivery" expenses, "taxes" and the like. For more than four years, the company's employees in Argentina had plied customs officials with gifts, including cash, jewelry, expensive dresses and even a handbag that retails for more than $10,000.

Violating any number of laws that govern international trade, upon learning about the crimes, the leaders of Ralph Lauren Corporation sounded the alarm. They could have tried to cover it up, or at the very least have hired an expensive public relations company to put an elaborately crafted spin on the story, attempting to shield the company from any possible fallout. But instead, within days of learning about the bribes, Ralph Lauren executives contacted U.S. authorities to explain what they had found and to offer further assistance in the federal investigation of their own business dealings.

. . . .

Building trust requires nothing more than telling the truth.

. . . .

By the time officials in the parent company caught on, the bribes had reached a total of nearly $600,000. In the end, Ralph Lauren Corporation was forced to pay penalties and fees of about $882,000 to the Justice Department and $732,000 to the Securities and Exchange Commission, but the trade-off was worth it. Like the Marine who took responsibility for falling asleep and accepted his punishment, Ralph Lauren showed it could be trusted. And all its leaders had to do was tell the truth. The penalties may have cost the company $1.6 million, but had they not been honest, it would have cost the company their reputation and the trust they have built up with all those who work with them. Profit wasn't worth violating their integrity.

Building trust requires nothing more than telling the truth. That's it. No complicated formula. For some reason too many people or leaders of organizations fail to tell the truth or opt to spin something to appear that they did nothing wrong. Again, our primitive brain, evaluating everything in terms of survival, can see through that. This is why we so often don't trust politicians or big corporations. It has nothing to do with politics or big business, per se. It has to do with the way that politicians and the leaders of corporations choose to talk to us.

Every single one of us should look at our managers or the leaders of the companies we work for and ask ourselves, "Would I want to be in a foxhole with you?" And the managers and the leaders of companies who rely on our hard work should, in turn, ask themselves, "How strong is our company if the answer is no?"

A Corporate Lesson in Telling the Truth

RESPONDING TO BACKLASH over a plan to charge customers five dollars per month to use their debit card to make purchases, Bank of America CEO Brian Moynihan proclaimed that the company had "a right to make a profit."

But such statements did little to quell the outrage felt by Bank of America customers across the country who rallied together and vowed to close their accounts with the bank in protest. There were demonstrations in Los Angeles and Boston, and a woman in Washington collected three hundred thousand signatures in a show of solidarity against the North Carolina company. Further fueling the anger was the realization that this fee would not apply to all Bank of America account holders. The most affluent would be exempt. It was primarily average checking account customers, many of whom lived paycheck to paycheck, who would be affected.

Bank of America leaders refused to divulge whether the number of account closings was higher than average following the announcement of their new policy. But on Tuesday, November 1, 2011, exactly thirty-three days after the announcement, the bank issued a press release stating that they had decided to drop the plan.

The leaders of large companies change their minds about the decisions they make all the time. We expect that both people and companies will make mistakes and dumb choices. We're perfectly at peace with that. Making all the right decisions is not what engenders trust between people or between people and organizations. Being honest does. And being honest is exactly what Bank of America did not do when they decided to squash the idea of adding the fee.

Bank of America first discussed the fee idea exclusively within business circles, and at the time, they were clear and direct about their motivations and intentions. They, among other banks, were very vocal in their opposition to the Dodd-Frank Act, which put limits on how banks could charge fees following the financial crisis. "The economics of offering a debit card have changed with recent regulations," a Bank of America spokeswoman said. It was widely reported and undisputed what these new fees were designed to do: to make up for the shortfall. Many banks were considering them—Bank of America was just the first to pull the trigger.

The company said one thing to the financial community, but another to the public. When they formally revealed the plan, they actually had the audacity to say that the proposed fees were designed to "help customers take full advantage of all the additional features like fraud protection." It's not even a good spin. That's like General Motors telling us they are going to charge us five dollars for every day we drive so that we can enjoy all the amazing features of their new car. But B of A customers didn't buy it. And so, in the face of public outrage, the bank changed their story. In a terse four-sentence press release, they attempted to undo the damage they had done to themselves.

CHARLOTTE, N.C., Nov 01, 2011 (BUSINESS WIRE)—

BANK OF AMERICA WILL NOT IMPLEMENT DEBIT USAGE FEE

In response to customer feedback and the changing competitive marketplace, Bank of America no longer intends to implement a debit usage fee.

"We have listened to our customers very closely over the last few weeks and recognize their concern with our proposed debit usage fee," said David Darnell, co-chief operating officer. "Our customers' voices are most important to us. As a result, we are not currently charging the fee and will not be moving forward with any additional plans to do so."

As a quick aside, "listening to customers" usually happens before decisions are made, not after. But let us not trifle with such things. The reality is, what the bank's executives were actually listening to were the sounds of TV anchors chastising, picketers shouting outside their offices and the money leaving their own accounts as customers reportedly closed theirs at uncomfortably higher than average levels.

The only thing that Bank of America needed to do to build trust with their customers—and, indeed, with Wall Street—was to tell the truth. That's all. What if the press release announcing the reversal of their decision had looked more like this:

CHARLOTTE, N.C., Nov 01, 2011—

BANK OF AMERICA DID NOT EXPECT SUCH A BACKLASH

In response to customer outcry and such a negative reaction in the press, Bank of America no longer intends to implement a debit usage fee.

"We are facing bigger economic challenges than we are used to," said David Darnell, co-chief operating officer. "In an effort to boost revenues, we thought we would try to implement a fee on debit card purchases. We expected some backlash, but not as much as we got. As a result, we will not be moving forward with any plans to charge any additional fees on debit card purchases for any of our customers. Further, we apologize for being short-sighted. We've certainly learned an important lesson about just how valuable our customers are and how much influence they can have over our financial standing."

Even though their decision would still have been completely counter to customer interests, simply being honest about it would have done more to engender trust. Bank of America actually would have enhanced their reputation had they simply told the truth. The trust we have for an organization is built the same way as the trust we have for individuals. We need to know what to expect so we can better navigate our social bonds and know with whom we can make ourselves vulnerable and with whom we can express weakness or turn our backs. It's not about winning or losing. All we want to know is if we can feel safe in a foxhole with you.

Like the Marine who wanted to "take responsibility for his actions" only after he got caught, there is a disturbing trend in modern business to do the same. When a company gets caught with its hand in the cookie jar, do the leaders have a meeting to discuss how to mitigate or avoid punishment or do they discuss the need to do the right thing based on a higher moral code . . . a code of ethics and integrity? Unlike the leaders of Ralph Lauren, the leaders of Bank of America chose to spin information to give the appearance of concern for their customers, when as plain as day, they were acting out of more concern for themselves.

Say your boss tells you that the company you work for has suddenly lost its biggest account and that, as a result, you and everybody else in your department are going to have to take a pay cut, perhaps even a furlough, as the company tries to regroup. Sure, it's going to be tough for a while, your boss says, but if you agree to stay on, you'll be compensated once things improve. Whom would you more likely believe with this information, an executive from Bank of America or an executive from the Ralph Lauren Corporation? As the Zen Buddhist saying goes, how you do anything is how you do everything.

CHAPTER 20

Leadership Lesson 4:
Friends Matter

To Win or to Serve

AT SOME POINT in the early 1990s, Newt Gingrich, Republican representative from Georgia's sixth congressional district, frustrated that the Democratic Party had controlled the House for decades, decided it was time to give the Republicans a shot at power and take the majority. The trouble was, he was tinkering with a system that wasn't really broken.

The two parties actually worked quite well together. Though the Democrats had the majority in Congress, unlike today, the primary goal wasn't to brag about who had control; it was to brag about who got things done. Knowing that whoever had the majority still needed the other party, the Democrats didn't take full credit every time something was accomplished. Efforts were made behind the scenes to allow for both parties to claim victories and appeal to their respective bases. Election after election, the Democrats kept the majority by default, not because they were better per se. When control was not the primary goal, things got accomplished and both parties were able to get their needs met by working together.

It was also common practice at that time for members of Congress, once elected, to move their families to Washington, D.C., returning to their home district offices as often as the congressional schedule permitted. In Washington, they existed in a small world in which their families went to the same churches and schools, regardless of their party affiliation. Democrats and Republicans would argue, debate and criticize each other in committees by day, then attend the same school events, backyard barbecues and cocktail parties by night. Despite their differences, relationships formed, as did the ability to trust and cooperate with each other.

Charles Gibson, former news anchor and fellow at Harvard's John F. Kennedy School of Government, recounts how George McGovern, Democratic senator from South Dakota, and Bob Dole, Republican senator from Kansas, would both take to the floor of the Senate and rail against each other's policies, then be seen behaving as the best of friends later that same day. In another example, Tip O'Neill, the outspoken Democratic Speaker of the House, had regular meetings with Republican leader Bob Michel. They worked together.

As Reagan's tax cuts were being debated in the early 1980s, Gibson recalls that O'Neill told Congress: "[The president] has no concern, no regard, no care for the little man in the country." In response, President Reagan accused O'Neill of "sheer demagoguery." Later, when the president called O'Neill to "smooth the waters," O'Neill is said to have replied, "Old buddy, that's politics. After six o'clock we can be friends, but before six, it's politics." These days, the politics seem to last all day and all night, leaving little time for the friendships.

And so it was. Members of opposite parties bridged the gap by forging friendships that gave them perspective; they felt a sense of a common purpose. Though divisions had always existed in Washington, for most of the sixties, seventies and eighties, Congress functioned—Democrats and Republicans had, for the most part, figured out how to cooperate. Which, as our biology and

anthropology help us to understand, happens most effectively
when we physically work together and get to know each other.

Gingrich, a man who seemed more obsessed with winning
than anything else, would set Congress on a new course, however. Cooperation was out. The new goal was control. The strategy he chose was to tear apart the existing system. To disrupt
the status quo, he worked to portray a system so corrupt that
only a complete overhaul could save it. And in 1994, he succeeded. The Republican Party took control of the House with
Gingrich at the helm as Speaker, and the hope for any cooperation between parties was over.

Once in charge, Gingrich promoted a whole range of changes
that completely altered the way things were done in Washington.
And it started with more fund-raising. One of the changes included
the idea that House members should spend the majority of their
time in their home districts, not in the capital. In the 1980s, nearly
two thirds of members of Congress lived in Washington, D.C. Today you'd be hard pressed to find more than a handful. Instead,
members fly into Washington for a short workweek, arriving at
Congress on Tuesday and returning to their home states on Thurs-
day evening. The result marks a major shift in relations between
Democrats and Republicans. Spending most of the week away
from where the work is in order to fund-raise, members of the two
parties now have even less opportunity to talk to each other, and
they certainly don't socialize together as routinely as the previous
generation of legislators. And with that, there's little opportunity to
develop trust.

Of course, there were many forces at play that led to the
deeply divided Congress we have today, and Gingrich's ascen-
dency was just one of them. Redistricting and highly politicized
media programming contributed to the polarization, as has
overreliance on the Internet. Why work face-to-face in Washington when you can send an e-mail from anywhere?

Members of Congress have gone from sharing power to
hoarding it. With no single guiding vision or purpose, we've

moved from governing as a selfless pursuit to governing for selfish gain. Just as business moved from serving the customer to serving the shareholder, Congress went from a culture of cooperation to a battle of wills.

All leaders, in order to truly lead, need to walk the halls and spend time with the people they serve, "eyeball leadership," as the Marines call it. The same goes for our elected officials. Yet that's not what's happening. Today, members of Congress say they're spending more time in their home districts in order to better serve their constituents, but they don't actually serve them by doing this. There's little evidence that, when back in their home states, our elected representatives are visiting factories, or working with the citizens to better understand their needs (except perhaps during election season). What they seem to be doing more of when they return home is fund-raising to help ensure their reelection. When we are disconnected from the people with whom we work, we spend more time focused on our own needs than the needs of the people for whom we're supposed to be responsible.

In a PowerPoint presentation shown to newly elected Democratic members of Congress, the DCCC (Democratic Congressional Campaign Committee) recommends a "model schedule" while members are in Washington: four hours spent making fund-raising calls, one to two hours for constituent visits, two hours for work on the floor or in committee, one hour for strategic outreach (breakfasts, meet and greets, and press) and one hour of recharge time. In fact, Tom Perriello, who served in Congress for one term, told the *Huffington Post* that the "four hours allocated to fundraising may even be 'low balling the figure so as not to scare the new Members too much.'"

Regardless of whether or not the members uphold the model schedule, it is just another example of the pressure to make the numbers, win elections and stay in power instead of building relationships, finding common ground and making progress for the common welfare. Like the CEO of a public company who cares more about winning and numbers than they do about the people who are doing the actual work, so too have our elected officials got their priorities backward.

It is not a surprise then that relationships in Congress today are in a shambles. Hostilities between the parties are at an all-time high. Veteran congressmen recount anecdotally that in the past about 80 percent of the debate about a new bill would happen behind closed doors in committee, and 20 percent on the floor for the camera. These days party leadership takes debates to the floor before attempting to get consensus in committee first.

Olympia Snowe, the Republican senator from Maine who served for thirty-three years, decided in 2012 not to stand for reelection, even though she was the easy favorite to win. In a statement given by Snowe and reported by one of her hometown papers, she explained, "I have had to consider how productive an additional term would be. Unfortunately, I do not realistically expect the partisanship of recent years in the Senate to change over the short term. So at this stage of my tenure in public service, I have concluded that I am not prepared to commit myself to an additional six years in the Senate." Snowe is just one of a growing number of people who, after devoting their lives to public service, are now leaving due to frustration with the caustic environment. If the "good guys" are leaving, that means that the future of our government is in the hands of the ones who either benefit from the current system or have the stomach to endure the excessive fund-raising, increasing short-sightedness and growing culture of self before service.

The result of such an aggressive atmosphere in our government is, as we would expect, a lack of trust and progress. A Gallup poll in January 2013 showed that the U.S. Congress had an approval rating among Americans of only 14 percent. That's lower than the approval rating of used-car salesmen or even Genghis Khan, the twelfth-century Mongolian emperor infamous for his slaughter of as many as 40 million people, most of them innocent civilians. It is not surprising that three quarters of Americans, the poll shows, believe "the way politics works in Washington" is harmful to the country. And based on all we know about the conditions necessary for trust, cooperation and progress to exist, they'd be right.

If as social animals we are most productive when we trust and cooperate, then a lack of trust and cooperation means less will get done. Congress is now considered largely ineffective as a governing body. At the time this book was written, the 112th Congress, the Congress that served from January 3, 2011, until January 3, 2013, was considered the most polarized Congress in history. It passed fewer laws than at any time since the 1940s—only 220. The Congress before that passed 383 bills into law and the Congress before that passed 460. If we accept that passing laws is a legitimate metric of cooperation, even the Congress that previously held the record of least productive, the 104th Congress, from 1995 to 1996, was more cooperative with the 333 bills they passed into law—over 100 more than the 112th.

The disregard for the human element of governing shows a steady downward trend in the ability of Congress to get anything done. And the effects of this are dramatic. According to political observers, the public largely blames the inability of members of Congress to work together for the economic crisis of 2008. A polarized Congress has been blamed for a lack of progress on the deficit, on reforming Social Security and on dealing with climate change, among a host of other things.

Some current members blame "the system" or the speed with which news is able to spread in a wired world for their struggles and low approval ratings. However, they ignore the fact that they *are* the system and the Internet doesn't do them harm; it simply reports on the harm they do. The problem is not politics, money or the media. They are all symptoms of the problem. The reason our Congress is as ineffective as it is, is just a matter of biology. If members of Congress don't spend any time together, if they don't get to know each other and the people they represent, the flow of the social chemicals is limited and the drive to raise money and win elections makes dopamine their primary incentive. The environment in which our legislators now work makes it difficult for them to trust each other or work together for the benefit of anyone but themselves.

Enemies Fight. Friends Cooperate.

THE MEMBERS OF Congress from the House Agriculture Committee were in Romania as part of a tour to learn more about trade policy and meet some of their European counterparts. It was only by chance that Bob Goodlatte, the long-serving Republican congressman from Virginia, and Stephanie Herseth Sandlin, a junior Democratic congresswoman from South Dakota, found themselves the only two people from the delegation with nothing to do after a day of meetings. And so they decided to do some souvenir shopping together.

Despite serving on the same committee, the two representatives served different parties. And by the unwritten rules of Congress, that meant they were adversaries. Until that day, their relationship could have been described as cordial at best.

There is something about getting together out of context that makes us more open to getting to know someone. Whether we're bonding with colleagues with whom we play on the company softball team, out to lunch or on a business trip with someone we don't know well, when the responsibilities of our jobs are not forcing us to work together, when our competing interests are put aside for a while, we seem to be quite open to seeing others as people rather than coworkers or competitors. This may be one of the reasons peace talks so often happen in serene environments where the two warring parties can go for a walk together.

And that's exactly what happened with Representative Herseth Sandlin and Representative Goodlatte. Without the weight of politics or their respective parties breathing down their necks, the two of them went exploring together. The Democrat and the Republican became Steph and Bob. And as it turned out, they really hit it off. Though they disagreed on many things at work, they had a lot in common as regular people. As we all know, it is the things we have in common with people that attract us to each other and are the basis of friendship.

By the modern standard, what happened between the two members of Congress with often opposing views is almost unheard of. Given how little time members spend in Washington, there is simply less opportunity to get together socially with people they like, let alone to try to form relationships with people they are expected to resent. But on this day in Romania, the seeds of friendship would be planted and later grow into something that would serve both representatives for years to come.

With the foundation laid, Representative Herseth Sandlin and Representative Goodlatte continued to get together for meals in Washington for no other reason than they enjoyed each other's company. They started to see and treat each other as human beings instead of adversaries. Like any two warring parties that eventually make peace, the two representatives learned that what they had in common was the basis of the trust they needed to talk about the things about which they disagreed. "We paid attention to each other," Herseth Sandlin recounted. "We listened to each other, and we compromised on bills we might not have otherwise."

Goodlatte and Herseth Sandlin still voted in opposition to each other more often than not. They didn't always see eye to eye on legislation, but they didn't need to. It was because of mutual respect and friendship that occasions arose when they agreed to do the right thing, even if it meant one of them would have to vote against the party line (which, unlike in a parliamentary system, is technically what we elect our representatives to do in America). Representative Goodlatte even voted for an amendment sponsored by Herseth Sandlin, "much to the disappointment of GOP leadership," she said. "That rarely happens these days." (It's worth noting that when Olympia Snowe voted to allow more debate on the subject of health-care reform her own party lambasted her publicly and threatened to pull her funding. Just because she voted to continue to *talk* about it.)

Cooperation doesn't mean agreement, it means working together to advance the greater good, to serve those who rely on our protection, not to rack up wins to serve the party or ourselves. What the two members of Congress built was a genuine appreciation and respect for each other. What they formed was nothing more than what we in the world outside of politics would call a friendship. That such a relationship should be considered extraordinary enough to serve as fodder for a book is somewhat disturbing. Getting to know the people with whom we work every day seems like it should be the normal way of doing things.

A few years before Goodlatte and Herseth Sandlin's experiment, a few forward-thinking members of Congress tried to do the same thing. Recognizing the caustic, relationship-lacking environment that consumes Washington politics, they called for a series of retreats with the aim of encouraging greater civility in Congress. The first was held in Hershey, Pennsylvania, and Dr. William Ury, world-renowned peace negotiator and coauthor of the book *Getting to Yes,* was there. He recalls several representatives telling him the same thing about the quality of relationships in Congress. "They had spent more time with members of the other party during those three days than they had in their entire careers," Ury recounted. Sadly, the retreats were soon canceled due to lack of interest. It turns out that friendship and trust can't be built over three days. It takes a regular commitment of (no big surprise here) time and energy.

"If there is conflict, without knowing each other it's very hard to make peace," says Ury. And Ury knows a thing or two about peace. Founder of the Harvard Negotiation Project, he is widely seen as one of the leading authorities on negotiating. He is often called upon to help negotiate peace deals among adversaries in various parts of the world. "We need them to understand each other," he says. "To humanize each other. And listen to each other."

Few would argue with Ury's sentiments. We know that for there to be peace between Israel and Palestine, the leaders must meet. They must talk. We know that for there to be peace between India and Pakistan, they must be willing to come to the table and to talk and to listen. When the parties refuse to talk, refuse to listen, refuse to even meet, then the odds are high that the conflict will only continue. How can our Congress have the credibility to tell the world how to make peace when they seem incapable of demonstrating how it's done?

Herseth Sandlin and Goodlatte are a model of what could be. If "the system" will not allow for one party to socialize with the other party, hope lies with the individual senators and representatives who have the courage to lead. If they are driven by the desire to serve their constituents and the country, then investing time and energy simply to get to know each other is essential. If, however, they are driven primarily by the desire to win elections and keep their party in power, then the current system is working just fine . . . for them . . . not anyone else.

Without retreats or formal engagements, all that is required is for a few progress-minded members in one party to personally reach out to a few progress-minded members of the other party to meet for a drink or a bite to eat with no agenda. If they care about the American people, it is anthropologically necessary for them to get together for no other reason than to get to know each other. Like any relationship, some will get along and some won't. But in time, cooperation will happen.

CHAPTER 21

Leadership Lesson 5:
Lead the People, Not the Numbers

Neutron Jack

TEN YEARS AFTER economist Milton Friedman wrote about the social responsibility of business, "to use its resources and engage in activities designed to increase its profits so long as it stays within the rules of the game," his words became the rallying cry of a new movement that would consume Wall Street and corporate America. The primacy of the customer was replaced with that of the shareholder, the true "owner" of the company (a self-serving definition that is often refuted by legal experts). The thinking was that by focusing on shareholder value, companies would build wealth, create jobs and fuel the economy. Everybody wins. But that's not what happened. By everybody, they meant only a few.

When we understand the history of the theory of shareholder value, the results aren't surprising. The 1940s saw the rise of "managerialism," a system that defined U.S. corporations as having a broad social purpose. For most of the twentieth century, the directors of large public corporations saw themselves as trustees and stewards charged with steering institutions in directions that served the public as they provided stable, lifelong jobs. It was a system that worked fairly well . . . until the challenges of the 1970s. In January 1973, the U.S. stock market reached past a peak before entering a two-year period of almost steady decline fueled by a number of events.

It started with President Richard Nixon's decision to abandon the gold standard, which led to inflation, among other challenges, followed by the Arab oil embargo in 1973, during which time the price of oil quadrupled. Add the impact of Watergate and the war in Vietnam and the U.S. economy stagnated. The market wouldn't hit bottom until December 1974, four months after Nixon's resignation, when the Dow reached a low of 577, a 45 percent drop from its high less than two years earlier. It was the beginning of a new era in which a company's share price had little to do with its overall performance.

As humans do when they are facing uncertainty and confusion, people went looking for answers. Corporate directors and stakeholders were eager to protect their interests and return to growth, and economists sought a simple metric for measuring corporate performance. They found it in a little-known theory called shareholder value.

Though Milton Friedman first proposed the general idea, it was a pair of academics—William Meckling, of the University of Rochester, and Michael Jensen, of the Harvard Business School—who spread it with a piece they published in the *Journal of Financial Economics* in 1976. It was the answer everyone was looking for, a formula that could solve the problems of a corporate America fed up with stagnation and falling profits.

In 2012, Professor Lynn Stout of Cornell Law School wrote a definitive work on the subject, *The Shareholder Value Myth,* in which she points out that shareholder value was instantly appealing to two influential groups: activist corporate raiders and company CEOs, the very groups that would stand to benefit most from it. And so it took hold. Carl Icahn and other corporate raiders began trolling for financially stricken companies to swallow (and there were a lot of them in those days). They typically went looking for companies whose stock was undervalued, bought up shares and then forced the board to cut expenses, usually through layoffs or by selling parts of the company. At the same time, the pay of corporate executives became directly linked to stock performance in the form of options and bonuses, thereby ensuring that executives were financially incentivized to put their priorities ahead of both customers and employees.

During the boom years of the 1980s and 1990s, titans like Jack Welch, then CEO at General Electric, and Roberto Goizueta, who ran Coca-Cola, were pioneers in building companies to maximize shareholder value. And for a time, it seemed to work—that is, for shareholders. Both companies made their shareholders (and their executives) a lot of money. Back in the managerialist period, CEOs were typically paid in fat salaries and small bonuses, while in this new period they would be paid according to stock price. The strategy gave rise to the first generation of billionaire CEOs who neither founded the company nor took it public. (Goizueta, in fact, holds the distinction of being the first American business executive to become a billionaire on the basis of stock holdings in a company he didn't found or take public; the second was Microsoft's former CEO Steve Ballmer.)

By the end of the 1980s, shareholder value had become a managing principle at GE, where Welch had been in charge since 1981. Every year, Welch would fire the bottom 10 percent of his GE managers, those whose divisions contributed the least to the company's share price, while rewarding the top 20 percent with stock options. This "rank and yank" system was in place for most of Welch's tenure at GE, and helped earn him the derogatory nickname "Neutron Jack."

Welch did, indeed, succeed at building a powerful company that made lots of money for its shareholders, and many companies still consider the "Welch Way" the route to higher profits. While he was running things, GE sales increased from $26.8

billion to $130 billion. The company's market cap rose by thirty times, making it the most valuable company in the world by the time of his departure.

There's no question what Welch achieved was remarkable, and that few others have achieved anything near it. However, if we compare GE's performance to the performance of the S&P 500 over the same time period, it makes the accomplishment seem less impressive. GE's trajectory matched the trajectory of the market for the time Welch was in power. It's like celebrating the rise of an oil company's stock as the price of oil increases. A rising tide lifts all ships. (This was a point not lost on Welch's successor, Jeffrey Immelt, who took over when Welch left in 2001, right before things got really rough: "Anybody could run a business in the 1990s," Immelt told the *Financial Times* in 2009. "A dog could have run a business.") It's also worth pointing out that during this period, half of GE's profits came not from its core industrial business but from its financial arm, GE Capital.

If we judge Welch by the kind of leadership that succeeds by focusing on profit before people, then he retains his title as Wall Street's hero. A man brilliant at developing systems to maximize short-term value. But great companies and great leaders are the ones able to succeed beyond any one leader and manage through hard times. What if we judge a leader not on what they do when they are holding the torch but on what happens after they pass it on? On that metric, Welch doesn't fare as well. A leader's legacy is only as strong as the foundation they leave behind that allows others to continue to advance the organization in their name. Legacy is not the memory of better times when the old leader was there. That's not legacy, that's nostalgia. The founding fathers of the United States have a strong legacy because the United States was built to last long beyond their lifetimes. GE was built to maximize the opportunity of the day, a day when the numbers mattered more than the people. It was not an opportunity built to last. And so it didn't.

Jim Collins and Jerry Porras make the case in their book,

Built to Last, that when the genius at the top leaves, they take all their expertise and genius with them. In contrast, when a leader has the humility to distribute power across the organization, the strength of the company becomes less dependent on one person and is thus better able to survive. In this model, instead of trying to command-and-control everything, the leaders devote all their energy to training, building and protecting their people—to managing the Circle of Safety—so that the people can command and control any situation themselves. That's the best way to protect the legacy of the leader and extend the success of the company for many years after the leader departs.

According to a study conducted by Dr. Natalia Lorinkova, who studies management and leadership at Wayne State University, "Teams led by a directive leader initially outperform those led by an empowering leader. However, despite lower early performance, teams led by an empowering leader experience higher performance improvement over time because of higher levels of team-learning, coordination, empowerment and mental model development." In other words, all of the benefits of higher performing teams are direct results of feeling safe among their own and believing that their leaders have their well-being at heart. Any other model is simply a gamble that the next genius will be as good as the one who left irrespective of how strong the rest of the company could be.

This gamble on the next-guy theory adds an unbalanced importance and uncomfortably high risk to succession planning. If the new leader can't command and control as effectively as their predecessor did, it is doubtful many inside the organization will put themselves at risk to advance the leader's vision; they will be too busy trying to protect themselves from each other.

At some companies, layoffs continue to be such a normal occurrence in the fourth or first quarters, when the company is trying to make its numbers, that some employees take extreme measures to protect themselves. A source at a large investment bank privy to this information told me that, like clockwork, during the period before the announcement of annual earnings, the number of internal complaints filed for harassment, discrimination and whistle-blowing protection suspiciously goes up. There is no obvious reason why there would be a season for complaints—one would expect an even distribution throughout the year. And there is no reason why harassment, discrimination and whistle-blowing protection should all happen at the same time.

It turns out that the number of internal complaints goes up right at the time when some companies start looking at their end-of-year numbers and making preparations for layoffs to meet their projections. It seems that at the end of the year, employees start filing complaints in an attempt to protect their bonuses and, at the same time, their jobs. It's not a culture that inspires people to give their blood, sweat and tears to the company, its leaders or each other. It's a culture of watching your own back . . . and so they do.

Welch and others, through the 1980s, pioneered using people as an expendable resource to the benefit of investors. Since then, it has become increasingly more common for companies to use layoffs to beef up their bottom line. It is considered an acceptable business practice today to lay off people, often ending their careers, simply to balance the books for the quarter or the year. If careers are to be ended, it should be for negligence or incompetence or as a last resort to save the company. But in our twenty-first-century version of capitalism, the expectation that we are working in meritocracies seems false. In many cases, it doesn't matter how hard we've worked; if the company falls a little short, people will have to be laid off. No hard feelings, it's just business. Can you imagine getting rid of one of your children because you made less money than you expected last year? Imagine how your kids would feel if that were the plan. Well, that's how it is in too many companies today.

By the mid-1990s, the transformation was complete. Shareholder primacy was now the mantra of corporate America. And with it came a host of new problems. Thanks to cultures with unbalanced levels of dopamine driving behavior and too much cortisol flowing, empathy had become limited and self-interest a dominant motivation. And with that we started to see an increase in stock manipulation, massive pay inequality and more than a fair share of accounting fraud. All of which continue to this day.

It seems reasonable that the leaders of companies should work hard to protect the interests of the companies' owners. However, a strong case can be made that the shareholders don't actually own the companies. In the view of Professor Stout, Friedman, the hero of modern capitalist economics, was simply wrong. There is no legal standing to the idea that shareholders are the true owners of corporations. They simply own shares, which are abstract representations. In legalese, corporations own themselves. And given that shareholders are not the true owners of corporations, corporations have no legal requirement to maximize share price, as many have claimed.

Professor Stout takes this thinking even further to argue that maximizing shareholder value has failed. Sure, it has fattened the pockets of the corporate elite, but in virtually every other way it has been bad for business and bad for the companies themselves. Employees are forced to work in atmospheres where short-term performance is valued above all else and where the well-being of people is almost always put second. The consequences of which are empirically bad for the company. And contrary to its claim, shareholder value maximization has done little or nothing for dispersed shareholders. According to research conducted by Roger Martin, the dean of the Rotman School of Management, shareholders who invested in the S&P 500 in the years prior to 1976 enjoyed real compound average annual returns of 7.5 percent. After 1976, the average dropped to 6.5 percent, he says, and has been even lower than that since 2000.

"There's a growing body of evidence that the companies that are most successful at maximizing shareholder value over time are those that aim toward goals other than maximizing shareholder value," Justin Fox and Jay Lorsch wrote in the July–August 2012 issue of the *Harvard Business Review*. "Employees and customers often know more about and have more of a long-term commitment to a company than shareholders do." Consider the case of British Petroleum. As examples go, I'll concede it is an extreme one, but it highlights what happens when people ignore the impact of their behavior on others.

Boom and Bust

ON THE NIGHT of April 20, 2010, the shareholders' value exploded into the news—quite literally. This was the day an explosion aboard the Deepwater Horizon oil rig killed eleven workers and caused five million barrels of sticky black crude oil to start spewing into the Gulf of Mexico—creating an environmental and financial disaster that would take far longer to fix than the five months it took to cap the well.

How could a catastrophe of such epic proportions happen? Accidents are a normal outcome of human carelessness or mistakes. And we all make mistakes. But that so many would later call the accident inevitable means this was more than an isolated error. As it turns out, BP had a long practice of cutting corners in safety in order to stay on schedule and on budget. After an explosion in 2005 at BP's Texas City refinery killed fifteen, the company reluctantly admitted it had ignored safety procedures to keep costs down. During the three years prior to the Deepwater explosion, BP had racked up 760 "egregious, willful" safety violations, according to OSHA records. Over the same period, Sunoco and ConocoPhillips had each racked up 8, while Exxon had only 1 comparable citation. A survey of workers on the Deepwater, all of whom worked for either BP or Transocean, the rig's owner, taken just weeks before the blast, showed there was an overall feeling among workers that the Deepwater rig was entirely unsafe. The data was there in front of the owners, but they wouldn't listen. Blinded by their dopamine-driven focus, they were simply too shortsighted to heed the warnings.

By the spring of 2005, the Deepwater Horizon project was already more than six weeks behind schedule and $58 million over budget. The pressure on the company was intense. Each additional day's delay was costing another $1 million. Eventually, BP would plead guilty to eleven felony counts, in addition to which it faced more than a million claims filed by aggrieved parties. BP has already paid $713 million in lost tax revenues to Louisiana, Alabama, Florida and Texas. The company estimates the cost of overall settlements at $7.8 billion, on top of the $17.6 billion fine imposed for environmental violations.

Based on the fines alone, BP could have been twelve years behind schedule and still have lost less money than it has over the oil spill. As Professor Stout points out, BP would have done much better for its shareholders even if it had delayed well development for as long as a year in order to follow proper safety measures. Shares of BP were $59.88 in the week preceding the spill; on June 21, as the spill entered its third month, shares were $27.02. Nearly three years later, in February 2013, the shares had still not recovered, trading at about $40 a share. The shareholders, invested in multiple companies and industries, not only lost money if they had any holdings in BP, but the impact of BP's carelessness was felt throughout the industry.

A ban on drilling in the Gulf combined with the longer process for obtaining offshore oil and natural gas permits were estimated to cost the United States more than $24 billion in lost oil and natural gas investment, according to industry officials. (The same report, commissioned by the American Petroleum Industry, estimated the United States lost 72,000 jobs in 2010 and 90,000 jobs in 2011 as a result of the spill.) Add to that, if any shareholders, as part of their well-balanced portfolios, owned any property in the Gulf region or equity in companies that operated any business affected by tourism, including restaurants, construction, shipping and a host of other industries, their finances were harmed as well. If providing the shareholders the value they expect was BP's chief goal, it's a wonder why the loudest voices against BP, the ones demanding greater controls, weren't the oil companies themselves.

The rise of shareholder primacy and an overreliance on external, dopamine incentives to drive that primacy has put executives in the habit of thinking for the short term, a trend that is not surprising if you consider that the average tenure of a corporate CEO is five years. Consider GE: like many of the powerful financial companies of the 1980s and 1990s, it was not built for hard times. Nor was Enron. Or WorldCom. Or Tyco. These companies had something else in common as well: they all had hero CEOs who maximized shareholder value for the short term and managed the lives of human beings like they were numbers on a spreadsheet. But numbers never save anyone in hard times. People do.

Even Welch himself would eventually call the focus on shareholder value the "dumbest idea in the world," insisting to this day that he always saw shareholder value as an outcome, not a strategy. The emphasis businesses put on shareholder value was "misplaced," he said. "Your main constituencies are your employees, your customers and your products." (A few days after Welch spoke these words in 2009, eight years after his retirement, GE lost its AAA credit rating with Standard & Poor's, toppling it from its perch as one of the nation's most creditworthy companies.)

The perverse interpretation of shareholder-first has created cultures in which barely a single person working in any public company, large or small, feels protected by their leaders. Too many CEOs seem to skip the hard work of actually leading their employees. With an eye on short-term results, executives can't truly inspire workers. Wall Street's priorities maintain unreasonable power over executives and, by extension, entire company cultures. People in these companies fear they could lose their job if the stock takes a tumble. And to our primitive human brain, that feeling initiates instincts of survival. When fight or flight is the name of the game and no broad Circle of Safety exists, then kill or get fired is the best strategy. Feeling uncertain and insecure, our ability to create relationships and trust in any scalable or meaningful way is near impossible. And when that happens, our work suffers, the culture suffers and the whole organization suffers. . . .

But not so fast. It is also important to note that we, the shareholders, are just as susceptible to the lure of profits over people. During the dot-com bubble, we were the ones investing based on tips from our friends. Research was something we largely ignored. With dopamine driving our need for instant wealth, we lunged at opportunities without taking the time to check out all the facts. Worse, fearing we would miss out, we seemed to blindly trust information regardless of the source. We cannot get away with simply pointing a finger at people like Welch or BP or the theory of shareholder value when we have behaved just as irresponsibly to make a quick buck.

Leadership by the People

THE PERFORMANCE OF a company is closely tied to the personality and values of the person at the top. And the personality and values of the person at the top set the tone of the culture. A man who has penned five books about leadership and put his own face on the cover of all of them, Welch, it's fair to say, liked his celebrity . . . and the culture of his company followed. In Jack Welch's GE, people were pitted against each other. They were driven to do whatever they could to make themselves look good. A priority was put on the thrills of dopamine achievement, capped off with a selfish love of serotonin-fueled status. Being number one was all that mattered. Ooey-gooey oxytocin be damned.

James Sinegal is different. He ran his company completely the opposite of how Jack Welch ran his. Most people don't even know who Sinegal is. He doesn't put his own face on things and he would rather his people get the credit instead of him. The co-founder of Costco, Sinegal ran the company from 1983 until his retirement in January 2012. Unlike Welch, Sinegal believed in a balanced culture, one in which looking after people was the priority. Sinegal knew that if the company treated their employees like family, their employees would reciprocate with trust and loyalty. He rejected the widely held notion that to succeed in retail, particularly in the warehouse sector, companies need to keep salaries low and employee benefits to a minimum. His people-first attitude was the foundation for a culture that allows the social chemicals to operate as they were intended. And this, in turn, allows trust and cooperation to develop. Workers are praised for finding solutions and better ways of doing things. They look out for each other rather than competing against each other.

Both Sinegal and his successor, Craig Jelinek, have taken heat from more than a few Wall Street analysts for this approach. Back in 2005, when Sinegal refused to pass on a greater percentage of health-care costs to employees, Emme Kozloff, an analyst at Sanford C. Bernstein & Co., faulted him for being "too benevolent" (a description I suspect Sinegal quietly appreciated). Ignoring less than selfless counsel from those outside the company is one of the factors that make CEOs like Sinegal leaders and not followers.

GE VS. COSTCO

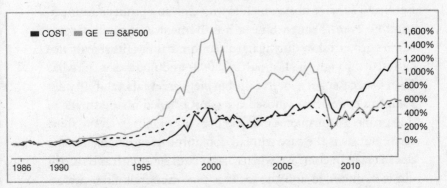

It should come as no surprise at this point that the empathy leaders like Sinegal have for their employees is, in fact, good for business. If you had invested in GE and Costco in January of 1986—just after Costco went public and only a few years into Welch's tenure as CEO of GE—at the time this book was written in October 2013, you would have made about 600 percent on your investment in GE (about the same as the S&P average). In the same period, you would have made nearly 1,200 percent investing in Costco. Though GE's highs reached levels of 1,600 percent on the initial investment, it was a roller coaster to get there and there was no guarantee you would have timed that sale just right before the decline. However, in Costco, you would have enjoyed a comparatively steady, even-keeled ride, even through the rough waters of a difficult economy. This further confirms Dr. Lorinkova's research that distributing power, though not as good in the short term, is much better over time. Good leadership is like exercise. We do not see any improvement to our bodies with day-to-day comparisons. In fact, if we only compare the way our bodies look on a given day to how they looked the previous day, we would think our efforts had been wasted. It's only when we compare pictures of ourselves over a period of weeks or months that we can see a stark difference. The impact of leadership is also best judged over time.

Unlike Welch, Sinegal, by cultivating a strong Circle of Safety, built his company for bad times as well as for good ones. He also built it to survive him, which is why Costco's profits continued to grow even through Sinegal's retirement. Certainly, Costco saw its growth slow during hard economic times (its share price suffered through the last half of 2008) and not every store has been a success. But a look at the big picture reveals a stability not found in companies whose leadership is ruled by the thrills of dopamine. Performance can and does boost morale in the short term. But, as is the case with all dopamine rewards, that feeling doesn't last. In contrast, when a balance of serotonin and oxytocin is maintained and the focus is put on morale first, performance will follow and the strong feelings will last. When people feel good about working at the company they will work harder for the company . . . in that order.

Costco has succeeded *because* it recognizes employees are like family, not in spite of this fact. That Costco is an amazing place to work actually drives the company's performance. In other words, what's good for employees really is good for Costco shareholders. Today, Costco is the second largest retailer in the country, the seventh largest in the world. And it shows no signs of slowing down. "Wall Street is in the business of making money between now and next Tuesday," Sinegal once said. "We're in the business of building an organization, an institution that we hope will be here 50 years from now."

Even through the recession that started in 2008, the company posted profits of more than $1 billion a year, while continuing to have the highest wages in the retail business and providing company-subsidized health insurance to nearly 90 percent of its employees. Costco pays its workers an average of about $20 an hour (while the federal minimum wage is only $7.25 an hour). By comparison, Walmart's average wage for full-time employees in the U.S. is roughly $13 an hour, and the company provides healthcare insurance for only about half of its workers.

And that's not all. While Walmart and other major retailers have rallied behind an effort to defeat an increase in the federal minimum wage, Costco executives have been vocal in their support of it. "Instead of minimizing wages," said Jelinek, in a 2013 statement supporting an increase, "we know it's a lot more profitable in the long term to minimize employee turnover and maximize employee productivity, commitment and loyalty." The leaders of Costco believe every company should extend the Circle of Safety to every employee, including the ones at the lowest levels of the organization.

In the fall of 2009, the slowdown of the economy began to hit the retail sector hard, and Costco, like its competitors, began to feel the pressure. In April 2009, the company reported a 27 percent decline in sales. The industry began to retract and some chains announced layoffs. What did Sinegal do? He approved a $1.50-an-hour wage increase, spread out over three years. According to Costco CFO Richard Galanti, Sinegal was steadfast in his insistence that workers needed extra help during a recession, not the opposite. "This economy is bad," Sinegal is reported to have told Galanti. "We should be figuring out how to give them more, not less." That's not to say Costco has never had layoffs—it has. In early 2010, 160 employees out of 450 in a brand-new store in East Harlem, New York, received pink slips after the store's sales were disappointing. The difference between Costco and companies like Welch's GE is that Costco uses layoffs as a last resort, whereas the GEs of the world use them as routine strategy.

As a result of this attitude, turnover at Costco is extraordinarily low—less than 10 percent for hourly employees. Whereas people go to work for Walmart because they want a job, people go to work at Costco because they want a future and a sense of belonging to a team. The company also prefers to promote its longtime employees to executive positions rather than hire from outside and almost never goes looking for business school graduates for managers. According to *Bloomberg Businessweek*, more than two thirds of Costco's warehouse managers started as cashiers and the like. This is one of the protections the leaders of Costco have embraced to ensure that the Circle of Safety they have spent so long building stays intact. That those who benefit from it will stick around to keep it strong. This is the value of loyalty.

. . . .

Customers will never love a company until the employees love it first.

. . . .

Customers will never love a company until the employees love it first. Only when a critical mass of employees feel like their leaders are working to help defend them from dangers outside can the company then invite customers into the circle too. It is usually the people at the edges, the infantry, so to speak, who are the most vulnerable to the external dangers. They are also the ones who tend to have more contact with clients and customers. If they feel protected, then they will do all they can to serve the customers without fear of repercussions from the company's leaders.

It is a given that profit is the goal of any business, but to suggest it is the primary responsibility of a business is misguided. It is the leaders of companies that see profit as fuel for their cultures that will outlast their dopamine-addicted, cortisol-soaked competitors.

THE
ABYSS

[A SOCIETY OF ADDICTS]

CHAPTER 22

At the Center of All Our Problems Is Us

Enlightenment

Case 1. Mrs. _____ was confined on the 7th of May, at 5 o'clock, P.M., after a natural labor of six hours. At 12 o'clock at night, on the 9th (thirty-one hours after confinement), she was taken with severe chill, previous to which she was as comfortable as women usually are under the circumstances. She died on the 10th.

This was a typical case of puerperal fever, an epidemic that was sweeping across Europe and America in the late eighteenth and early nineteenth centuries. Though fatalities resulting from complications during childbirth were not uncommon in those days, sometimes affecting as many as 6 percent to 12 percent of childbirths, this was much worse. At the height of the epidemic, puerperal fever was responsible for killing as many as 70 percent to 80 percent of women who gave birth in some hospitals. The symptoms, which included fever and abdominal pain, would strike only days after a mother gave birth. Death often followed shortly after. So devastating were the effects of the disease that it was called the Black Death of Childbed.

Needless to say, the intensity and pervasiveness of puerperal fever sent shockwaves through the medical community and caused a considerable amount of anxiety among the doctors of the day who were attempting to convince people that their hospital care was far superior to the care people relied on at home. The good news was that this was the age of the Enlightenment in Europe and America, a period that saw the rise of an intellectual class determined to reform society by replacing tradition and faith with science and rational analysis. Also known as the Age of Reason, it was a time when empirical data was the name of the game and expertise was the currency.

"Enlightened" physicians of the day drew from complex theories based on their own experiences and studies to explain the puerperal fever epidemic and offer sometimes equally complex ideas for how to prevent its spread. But for all their good intentions, for all their science and data, for all the complex models they developed, the doctors failed to consider one significant factor in the spread of puerperal fever: themselves.

In an earnest attempt to advance their thinking and figure out a solution to this scourge, it was common for intellectually driven surgeons to perform autopsies in the morning, study the victims for clues, then attend to patients in the afternoon. The idea of germs, however, was not yet well understood, and the surgeons frequently did not properly wash their hands or sterilize their instruments. It was not until 1843 that an American physician in Boston, Dr. Oliver Wendell Holmes, father of Supreme Court Justice Oliver Wendell Holmes Jr., proposed in an essay in the *New England Quarterly Journal of Medicine and Surgery* that it was the doctors themselves who were responsible for the spread of the disease. He insisted that doctors had a moral obligation to purify their instruments and burn the clothing they wore when administering care to infected women.

Though it originally went largely unnoticed, Dr. Holmes's essay did stir controversy among some of his peers. He came under attack from many of those he accused of doing accidental harm.

"Doctors are not the cause," said one critic. "They are gentle-men!" But the body of evidence Holmes had collected was hard to dispute. The more doctors performed autopsies on women killed by the deadly disease, the more women were infected. Some of the doctors performing the autopsies even contracted the disease themselves.

Still, it wasn't until twelve years after his original essay was published that the rest of the medical community accepted responsibility and began adequate sterilization practices. Only after the men who claimed to offer the solution accepted that the way they conducted their business was part of the problem did puerperal fever all but disappear.

The corollary between the spread of puerperal fever and the dangerous disease afflicting our business culture today is disturbingly close. We live in a new age of Enlightenment. Only now, our men of science are men of business and economics who rely on metrics, drives for efficiency, Lean, Six Sigma, calculations of returns on investment and empirical data as the preferred means to guide decisions. And with all our numbers and systems, we require a greater reliance on managers to manage them. And like our inability to see the forest for the trees, sometimes we can't see beyond the system—or the resource to be managed—to see the people doing all the work. The bigger the scale, the more abstract things become. And the more abstract things become, the more we rely on numbers to keep track of it all. It makes perfect sense. The fact that the conditions that existed before each of our stock market crashes (except for the oil crisis in the 1970s) were nearly identical cannot be mere coincidence. Like Dr. Holmes, we need to look to ourselves for answers.

. . . .

All managers of metrics have an opportunity to become leaders of people.

. . . .

Leadership is about taking responsibility for lives and not numbers. Managers look after our numbers and our results and leaders look after us. All managers of metrics have an opportunity to become leaders of people. Just as every doctor in our country learned the importance of sterilizing their instruments, so too must every leader of every organization do the little things necessary to protect their people. But first, they have to admit they are at the root of the problem.

A Very Modern Addiction

IT WAS THE most incredible feeling. It worked like magic. Any sense of despair or discomfort, any unease or insecurity, any fears or anxieties, even feelings of intimidation caused by another person or situation, were gone. He felt like he was in a "state repaired," as he called it. He felt that he could do anything. He felt like he was the person he wanted to be. This is how Jon felt when he drank.

"Dutch courage," some call it. That boost of confidence we can get from a couple of drinks. If a guy is at a bar with a couple of friends and he makes eye contact with someone he finds attractive on the other side of the room, all he needs to do is walk over and introduce himself. But that can be intimidating to a lot of men. A drink or two is all it takes to calm the nerves and find the courage to walk across the room.

Now multiply the anxiety and the courage needed to face the world by an exponential amount and we can start to understand the power and importance alcohol plays in an alcoholic's life. Thanks to the dopamine released by the alcohol, the feelings of struggle, intimidation, fear, anxiety and paranoia go away when they drink. This is one of the reasons taking control of alcoholism is so difficult. All the problems an alcoholic may face— stress at work, stress in a relationship, stress with finances and any feelings of inadequacy—all get worse and more difficult to confront when sober. "Others have a drink and go home," explained one alcoholic, "I had to drink to leave home."

For a huge number of those affected by the disease of alcoholism, their drinking began when they were teenagers. It is a time in our lives when almost all of us have to deal with feelings of insecurity and inadequacy. It is a time when we transition from needing the approval of our parents to needing the approval of our peers—a need that lasts a lifetime.

Social awareness and our desire to "belong" or "fit in" are part of our anthropological growth. We all want to feel like we are a welcome and valuable part of a group. Concern for what others think about us is a natural part of our becoming social, and it is necessary for our survival as a species that lives in groups (even if it is confounding for our parents during those teenage years). Combined with our budding sexuality and changing bodies, the social anxiety, sense of confusion and self-doubt during this time can be, for many adolescents, overwhelming.

This is the reason for supportive parents, teachers, friends and community. This is, in part, the value of the family dinner, team sports, hobbies and extracurricular activities. It is the strong support networks we build during this fragile period that teach us that we need others to help us cope and survive. But some teenagers accidentally discover that the magical forces of alcohol can be a much quicker way to find strength and confidence. Left unchecked, alcohol can become a substitute for relying on other people for support during periods of self-doubt. This is important because the way we learn to deal with our struggles and anxieties during adolescence is likely to become the way we deal with these challenges for the rest of our adult lives.

Using alcohol or cigarettes or binge eating to "put our minds at rest" is highly effective. These activities can all be done alone, without the help or support of anyone around us. They all work immediately or close to it. In other words, it doesn't require much work to find that calm or relief we get when we drink or smoke—it happens basically at the same time we drink or smoke.

The pleasure we derive from alcohol or nicotine or food all comes from dopamine. Dopamine is the chemical that is released when we accomplish something or find something we are looking for. It is one of our internal incentives designed to encourage us to look for food, finish building a shelter and generally make progress as a species. It is designed to keep us engaging in behaviors that are supposed to be in the interest of our survival and prosperity.

Mother Nature could not have imagined or prepared us for a time when chemicals like nicotine and alcohol would be available to short-circuit our reward systems. Dopamine was built for a time when food was not so readily available. Our bodies weren't built for a food-whenever-we-want-it world. Bingeing, gambling, drinking and smoking are all, ostensibly, dopamine addictions. They are easy ways to get the shot of dopamine we love and crave. And when we are unable to keep our desire for those dopamine bursts in check, they become addictions. We reach a point where a chemical designed to help keep us alive actually rewards us for engaging in behaviors that can harm us. This is exactly what has been happening in our corporate cultures where incentive programs create environments ripe for a new kind of dopamine-driven addiction. We are addicted to performance.

Have a Dopamine Addiction. You Earned It!

OUR PALEOLITHIC ANCESTORS prepared for the hunt, excited about what the day might bring. Their ability to imagine what their goal looks like and the rewards it will confer on them gives them their first shot of dopamine as they set off. One of the hunters finds some clues to indicate that a gazelle has been in the area—there's another shot of dopamine to encourage them to keep going. One spots a gazelle in the distance—then, a bigger shot of dopamine as they track the animal for the next few hours. Finally, they get a rush of adrenaline and excitement and, at the point of the kill, dopamine surges through their bodies, giving them a huge sense of accomplishment. They congratulate one another and thank their trusted leader, serotonin now coursing through everyone's veins. They slap and hug one another, feeling intense bonds of brotherhood with those who have been out in the muck with them for these few days. The oxytocin reinforces their bond. The fearless hunters bring the food back to the tribe, who shower them with praise and respect; the serotonin flows again. The rest of the tribe feels looked after and grateful for the risks the hunters took for them—and everyone feels good and enjoys a tasty meal together.

Like our prehistoric predecessors seeking food, in the business world today we receive a burst of dopamine with each marker we hit on the way toward our end goal. Unfortunately, unlike our ancestors, we are working within environments in which the reward systems are unbalanced. Dopamine-releasing incentives predominate. Our incentive structures are almost entirely based on hitting goals and getting financial rewards for doing so. What's more, they are usually set up to reward individual performance on achieving short-term goals—a month, quarter or year. They can even end up pitting coworkers against one another, accidentally promoting behaviors that undermine the progress of the group as a whole.

One of my favorite examples comes from the heady days of America Online (AOL). The company would routinely send out CDs in an attempt to get people to sign up for its product. One group within the company, responsible for acquisitions, was given financial incentives for hitting subscription goals. And so all tactics were designed to do just that: sign people up. There were offers of 100 free hours in the first month, which became 250 free hours, then even 700 hours. I remember when the offer got to

1,000 free hours, as long as they were used in the first 45 days (which left 1.7 hours of sleep per night for anyone who could take advantage of the promotion). It worked. Whatever tactics the acquisition group members developed were designed to do one thing and one thing only—maximize their bonus. The problem was there was another group responsible for retention; they had to find ways to get all the people who had canceled their subscriptions to come back. By creating a system in which each group was preoccupied with its own metrics without concern for anyone else's or even what would serve the company best, the leaders of AOL had effectively incentivized their people to find ways to cost the company more money.

For the most part, the incentive structures we offer inside our companies do not reward us for cooperating, sharing information or reaching across the company to offer or ask for help. In other words, there is little positive reinforcement when it comes to behaviors and actions critical to maintaining the Circle of Safety. Whether intentionally or not, they are designed not only to allow dopamine addiction to happen, but to cultivate and encourage it. And like all addictions, this one has its consequences. Our judgment gets cloudy, we become less concerned with outsiders, and selfishness takes hold. We become obsessed with finding our next hit and we won't let anyone or anything stand in our way.

CHAPTER 23

At Any Expense

There are regulations to manage the drilling of oil so that we can reap the benefits of the resource while also preserving the land from which we extract it. Other regulations keep car and machine emissions in check to ensure that we can have our conveniences and still maintain air quality. This is what good regulations do: they attempt to balance the benefit and the cost of that benefit. It is an inexact science, but few would disagree that imbalance one way or the other would be damaging to commerce or our lives. And so the process of trying to maintain that balance continues in earnest.

In the early twentieth century, the electromagnetic spectrum was viewed as a publicly owned natural resource, and a scarce one at that. With the arrival of radio, the broadcast industry was a bit like the Wild West, with too many broadcasters attempting to be heard on a limited number of wavelengths. And so Congress passed the Radio Act of 1927 to help organize the system. The Act was later replaced by the Communications Act of 1934, which also introduced the FCC, the Federal Communications Commission, as part of Franklin D. Roosevelt's New Deal. The new act and the new commission also took responsibility for the new medium of television and, as with radio, did the work of helping the broadcast industry grow while also protecting the public's access to information.

One of the ways in which the FCC could regulate the limited resource was to require broadcasters to have a license to broadcast on the public spectrum. One of the requirements to obtain a broadcast license was for the networks to provide public service programming for the community from whose airwaves they were profiting. The networks feared they would lose their licenses to operate if they did not comply. And thus was born the evening news: programming meant to serve the public interest apart from the commercial interest of the rest of network programming. Though the networks didn't make a lot of money from the news, they did gain something just as important to their businesses, something that money couldn't buy: a reputation for integrity.

Walter Cronkite, who served as anchorman of the *CBS Evening News* from 1962 to 1981, was considered "the most trusted man in America," a reputation that clearly benefited the entire CBS organization. Both Cronkite and the other newsmen of the day thought of themselves as having a mission. "We were sort of driven during the 1960s by this quasi-religious drive to give people the information they needed to have," says Ted Koppel, the award-winning newsman and former host of *Nightline*. The news fulfilled an obligation to the public. It was ostensibly "the loss leader that permitted NBC, CBS and ABC to justify the enormous profits made by their entertainment divisions," Koppel explains. "It never occurred to the network brass that news programming could be profitable." The system of give and take was balanced.

But near the end of 1979 something happened. On November 4, a group of Islamist students and militants stormed the American embassy in Tehran and took captive fifty-two Americans. Not long after, ABC News debuted *America Held Hostage: The Iran Crisis,* a series developed expressly to cover developments in the hostage crisis. Later renamed *Nightline,* the show Ted

Koppel anchored for twenty-five years gave Americans an update on the crisis every night of the 444-day ordeal. The program was instantly popular and, for the first time in news history, the network executives took notice. Instead of leaving the news alone to be run by cause-driven, idealistic journalists, they began to see the news as a profit center, and so they started to get more involved.

Though programs like *60 Minutes*, which had already been on the air for more than a decade, were profitable, they didn't air every night. They weren't the nightly news. What's more, this was a different time. It was now the 1980s. America's wealth and affluence were at an all-time high and our desire for more wealth and affluence became a force that would drive nearly every facet of life in the country for the decade and beyond, including in broadcast television. Our craving for dopamine was on the rise. The balance was about to tip.

With the end of the Iran hostage crisis came the Reagan administration, and with it a new broadcast sheriff moved into town, newly appointed FCC chairman Mark Fowler. Fowler, and many of his supporters, saw broadcast television—including television news—as just another business trying to make a buck. With the advent of cable television and the introduction of CNN, the news began to transform from a public service and the jewel in the crown of the networks into a twenty-four-hour opportunity to get more jewels.

Any obstacle that stood in the way of the networks' achieving another hit had to be eliminated. The job of the regulator was no longer to provide protection but to help drive profit. One by one, sometimes with the support of Congress and sometimes acting alone, Fowler and the FCC slowly dismantled all the standards to which networks needed to adhere to qualify for a broadcast license, standards that aimed to maintain at least some sense of balance by serving the public good. For starters, the time that networks had to renew their licenses was extended from three to five years, meaning the old fear of losing a license became less of a concern. The number of stations a single company could own went from seven to twelve, giving each holding company a greater opportunity to try to seize more market share. Any provisions for how much advertising could be carried were also eliminated.

Fowler's FCC even went so far as to abolish the guidelines that set the minimum amount of non-entertainment programming a network was required to air as a condition of its ability to profit from the public's airwaves. The very purpose of the 1934 Act, to reel in the Wild West of the industry and ensure that each network would also offer a public service, was now destroyed. And it didn't stop there. Perhaps the greatest casualty in the network and TV news business came in 1987 with the elimination of the Fairness Doctrine.

The Fairness Doctrine was introduced in 1949 to prevent a broadcaster from using a network to advocate one perspective. The doctrine provided that any broadcaster granted a license by the FCC would, as a condition of its license, agree not only to discuss controversial topics that would be in the interest of the public, but also to ensure that any views expressed would be balanced by opposing voices. With that provision having been eliminated, our modern networks now have the right to take a partisan perspective and be as polarizing as they like—whatever is good for business. What the Committee for the Fair Broadcasting of Controversial Issues in 1973 called indispensable and the "single most important requirement of operation in the public interest" had been disposed of. The path was now completely cleared for news, as a service, to be replaced by news as another platform on which to sell advertising. As the pursuit of greater abundance continued throughout the 1980s, the destruction of the industry's trust-building elements seemed unstoppable. And the dopamine flowed.

No one disputes the right of a company's leaders to grow their business in any way they choose as long as the means they choose are not harmful to the people they claim to serve. The problem is that the news business seems to have forgotten the people it is supposed to serve. If we consider the current state of television news, we get a perfect view of what happens when the drive to be first or to boost ratings is put ahead of the drive to serve the public interest. Among the worst symptoms is the media's willingness to woefully underreport important stories while it overindulges the kinds of stories that might entertain but hardly inform. Now more than ever, the mission of delivering information has become the business of delivering news.

What has happened is not because of journalists. In fact, a good many of them are still driven by the same "quasi-religious" commitment to reporting the truth that Koppel described. The problem lies with the media executives who see the dissemination of information as part of their business portfolios and not as something driven by mission. These executives quickly defend their products as fulfilling their obligation to provide a public service. But their claims are untenable. It is a clear conflict of interest if they count the Nielsen ratings and set advertising rates accordingly. Like a doctor who prescribes the drugs their patients ask for and not just the ones they need, Koppel says that news organizations went from delivering the news you need, even if you don't want it, to the news you want even if you don't need it. He laments the bygone days when being a part of a news organization meant something, when it was more of a noble pursuit than a commercial pursuit—a time when newsrooms made the news interesting instead of what they do today: make interesting news.

Whether it is a congressman courting donors instead of spending more time responding to the needs of constituents or a leader of a company who opts to sell a product they know might have harmful ingredients because it is profitable, the race to win has always existed and has always caused problems. In healthy organizations, as in a healthy society, the drive to win should not precede the desire to take care of the very people we claim to serve.

More! More! More!

BEFORE THE STOCK market crashed in 1929, there were twenty-five thousand banks in America. However, so many of them were built on such unstable foundations that roughly half of them went out of business in the years immediately following the crash. In 1933, Congress passed the Glass-Steagall Act, then known as the Banking Act of 1933, in an attempt to curb the excessive risk taking and speculation of the banking industry so that future generations would not find themselves in the same predicament. In addition to the introduction of the Federal Deposit Insurance Corporation (FDIC), an independent body that "preserves and promotes public confidence in the US financial system," other provisions were instituted to reduce the risk the public and the country would have to bear as the banks looked to advance their own interests.

One of the most significant provisions of the Act separated commercial banking from investment banking. Commercial banks exist to offer what would be considered traditional banking services: receiving deposits, cashing checks, offering loans and so on. Investment banks, in contrast, are able to issue securities to help a client raise capital as well as offer other services, including the trading of equities, commodities and other financial instruments. Seeing that commercial banks were depositories for personal and business funds, Congress, at the time, decided that those funds should be off limits to any investment bank to use for their own speculative and risk-taking ventures.

Unfortunately, the future generations our predecessors were trying to protect were less reluctant to risk the public interest to pave the way for new revenue streams. And so, in 1999, at the height of the dot-com boom, during a time of wild speculation, the majority of the Glass-Steagall Act was repealed.

The repeal of the Act was justified, as then Treasury Secretary Lawrence Summers said, to "enable American companies to compete in the new economy." This is political rhetoric to disguise the true intention: to remove regulations specifically designed to protect the public welfare in order to largely help one industry (banking) get bigger so that one group (bankers) could get more hits of dopamine.

If "competing in the new economy" means creating conditions for stock market crashes, then the politicians and the banking lobbies did a great job. With the Act in place, very few large banks failed between 1933 and 1999, and there have been only three significant stock market crashes in the United States since the crash that caused the Great Depression in 1929. Again, there was one crash in 1973, which was the result of a sudden rise in the price of oil and not a banking crisis. Another in 2000 was due to careless betting on the dot-com bubble. The third crash in 2008 resulted from the excessive speculation and risk taking on the part of the banking industry, as well as the use of mortgage-backed securities. The conditions for the 2008 crash were fueled by companies like Citigroup, previously a commercial bank, and the American International Group (AIG), an insurance company dealing in securities, a practice that would have been forbidden if the Banking Act of 1933 had not been eviscerated less than a decade before.

The repeal of most of Glass-Steagall is one of the more obvious and extreme examples of the attempts of some me-first Boomers to bend or break the laws in the name of self-gain. It's an example of what happens when our leaders put their interests ahead of those they are supposed to protect. (On a side note, the events during this period of Destructive Abundance all happened under the watchful eye of America's first Baby Boomer president, Bill Clinton, born August 19, 1946.) Addiction has a terrible way of making us lose sight of reality.

Like an addict who wakes up regretting what they did under the influence the night before, there are many of the Boomer generation who are now looking back at the destruction accidentally wrought under their watch. And for some of those in charge at the time, that destruction seems to have had a humbling effect. In an interview with Bloomberg Television in 2010, David Komansky, the former CEO of Merrill Lynch whom Stanley O'Neal replaced, said that it was a mistake to repeal Glass-Steagall. "Unfortunately, I was one of the people who led the charge to get Glass-Steagall repealed," he said. "Of course, when I was running a firm, I didn't want them to strictly enforce [the rules]." Komansky now concedes, "I regret those activities and wish we hadn't done that." John Reed, the former co-CEO of Citigroup Inc., also said that it was a bad idea to repeal Glass-Steagall. What is it about former CEOs that they are suddenly able to have the kind of sober clarity we wished they had had when they were in charge? I understand that we all have 20/20 hindsight, but don't we pay these leaders for their vision and foresight?

Beginning in earnest in the 1980s and 1990s, some members of the Boomer generation oversaw the steady dismantling of the very controls that were designed to protect us from excess, imbalance and addiction in our system. The leaders of companies and leaders in government created a strong inner circle with little regard for the protections that are supposed to be offered to others. Just as leaders of any organization are supposed to look after those in their care (which ultimately makes their organizations stronger), leaders of companies are also supposed to consider the care of the environment in which they operate. This includes the economy writ large and even civilized society. The Circle of Safety built to make as many Americans as possible feel safe is now slowly breaking apart, leaving us exposed to greater danger. It weakens a country, just as it weakens a company, when we have to focus on protecting ourselves from ourselves instead of working together to protect and advance the country as a whole. And if we think the next generation is equipped to fix the problems of the generation before them, we must remind ourselves that they are dealing with addictions of their own.

CHAPTER 24

The Abstract Generation

(Revised and Expanded)

The Biggest Losers

THIS BE THE VERSE

They fuck you up, your mum and dad.
They may not mean to, but they do.
They fill you with the faults they had
And add some extra, just for you.
But they were fucked up in their turn
By fools in old-style hats and coats,
Who half the time were soppy-stern
And half at one another's throats.
Man hands on misery to man.
It deepens like a coastal shelf.
Get out as early as you can,
And don't have any kids yourself.

PHILIP LARKIN'S 1971 poem paints a bit of a dreary picture of parenting. But, sadly, there is some truth in it. The period of Destructive Abundance in which we are currently living is due in large part to the good intentions of our parents and their parents before them.

The Boomer generation, the very generation who throughout the 1980s and 1990s worked to reinvent business to suit the times, dismantled many of the protections we had in the name of individual advancement and corporate profitability. At the same time, they were embracing new ideas about how to raise their children, which included additional focus on individualism and personal achievement. In perhaps the greatest irony of this period, however, the parenting strategies that Boomers popularized actually left many of their children less prepared to work in the corporate environments they themselves built, ones in which Circles of Safety are the exception rather than the rule.

The Greatest Generation, raised during the Great Depression and wartime rationing, wanted to ensure that their children did not suffer or miss out on their youth as they did. This is good. This is what all parents want—for their children to avoid their hardships and prosper. And so that's how the Boomers were raised—to believe that they shouldn't have to go without. Which, as a philosophy, is perfectly fine and reasonable. But given the size of the generation and abundance of resources that surrounded them, the philosophy got a little distorted. When you consider the rising wealth and affluence of their childhood, combined (for good reasons) with a cynicism toward government in the 1970s, followed by the boom years of the 1980s and 1990s, it's easy to see how the Boomers earned their reputation as the Me Generation. Me before We.

Putting the protection of ideas and wealth before the sharing of them is now standard. A New Jersey–based accountant told me that he sees a clear difference between his older clients and his younger ones. "My older clients want to work within the confines of the tax code to do what is fair," he explained. "They are willing to simply pay the tax they owe. The next generation spends lots of time looking to exploit every loophole and nuance in the tax code to reduce their responsibility to as little as possible."

When the Baby Boomers started having children of their own, they raised their children to be cynical about those in charge.

"Don't let people get things from you if they aren't willing to compensate you for it," went the thinking. "Don't let anything stand in the way of what you want." Again, all reasonable philosophies if the circumstances today were the same as when they were younger. But they aren't. And so a few good ideas got a little twisted for the Boomers' kids. It was impossible for anyone to predict how parenting strategies developed in the 1980s and 1990s would impact children in the age of the Internet.

Both generations X and Y grew up to believe they could get whatever they want. Gen X, growing up before the Internet, interpreted that lesson as putting your head down and getting to work. An overlooked and forgotten generation, Gen Xers didn't really rebel against anything or stand for much in their youth. Sure, there was the Cold War, but it was the nicer, gentler version of the Cold War than existed in the 1960s and 1970s. Gen Xers didn't grow up practicing drills at school in case of nuclear attack. Growing up in the 1980s was a good life. The 1990s and the new millennium saw even more boom years. Dot-com. E-commerce. E-mail. E-dating. Free overnight shipping. No waiting. Get it now! All of which had an impact on the generation that came of age at this time.

Born in the early 1980s through the early 2000s, members of Gen Y are also referred to as Millennials because they were the first generation to come of age in the twenty-first century. They are the first generation to grow up with the Internet, smart phones and social media. Millennials are often accused of being superficial, lazy and disrespectful. These kinds of complaints aren't new, however. Similar charges seem to be leveled at each succeeding generation. "Kids these days" is a phrase that never goes out of style.

It is true that by the very nature of youth, young people across generations do share some tendencies—they often reject the advice of those with gray hair, are generally quick to embrace new ideas and technologies and want to carve out their own distinct identities in the world. It's not surprising that their elders find them difficult to understand or fear that they are threats to the traditional ways of doing things. The response by Boomers, and even some older Gen Xers, to Millennials is no different.

For those who think that generalizations cannot be made about one generation or another, the fact is, the experiences we have during our formative years shape us into who we are, not just as individuals, but as a collective, too. Of course, there are exceptions to the rule and generational divides are not as hard set as some often claim. However, when cataclysmic events like the Vietnam War or 9/11 occur, or when life-changing technologies, like the lightbulb or the Internet, are introduced, there is an undeniable societal impact on the people living at that time. And that impact will vary depending on, among other factors, the age of those affected. Many of those children of the 1930s and 1940s, for example, who grew up with the poverty of the Great Depression and rationing of World War II, developed lifelong tendencies toward frugality and conservation. For some, this showed up as a need to squeeze every last bit of toothpaste out of the tube; for others it was coupon clipping. But the shared pattern seems to have the same source—they all experienced some degree of economic hardship at a formative time in their lives.

Like the generations who preceded them, Millennials have been impacted by the dominant events and technologies of their youth. As a result, we are starting to hear some new and quite specific complaints about the Millennial Generation that we cannot as easily write off as "kids just being kids." These go beyond the same recycled grievances every generation has about the next. These are unique characterizations that are, significantly, attached to the behavior and performance of Millennials in the workplace. Many employers complain that their Millennial employees, for example, are poor communicators, lack the instinct to be proactive, cannot handle critical feedback, are impatient, are unable to commit, and the big one: have a sense of entitlement.

Of the many, many stories I've heard about Millennial employees, one story perfectly captures the "entitled" attitude they are accused of having. Courtney, a young, entry-level employee, was hired as a part-time personal assistant. She was paid $20 per hour to be on-site and on call for the occasional errand (for example, fetching coffee, picking up lunch, and so on). Knowing that she was a performing artist, Courtney's employer encouraged her to research casting calls online when she wasn't needed. She could also read a book, surf social media or stream a movie, if she wanted. The point is, the majority of the time that she was paid to be at work was basically her own, to do with as she pleased. As if that were not enough, she also had flexible hours. She got to choose the days and times she worked based on her audition and rehearsal schedule. After some time, Courtney asked for a raise. She wanted $30 per hour. When asked to make her case for a 50 percent pay increase, she made one simple argument: "That's what I think I'm worth." She was not invited back to work again.

This story is not unique. There seems to be a disproportionately high number of employers who feel that their entry-level Millennial employees are making unreasonable demands. Across companies big and small, employers share tales not just about requests for unjustified pay increases, but also things like premature promotions, customized schedules and open access to senior executives.

But I have also spoken with countless Millennials, and things look a little different from their point of view. Many of them admit that not all the stereotypes about them are completely off base, at least in comparative terms. In a Pew survey, for example, the majority of younger people credited older generations with having a stronger work ethic, higher moral values and greater respect for others. The Millennials I have talked to also cop to getting bored easily and say that they don't have a desire to stay with one organization for the whole of their careers. Yet most of them say that they want to work hard and are willing to work hard. This is most evident in their entrepreneurial spirit. Millennials are founding their own businesses at much younger ages than older generations. Boomers started their companies at an average age of thirty-five, whereas the average age at which a Millennial takes the plunge is twenty-seven.

When they are accused of lacking work ethic, many Millennials will respond that their bosses don't share their conception of time as it relates to productivity. They don't need to work specific hours in the office—technology allows them to work remotely whenever they feel like it. Unlike older generations who are missing out on life because they are chained to their desks, Millennials have found a way to do both. And why shouldn't they be entitled? Why shouldn't they expect to earn more, have greater responsibility and advance up the ranks quickly? Almost everyone agrees that they are, generally speaking, more connected and technologically savvy than their Boomer bosses. Millennials are also poised to be the most educated generation in history.

Rare are the meetings or events that I attend, however, that someone doesn't ask a question about Millennials. There seem to be a huge number of employers, including many Millennial employers, who struggle when it comes to leading their youngest workers. They express frustration about the generation's lack of resourcefulness, poor writing skills and demands for early promotions. They also express exasperation that if their Millennial employees don't get what they want when they want it, many simply quit.

But the knife cuts both ways. I hear just as many complaints from Millennials about their frustration with their employers. They express dismay that their bosses don't understand them or their lifestyles, give them enough feedback, take full advantage of their skills or show enough appreciation for their work. They would also like the companies they work for to have a greater sense of purpose and offer them a work environment in which they can find fulfillment and feel like they are making an impact in the world.

Any debate over which side is "right" could go on forever. If I were to describe my observations about Millennials in entirely negative terms, for example, a good number of Gen Xers and Boomers would nod their heads in agreement, while Millennials would lash out at me for making broad generalizations. However, if I were only to shower Millennials with praise and frame everything they do as a strength or advantage, I expect a lot fewer Millennials would accuse me of making gross generalizations about them. Though I would expect more Gen Xers and Boomers would scowl and think me an apologist. Both sides have valid points based on their own experiences. Regardless of the lens through which we choose to see things, it seems to me that the only responsible thing for us to do is try to understand what's going on and use any insights as the basis for a course of action. What both sides of the argument must appreciate is the mutual value of trying to understand the factors that make Millennials who they are. If for no other reason than it will help employers better lead their Millennial employees and it will help Millennials find that sense of career fulfillment that seems so elusive.

There appear to be three dominant factors that impacted, and continue to impact, Millennials most significantly as they grew up: over-parenting, ubiquitous technology and greater opportunities for instant gratification. The effects of all three are both exacerbated by and sometimes in conflict with the corporate environments in which they now work.

Eat Dirt. It's Good for You.

EVERY PARENT GRAPPLES with this critical decision—whether to swoop in to help their kids or to let them struggle, fall or fail. One communicates love and support; the other teaches self-reliance and grit. Both are important, but a growing body of evidence suggests that the parents of the Millennial Generation may have erred on the side of over-coddling their kids and accidentally tipped the delicate balance between the two.

Every parent wants to protect their child from the dangers of the world, from bad people, sharp objects, hot things and, of course, that powerful but unseen enemy—bacteria. Thank goodness we have antibacterial products like Purell to kill all those nasty germs. Thanks to pocket-size potions of protection, we can now sanitize our children after they pick up every stick, press every elevator button or climb the jungle gym that all the other kids have had their hands on, too. But should we? A September 2015 issue of the journal *Science* reported that kids who grow up in less sanitized environments in which they have early exposure to animals, plants, dirt and microbes actually grow up with fewer allergies. In other words, when it comes to protecting our kids, sometimes less is more.

Many parents of Millennials admit they may have been overprotective of their children in far too many areas of life. Most common among professional and well-off families, so-called helicopter parents did everything within their power to ensure that their kids avoided catching a cold on the playground. They also worked to safeguard them against everything from broken bones and hurt feelings to academic failure. I know of one mother who actually put kneepads on a child who was learning to walk. Stories abound of parents who demanded teachers give their children higher grades, wangled invites to birthday parties or wrote their teenagers' college application essays.

Most teachers, coaches, doctors and therapists will tell you that parental involvement is a wonderful thing. But, again, it's all about balance. Too little involvement is bad . . . and so is too much. By rushing in to dispute every subpar grade, force friendships between kids who don't actually get along or do their work for them, helicopter parents were doing what seemed right for their kids in the short term, without necessarily considering the long-term impact of their behavior. Jessica Lahey, talking about her own children in *The Gift of Failure*, admits, "I'd so successfully researched, planned and constructed their comfortable childhoods that I'd failed to teach them how to adapt to the world on *its* terms."

A former Stanford dean, Julie Lythcott-Haims, wrote a book called *How to Raise an Adult*, in which she discusses the growing phenomenon of "parents on college campuses, virtually and literally." She is not the only one to tell stories about parents who continue to hover even after their children go off to university— a time that should be a transition to independent, adult living. I heard one story of an undergrad who has a webcam set up in his dorm room so his parents can make sure he gets up in time for class in the morning.

Lythcott-Haims offers an uncomfortable picture of college-aged students who are so overly reliant on their parents that they struggle to handle things like paying their own bills, doing their own laundry or making simple decisions on their own. All that over-parenting has also made many of them desperately afraid of failure and uncertain how to handle conflict or setbacks. "[They seem] to be scanning the sidelines for Mom and Dad," she writes, unable to cope with the normal ups and downs of life. And having not yet learned those skills, they graduate from college and enter the workforce.

Lythcott-Haims offers a degree of credibility to so many employers' accusations that the Millennials in their companies seem unprepared, and lack initiative and resourcefulness. Her observations also explain why Millennials feel that they lack decent mentorship at work or that their bosses don't give them enough direction. Two sides of the same coin. Where their parents helped them while growing up, a good deal of Millennials now look to their bosses to do the same.

Compare this to the experience Richard Branson had as a boy. In a *Time* magazine interview, Eve Branson, Richard's mother, tells the story of how she helped her then seven-year-old son overcome his severe shyness. When driving home from a nearby village one day, Eve pulled the car over three miles from their house and told Richard to get out. "You will now walk home," she said. "You will have to talk to people to find your way home." After ten hours, Richard finally made it back.

As Eve explained, the reason it took him so long was because she forgot to account for the fact that he would stop to examine all the bugs and rocks along the way. We all know the rest of the story. Branson went on to become one of the most successful and famous entrepreneurs in the world.

Mary Mazzio, who interviewed Branson's mother for the *Time* article, also produced a documentary called *Lemonade Stories*, in which Eve and other mothers of successful entrepreneurs talk about their children's upbringings. Their stories made an impression on Mazzio, herself a mother. "It occurs to me," she concludes, "that if American parents want to raise children who think entrepreneurially, have initiative and become innovative and truly independent adults, it might serve us all well if we stepped back and let our sweet darlings make mistakes and fall on their faces from time to time." Though Mazzio's advice to parents could be transformative for our youngest generation (Gen Z), it's too little, too late for the over-protected Millennials who are now in the workforce.

In his 1969 book *The Psychology of Self-Esteem*, Nathaniel Branden theorized that "the higher the level of a man's self-esteem, the higher the goals he sets for himself and the more demanding the challenges he tends to seek." Boomer parents grabbed on to the idea that confidence was the key to their children's future success . . . and the "Self-Esteem Movement" was born, emerging in full-blown form in the 1980s. For a good many Millennials, excessive positive affirmation was now piled on top of excessive protection from failure and criticism.

Unfortunately, despite their best intentions, many parents oversimplified things at bit. While Branden and others pointed to the interdependence of self-esteem and traits like perseverance, self-responsibility and the ability to problem-solve, most parents attempted to instill self-esteem in their children chiefly through verbal praise and extrinsic rewards. Many raised their kids by constantly telling them that they were unique and special, that they *could* do anything they wanted and *would*, without doubt, do amazing things. Everyone was a winner. Come in first in the race—here's your trophy. Come in last? Here's your trophy, too. In fact, here's a trophy for everyone!

Few can argue that self-confidence matters and without question positive affirmation helps build it. However, all good things in moderation. A glass of red wine per day is good for us, but that doesn't mean that a bottle of red wine per day is better. In the same way, positively affirming kids' talents and encouraging their attempts is indeed good for them. But that doesn't mean that telling our kids they are great at everything is necessarily better. The use and overuse of extrinsic rewards follow the same logic. Giving out awards is good. Giving out awards to everyone who participates is not necessarily better.

The thinking behind participation awards, another hallmark of Millennial childhood, is that it can boost confidence and keep students engaged in something they might otherwise quit because, for example, they feel they are not "good at it." Unfortunately, the unintended consequences may outweigh the perceived benefits. Research shows that more extrinsic rewards do not add up to greater inner drive. In fact, they have the opposite effect—a decline in intrinsic motivation. Nor do extrinsic rewards motivate children, or any of us, in the long term. The most they provide is a short-term lift. If children see the reward as the only reason for doing something, studies show that once the reward is gone, they will have even less interest in the activity than they did when they started. This is the same reason why extrinsic, dopamine-based rewards systems, like hit-the-goal-get-bonus, when used as the primary means of incentivizing behavior in a work environment, can't and don't breed trust, loyalty or commitment.

Rewards for basic participation have other adverse effects as well. They not only deny children the chance to learn important lessons about adversity, loss and resilience, but they can also encourage complacency and overconfidence. There is little incentive to do more or to get better at something, the studies reveal, if all we have to do to get a trophy is show up. What we call "entitlement" could actually be a mismatch between the reality of what Millennials experienced in their youth and what they later experience in the workplace. In the real world, we get nothing for coming in last. Sometimes we don't even get anything for coming in first.

Even when they made mistakes while growing up, too many Millennials were not forced to take personal responsibility for their behavior. One veteran teacher, who now teaches other teachers how to teach, told me a story about how a fight broke out in a new teacher's classroom. The new teacher broke up the fight, but he decided not to report the incident to the principal. The next day, a parent of one of the students involved in the fight came to school and complained to administrators that the teacher's classroom was in "chaos." Without the years of experience that may have at least helped shield a more senior teacher, the first-year teacher was fired. The incident continues to follow him in his career. The students, on the other hand, suffered little to no repercussions. Consistent with the patterns of "you can do no wrong," it was the parents' instinct to blame the teacher and the school before holding the children accountable.

Stories like these help us understand the circumstances in which many Millennials were raised and why so many of them seem to their employers to have an insatiable appetite for appreciation. They also provide some context for why so many Millennials in the workplace seem to struggle with criticism. A group raised to think they are special, used to having their parents guide, support and intervene at any sign of struggle or setback, and accustomed to regular praise and rewards find few of those things in corporate culture. At work they are not treated as special. Their parents can't get them a promotion. Their bosses do not shower them with praise and aren't always there to guide them or explain everything. In other words, work isn't giving them the very things upon which their self-esteem is built.

Fully aware that their bosses aren't necessarily giving them

what they need, many Millennials are leaning on their connect-
edness to help cope or vent about their experiences. They text
with friends, they take little breaks to see what others are up to
on Instagram or Snapchat while finding things they can share
about what they are doing. However, their "advanced techno-
logical skills" may only be making things worse.

The Distracted Generation

IMAGINE YOU ARE sitting on a plane flying at 35,000 feet and
525 miles per hour from New York to Seattle. It's a calm flight.
There's no turbulence. It's a clear day and the captain predicts
that the whole flight will be a smooth one. Both the captain and
the copilot are seasoned pilots with many, many years of experience, and the aircraft is equipped with the most modern avionics and warning systems. As required by the FAA, both pilots fly
the airline's simulator a few times a year to practice dealing with
various emergencies. A hundred miles away, in a dark room in
a building with no windows, sits an air traffic controller with
ten years' experience looking down a scope monitoring all the
air traffic in his assigned sector. Your flight is currently on his
scope.

Now imagine that the controller has his cell phone next to
him. He is not allowed to make calls while he is on duty, but he
can send and receive text messages or access his e-mail. Imagine
that he is relaying coordinates to your flight, checking his messages, relaying coordinates to another flight, checking his phone
again. Seems fair, right?

As plain as the nose is on my face, I am confident that the
vast majority of us would not be very comfortable with this scenario. We would prefer that that air traffic controller check his
e-mail or send his text messages during his breaks. I think we
would all feel much better if access to the Internet and a personal cell phone were completely forbidden when an air traffic

controller is on duty . . . which they are. Only because our lives are at stake do we see this example as stark. So, if we take the life-and-death part away, why would we think that we can do our work, check our phones, write a paragraph, send a text, write another paragraph, send another text, without the same damage to our ability to concentrate?

Many Millennials think that because they grew up with all these technologies they are better at multitasking, and they often use multiple devices at the same time. In the *Frontline* episode "Digital Nation," college students talk about multitasking in both social life and the classroom. "You are talking to your friend at the same time you're talking to your other friend, same time you're e-mailing another friend about what you're going to do tomorrow night," one student says. "School is just kind of the same. Like, you're paying attention in class to your professor, you're e-mailing another professor and you're looking up something else."

Many Millennials consider this behavior a way of increasing their productivity and expect that others should find it acceptable. Another student featured in the *Frontline* report says, "I feel like the professors here do have to accept that we can multitask very well."

Despite the Millennial insistence that they are high-functioning multitaskers, and a general acceptance among many non-Millennials that this may, in fact, be the case, the science suggests otherwise. According to brain researchers, true multitasking does not actually exist. Rather, what we are doing is "mental juggling" or "rapid toggling between tasks." In other words, we aren't doing two things at once, we are merely switching back and forth between things. This is an important distinction. Despite what multitaskers might think, transitioning between tasks does not happen quickly or smoothly, particularly if complex tasks are involved. It takes time for our brains to reset and return, reset and return. Multitasking, it turns out, does not make us faster or more efficient. It actually slows us down.

According to the American Psychological Association, "shifting between tasks can cost as much as 40 percent of someone's productive time." In studies of workplace behavior, University of California Irvine researchers found similar results. When a worker is interrupted, it takes them around twenty-three minutes to return to their original task. Now consider that the average worker is interrupted about every three minutes. The more external interruptions we experience, like a text or an e-mail alert, the more we engage in self-interruption, that is, interrupting ourselves mid-task to check our e-mail or phones without any notification from a ring or a bing. In other words, interruptions lead to more interruptions. And more interruptions not only reduce opportunities for focused, deep thought, but they also delay the completion of work and increase feelings of pressure and stress . . . which leads to even greater stress and more pressure. You get the point.

The problem with switching between tasks isn't just about productivity. In a Stanford University study of college students, self-proclaimed chronic multitaskers made more mistakes and remembered less than those who considered themselves infrequent multitaskers. Another Stanford study found evidence to suggest that chronic multitaskers were worse at analytical reasoning as well. MIT professor David Jones has noticed similar patterns in his classes. His students, on the whole, are not doing as well as they should be. "It's not that the students are dumb," he says, "it's not that they're not trying. I think they're trying in a way that's not as effective as it could be because they're distracted by everything else."

The evidence is indisputable. Despite what they or anyone else believes, with rare exceptions, those who think they are more productive because they are better at multitasking are just wrong. What they are better at is being distracted.

The number of children and young people diagnosed with attention deficit hyperactivity disorder (ADHD) shot up 66 percent between 2000 and 2010 and continued to rise between 2011 and 2014. Why the sudden and huge spike in a frontal lobe dysfunction over the course of a decade? The Centers for Disease Control defines those with ADHD as often having "trouble paying attention, controlling impulsive behaviors (may act without thinking about what the result will be), or being overly active."

I would submit that this huge spike is not simply because more people have ADHD than previous generations, though this could be true. Nor is it due to an increase in the number of parents having their children tested, though this could also be true. Though there are, of course, many genuine cases of ADHD, the sudden spike may be the result of something as simple as misdiagnosis. What I believe is likely happening is that more young people are developing an addiction to distraction, or rather, to the dopamine-producing effects of the digital technologies and online activities that are distracting them.

Just like people who are addicted to drinking, smoking and gambling, we can find our cravings for texts, "likes" or e-mail notifications difficult to resist. When our phones ding while we are driving, we *must* look immediately to see who just sent us a text, even though we all know it's dangerous to do so. When we are trying to get some work done and our phones vibrate across the desk, we break concentration and *have to* look now, now, now, even though we know we have a deadline. If e-mail is down or if we leave our phone at home, many of us actually start to get anxious. It's not just that our behavior seems to look like that of addicts, it may be that we actually are addicts. The biology is the same.

The dopamine hit we get from the bing, buzz, flash or beep of our phones feels good. We like how it feels when we get a notification that someone commented on one of our posts on Facebook or Instagram. Or, if we are feeling a little bit down or lonely, some of us will send out a quick text to a whole bunch of friends hoping that at least one of them will write back immediately. Because if they do, that little burst of dopamine makes us feel better. But once it wears off, we go back to how we felt . . .

and we crave another hit. This is particularly dangerous when it comes to the teenage brain.

We have strict age restrictions for alcohol, cigarettes and gambling because we know that the still forming brains and neural pathways of teenagers make them especially susceptible to addiction. More than 40 percent of children who discover alcohol before age fifteen will become alcoholics later in life. And the same percentage of adult alcoholics report that they drank regularly between the ages of fifteen and nineteen.

Brain researchers know that teenagers require more dopamine than adults to reach the same level of stimulation. Which means that teenagers need to indulge more than adults to experience the same effects. But because we do not formally recognize digital addiction in the United States, we have done little to restrict young people's access to dopamine-producing digital activity. Parents, even though they express serious misgivings about how much time their kids spend "in front of their screens," don't seem to be doing much to keep devices out of their kids' hands. According to the Pew Research Center, as of 2015, 88 percent of teenagers age thirteen to seventeen had access to cell phones or smart phones, a number that is more than double what it was in 2013. And our laws don't seem to be filling the gaps.

In both China and South Korea, Internet addiction is recognized, and in South Korea it's treated as a psychiatric disorder. The Korean government has responded by opening up free "Internet rescue camps" for kids. At the camps, kids experience the equivalent of detox. Their devices are taken away and they receive counseling. Korean schools are also working proactively against digital addiction. Starting in second grade, students are required to learn about responsible computer use and healthy digital habits. We have no such government help in America.

Though the Children's Online Privacy Protection Act of 1998 (COPPA) unintentionally shields kids under thirteen from addictive online activities, its specific intent was, as its name suggests, to protect their privacy by prohibiting Web sites and apps from collecting data on them. Though many social media sites refuse to allow those under age thirteen to sign up for accounts, they do so in large part to avoid the costs and complications of compliance with COPPA. A few services, like YouTube, require someone to be at least eighteen to have an account, but these restrictions are usually set up to guard young people from inappropriate material, and can often be waived with a parent's permission or a simple click of a button "acknowledging" the user is of age. The bottom line is that thirteen-to-eighteen-year-olds are left almost completely vulnerable to the addictive qualities of dopamine-releasing activities online and on their devices at the very moment they are most susceptible to them. Of course, not all kids who use smartphones or engage in social media will form addictions, but the risk is real and significant. And even if they don't form addictions, their developing brains will, without question, be affected.

"How a young person chooses to spend their time will have a profound effect on what their brain will be like for the rest of their lives," says a leading neuroscientist from the Semel Institute at UCLA. In the best-case scenario, young people's brains will change such that the benefits of social media, smartphones, and other devices outweigh the negatives. In the worst case, we will have a generation in which a disproportionately high number of people lack the coping skills necessary to deal with stress as adults. Sadly, the evidence already seems to be tilting toward the latter.

When we're very young, the only approval we need is the approval of our parents. As we go through adolescence we make a transition to needing the approval of our peers. A highly stressful and anxious period in our lives, this transition is *supposed* to teach us to rely on our friends to cope with the stress. Though it may be frustrating for our parents when we start to care more about what our friends think than what they think, it is very important for us. It allows us to build the skills we need to make friends and form trusting relationships beyond our immediate families so that we may become valuable and trusted members of the broader tribe.

Some teenagers, quite by accident, discover that alcohol can help them cope with their teenage angst. We know that sometimes our wires can get crossed and the wrong behaviors can be incentivized. Someone who finds the dopamine- and serotonin-releasing effects of alcohol as a teenager can become conditioned to look to alcohol to suppress emotional pain instead of adopting other, healthier coping mechanisms. For some, that connection becomes hardwired in their brains and for the rest of their lives, when they suffer significant stress, they will not turn to a person for help, they will turn to the bottle.

Again, the biology and the mechanics of addiction are exactly the same for most other dopamine-producing things, like gambling, smoking, texting and engaging with social media. When our children are conditioned to look for a digital hit when they are stressed, for the rest of their lives, when they suffer social stress, financial stress or career stress, they will turn not to a person for support but to a device.

I Want an Oompa Loompa Now!

THIS IS A high-speed world. Gone are the days when we checked stock prices in the morning newspaper. Now everyone can study their investments in real time. Companies track their success in months and quarters, not years. Why should we wait when we can have what we want when we want it? You want to buy something? You go on Amazon . . . it arrives the next day. You want to watch a movie? You don't have to check movie times, just log on and stream it now. You want to watch a TV show? You don't have to wait week to week to week for the next episode. Binge! Even our social lives can be satisfied instantly. You want to go on a date? Just swipe right. No more awkward conversations with strangers required!

For Millennials who came of age in this world of instant grat-ification, seeing what you want and getting it when you want it is normal. For many, it's a baseline expectation. And that's all fine and good if we are talking about shopping and movies. However, when it comes to finding a feeling of fulfillment in one's life or career, things get more complicated.

As a generation, Millennials tend to be socially conscious. They care about the world around them, and they want to make an impact, both personally and professionally. According to the 2015 annual Deloitte Millennial Survey, 90 percent of Millenni-als, globally, want to use their skills for good, and six in ten report a "sense of purpose" as the reason they chose to work for their current employer. I love this about Millennials. I wish more of us cared as much as they do. The issue isn't the goal, it's the expecta-tions they have about the time it takes to achieve that goal.

While doing research for this book, I kept meeting amazing, wonderful, smart, driven and optimistic Millennials who quickly became disillusioned with their entry- or junior-level positions because they didn't feel like they were making a real difference. After only a few months in their jobs, many were considering quitting. Rather than questioning their expecta-tions or giving things some time, they assumed the job was the problem. At a different company, perhaps at one they started themselves, they reasoned, things would be better. Impact and fulfillment would be there on day one . . . or at least after a few weeks.

Millennials aren't just looking for work to provide them with the fulfillment that comes from doing good in the world. Many of them donate and volunteer. More, in fact, than you might suspect. Although the data shows that Millennials' charitable activities become more focused and longer lasting as they get older, most younger Millennials seem to take a scattered, almost random approach. Because of their impulse for instant gratifi-cation, the slow plod of service has been replaced with a quick burst of drive-by philanthropy.

"Giving," it seems, has become another area in which Millennials try to multitask. Bouncing from one cause to another, giving a little here and a little there, they feel like they can make a difference in lots of places . . . sometimes all at once. Just as the Internet, social media and their cell phones help them multitask in their social and academic lives, so too are they deployed in the name of service. Now we can text a donation, forward an e-mail, post a video, wear a colored wristband, add a filter to our avatar, "like" a cause we care about, show solidarity on Instagram, hashtag our opinion, shop from a socially conscious brand and sign an online petition all while heading to brunch in an Uber (unless we're boycotting them this month to express our political views, #boycott). In an instant, the desire to do real good in the world starts to look like a lot of disconnected, symbolic gestures that don't add up to much—for the giver or for the cause.

In 2014, the ALS Association encouraged people to take the Ice Bucket Challenge, a social media–driven campaign to raise awareness (and hopefully money) for their charity. The idea was that you would have a bucket of ice water dumped on your head and you would post a video of it on social media, then nominate friends to do the same. Like any fad or viral video, no one could have predicted how popular it was going to be. More than seventeen million people, including an exceptionally high number of Millennials, participated. The ALS Association brought attention to the cause and raised $115 million more that year, a nearly 500 percent increase in the amount they raised the previous year. Yet that money came from just two and a half million people. In other words, the overwhelming majority of people who participated did not make donations. And perhaps that doesn't matter. The success of the effort or how to create a successful online campaign is not the discussion. How an addiction to devices and virtual approval affects our behavior and the feelings we have about ourselves is.

The cynic in me doubts that most who participated in the Ice Bucket Challenge have a deep sense of commitment to help eradicate Lou Gehrig's disease in the world (or even how many people who participated knew that Lou Gehrig's disease and ALS are the same thing . . . or what the disease does to the human body). It's safe to say that the overwhelming majority who took part in the Ice Bucket Challenge probably didn't participate to be a part of a cause that deeply mattered to them. We participated in the campaign because it was fun and it felt good to be a part of a media sensation or we were uncomfortable with the thought that we would be "the one" of our friends who didn't do it (remember, this is the generation that gave us FOMO—fear of missing out).

It's hard to fault anyone who participated in the challenge, given the results, and we must assume that most of them participated with the best of intentions. However, let's just call a spade a spade. This kind of "activism" does not contribute to the longer-term financial prospects of an organization nor does it generate ongoing relationships between the organization and participants. Though the ALS Association ran the Ice Bucket Challenge again the following year, the *total* revenues were almost exactly the same as they were the year before the original campaign. In other words—it worked once, then everything went back, for the most part, to the way it used to be.

I'm not suggesting we should stop doing these kinds of things. We absolutely should. But we do need to recognize that they are not the way to achieve systemic change in the world or a lasting sense of fulfillment in ourselves. These things, as I've said before, require a single-minded, ongoing commitment of time and energy.

From the 1848 gathering at Seneca Falls, which is seen as the official launch of the women's suffrage movement in the United States, to the ratification of the Nineteenth Amendment in 1920, it took seventy-two years for women to win the right to vote. The majority of the founders and leaders of the movement, women like Susan B. Anthony, Elizabeth Cady Stanton and Lucretia Mott, died before, some long before, a single woman ever exercised that right. However, even if they never lived to see their dream come alive, I can almost guarantee that those leaders of the movement felt quite fulfilled at the end of their lives because of the cause they helped to advance for theirs and future generations—a cause that didn't end when the first women voted, but will continue as long as women are denied equal rights in other areas of life, too.

This is what it means to be a part of something bigger than ourselves. That we are a part of a movement that will live on beyond the goals we set or the lives of the people who set them. It's the camaraderie and shared purpose, as much as the milestones we set, that give our lives meaning. It is only by committing to a path, remaining steadfast on that journey, sticking it out through thick and thin and marching shoulder-to-shoulder with those who share our values and our vision that we can ever find that deep sense of joy, satisfaction and fulfillment in our lives. This is as true for our careers as it is for our social movements.

It's as if many Millennials are standing at the foot of a mountain and they can see what they want—to make an impact or find fulfillment—they can see the summit. What many can't seem to see is the mountain. This has nothing to do with an older generation insisting that the younger generation "do their time." Though we may all advance up the mountain at different paces, some of us faster and some of us slower, there's still no avoiding the mountain.

When Millennials stand at the foot of that mountain, looking up at the thing they want to achieve, they, like all of us, must remember that the summit serves only to set the direction in which we will march. Opportunities to lead and feelings of safety and belonging do not suddenly appear when we reach the mountain peak. These are the things we find and develop on the journey up. The sometimes long, sometimes arduous journey. And as if I haven't beaten this analogy to death enough, there is no cell service on the mountain, so get used to appreciating the little and the big wins without posting any selfies anywhere.

I will concede that impatience is perhaps only part of the reason so many Millennials quit their jobs so quickly. The other part is that too many companies don't have a clear sense of purpose, cause or belief to offer them. Too many company mission and vision statements talk about being the best, the biggest or the most respected—all goals that are self-centered and offer zero contribution to the world. How are Millennials ever to live their Why if the companies that court them don't have a sense of Why themselves?

If you want to ignore or discount everything I have said to this point—if you think I'm completely off base with my discussion about parenting styles, if you think multitasking is real and that we suffer no imbalance in our lives whatsoever; if you think Millennials are absolutely right to quit as soon as they suspect "this place isn't for me"; if you're an employer who wants to blame everything on Millennials themselves, or a Millennial who thinks your boss "doesn't get it," I beg you to at least take this last piece to heart.

The Dire Scenario

YOU MAY HAVE noticed a recurring theme throughout this book and this chapter—the importance of relationships not only to our survival, but also to our sense of fulfillment. This is no less true for human beings working in the modern workplace than it was for human beings living in tribes fifty thousand years ago.

I find it frightening that Millennials have grown up, and that the youngest generation is now growing up, in a world that seems dead-set on denying them the opportunity to build such deep, meaningful relationships. Addiction, in any form, undermines relationships. The desire for instant gratification allows no time for relationships to develop. Digital communication can stand in the way of deepening our relationships. And social media can deny us the chance to create real relationships to begin with. Perhaps even worse, it can be devastating to our own sense of self-worth.

While it is hard for many of us, regardless of age, to build relationships of value, research suggests that the Millennial generation may be struggling more than most. Teenagers are socializing less in real life, while engaging in social media more. The pattern continues into college, where there is less chance that they will form "tangible relationships" with their peers.

The number of Millennials of all ages who engage with social media, and the amount of time they spend with it, is astounding. A nationwide study by the Pew Research Center finds that social media usage among eighteen- to twenty-nine-year-olds has increased by almost 1,000 percent in less than a decade. By some estimates more than 98 percent of college students participate in social networking online, and a 2014 survey done by UCLA showed that 27 percent of undergrads are on social media more than six hours a week. Meanwhile, a 2015 survey by Common Sense Media shows that 60 percent of teens, thirteen to eighteen years old, are on social media daily for, on average, more than an hour.

Of course, social media is amazing in many ways. It allows us to stay in touch with friends and family across the globe. And I cannot dispute that for some young people, especially the very shy, engaging in social media can help them feel like they have some sort of connection to a group. Some teens say that social media acts as a gateway to real life friendships. Others say that social media gives them a place where they feel freer to be their true selves. A full one in three teens say they feel more accepted online than in the real world.

But such relationships rarely go beyond the superficial. There is no getting away from the truth: there is simply nothing that can replace real, face-to-face human interaction. Perhaps this is the reason one Millennial I spoke with admitted that he "struggles to form deep, meaningful friendships." Not only are virtual relationships a poor substitute for real ones, but social media can actually make us feel lonelier. As one student at Franklin and Marshall College put it, "Social media is a really easy way to feel excluded. Facebook, Instagram and Snapchat make me hyper-aware of the activities I wasn't invited to partake in and less involved in the activities that are actually in front of me."

And feeling left out is just the beginning. Studies have shown that people who spend excessive time on social media experience higher rates of depression and anxiety. A 2013 study by social scientists at the University of Michigan, for instance, tracked the use of Facebook by eighty-two young adults over a two-week period. At the end of the period, the subjects who had spent the most time overall on the network reported less satisfaction with their lives. "Rather than enhancing well-being . . . ," Facebook, the study concluded, "may undermine it."

When we are immersed in a Facebook-Instagram-Snapchat world, where everyone's lives are on display, it's hard not to compare ourselves to others. And it's easy to become envious and doubt the quality of our own lives when our friends' posts come off like a highlight reel of the year's best movies. True or not, exaggerated or not, filtered or not, what they see on social media makes many of the Millennials I've spoken with feel like they are in competition with their peers. One Millennial who is currently out of work told me that she jumps at opportunities to engage in networking or social events just so that she can have something to post online that makes her appear to be "keeping up." In an unfortunate twist, the drive for real, individual accomplishments seems to have turned into a game of virtual one-upmanship, based on the illusion of perfection.

Millennials have become well practiced at curating their lives. They know better than anyone how to manage their personal brands and present themselves as they want to be seen . . . not necessarily as they are. They may look confident. They may sound like they have all the answers and know exactly how to navigate their lives and the world. However, behind the filter, many are plagued by more self-doubt and uncertainty than they let on.

Though there is no hard evidence of a direct causal relationship, the correlation between increased use of social media among Millennials and rising rates of depression and anxiety is hard to ignore. Universities today are experiencing what some are calling an "epidemic" of depression among students, and as many as one in six college students have been diagnosed with or treated for anxiety. For teens, the situation is even more concerning. The National Institute of Mental Health reports that in 2015, the number of young people between the ages of twelve and seventeen who experienced a major depressive episode increased nearly 50 percent from what it was in 2005. In fact, teenagers now suffer depression at a rate twice that of adults. This is especially disconcerting given that depression—along with social isolation—is a major indicator of suicide risk.

Suicide is already the second leading cause of death among people fifteen to twenty-four, and that does not account for the number of young people who attempt suicide, which by some counts is as high as 25 to 1. Even more disturbing is the trend among kids ten to fourteen. In the period between 1999 and 2014, the percent increase in the suicide rate for girls in this age group *tripled*! It was the single biggest increase, by far, in any age group, male or female. Boys ten to fourteen fared better, but still had the second biggest increase among men. The fact that teenage girls use social media almost twice as much as teenage boys (one hour thirty two minutes versus fifty two minutes per day) and have a rate of depression nearly five times that of their male counterparts does not bode well for this trend reversing itself any time soon.

As if the increasing rates of suicide among young people aren't bad enough, over the past several decades, we have also witnessed the rise of the truly terrifying phenomenon of school shootings. In the period from 1969 to 1978, sixteen school shootings occurred in the United States. That number rose to sixty-three between 1999 and 2008. The next decade, though not even over at the writing of this book, has already surpassed these numbers. Between 2013 and 2017 alone, there have been more than two hundred school shootings. Studies treat the data in various ways—some define school shootings as incidents in which shots were fired, others are limited to multivictim events—but all the data show a clear and consistent increase that does not appear to be subsiding. What's more, many of the perpetrators are, themselves, students. A major FBI review of active shooting incidences from 2000 to 2013 indicates that all but three of twenty middle and high school events were carried out by students ages twelve to nineteen.

It is difficult to ascribe school shootings to a single cause. Nonetheless, one persistent observation in studies is the number of adolescent shooters who hold low social status within their peer groups and struggle for recognition. Many are victims of bullying, teasing, or social exclusion. They perceive themselves as outcasts, who are marginalized within communities to which they want to belong. Depression, substance abuse or psychological disorders can, in turn, exacerbate their feelings of loneliness and rejection.

Sick gazelles are pushed to the edge of the herd, pushed out of the Circle of Safety, so the lions might eat the weaker ones instead of the stronger ones. Our primitive mammal brain leads us to the same conclusion. When we feel like we are outside a Circle of Safety, with no sense of belonging and no sense that others love and care for us, we feel out of control, abandoned and left for dead. And when we feel that isolated, we become desperate.

I do not believe that there are digital solutions to these very real issues that Millennials, and the generation to follow, face. There's no app to fix addiction, depression, suicide or other antisocial behavior. These are human problems that require human solutions. (I offer some ideas for parents, Millennials and leaders of companies on page 292 at the back of this book that may help us take steps to reverse the trends.)

The kids who are still growing up require parents and caregivers who help them develop self-esteem with intrinsic motivation at its foundation, teach problem-solving and non-digital coping strategies and take more control over access to smartphones and social media. The Millennials who are entering or are already in the workforce require employers who are empathetic, understand the challenges that this generation faces, create Circles of Safety and find ways to make the most of the many positive attributes and unique skills that Millennials bring to the table. And for the Millennials themselves, it means taking personal accountability, being willing to turn off their phones or disconnect from social media from time to time to engage in the kind of face-to-face human interaction that leads to real connection and meaningful relationships. Only then will they find the fulfillment they are looking for. We must stop blaming each other and start helping each other.

It would seem that in the dire scenario, we are our own best hope.

[BECOMING A LEADER]

CHAPTER 25

Step 12

It seems our chances look grim. As animals made for cooperation with a need to trust, too many of us are working in environments that bring out the worst in us. We have become
cynical, paranoid, selfish and open to addiction. Our health and,
worse, our humanity, are at risk. But we cannot hide behind
excuses. We can't blame the media, the Internet or "the system."
We can't blame "the corporations" or Wall Street or even government anymore. We are not victims of our situation. We are
the architects of it.

But it isn't dangers outside that will see to our demise. Those
dangers are constant and will never go away. Civilizations don't
usually die from murder, to paraphrase the famous British his-
torian Arnold Toynbee. Civilizations die from suicide. It is increasing dangers inside our organizations that threaten us most.
And fortunately, those dangers are well within our control.

For over seventy-five years, Alcoholics Anonymous (AA) has
successfully helped people beat the dopamine addiction of alcoholism. Most of us have heard of their twelve-step program to

recovery and most of us know the first step—admitting we have a problem.

We admit that a good too many of our organizational cultures have a systemic addiction to performance and making the numbers. An addiction, like all addictions, that offers fleeting highs and often comes at significant cost to our health and our relationships. Further complicating our addiction is our ability to raise our status with celebrity or wealth alone, ignoring the anthropological requirements of alpha status. But admitting we have an addiction is only step one. Now, as in Alcoholics Anonymous, we begin the hard work of recovery. We need to do the work and make the sacrifices required to change the systems that pit us against each other and build new ones that inspire us to help each other. Something we will not be able to do alone.

"You wanna know the whole secret to AA?" Jon, a recovering alcoholic, asked me. "You wanna know who actually gets sober and who doesn't?"

Few if any of the alcoholics enrolled in AA will find sobriety until they complete Step Twelve. Even if they make it through all the other eleven steps, those who do not complete Step Twelve are very likely to drink again. It is those who complete Step Twelve who overcome the addiction.

Step Twelve is the commitment to help another alcoholic beat the disease. Step Twelve is all about service. And it is service that is the key to breaking our dopamine addictions in our organizations too. I'm not talking about serving our customers, employees or shareholders. I'm not talking about abstractions of people. I mean service to the real, living, knowable human beings with whom we work every day.

There is a reason why AA meetings happen in church basements and recreational centers and not in online chat rooms. And there is a reason why, when an alcoholic wants to reach out to their sponsor, the other alcoholic committed to helping them, they don't send an e-mail, they pick up the phone and call. It's because the connections required to beat addiction must be real. They cannot be virtual.

The whole purpose of AA meetings is to make people feel safe. The people who share the struggle, who come together to help and be helped, are warm and friendly and welcoming. For many alcoholics, the connections last well after the meetings are over. As Jon told me, the connections he made helped him feel less alone and the stories he heard gave him hope.

"Alcoholism is like a pack of wolves trying to attack you," Jon says. "If you get in the program and stay in the group, then you won't be attacked. The group will keep you safe." In other words, Alcoholics Anonymous is like a family, a tribe or a platoon. It is Aesop's oxen standing tail to tail, protecting one another from the lion. Alcoholics Anonymous is a perfectly formed Circle of Safety.

In Oxytocin We Trust

CONFRONTING THE THREATS we face in the world cannot be done alone, at least not very effectively. It takes the help and support of others—others who believe in us. Just as dopamine-addicted companies won't be able to self-regulate, addicts who try to follow the steps themselves, who try to monitor their own progress, usually fail. Alcoholics don't succeed just for themselves. They also want to succeed for the person who gives their time and energy to their success: their sponsor. This is how serotonin is supposed to work. It doesn't just raise our status, it reinforces caring, mentoring relationships.

And then there is oxytocin. Those feelings of trust and love, all those warm and fuzzies, as it turns out, are critical to helping us beat addiction. Preliminary findings from a 2012 study conducted by researchers in the Department of Psychiatry at the University of North Carolina at Chapel Hill show that the presence of oxytocin actually fights withdrawal symptoms in alcoholics and heroin addicts. There is evidence, in fact, that increased levels of oxytocin may even prevent physical dependence from happening in the first place. The evidence is strong that a healthy release of oxytocin, through acts of service, sacrifice and selflessness on behalf of others, might actually reduce the possibility of a corporate culture becoming toxic in the first place.

Oxytocin is so powerful that the bonds of trust and love we form not only help us beat or ward off addiction, they actually help us live longer. According to another 2012 study, this one conducted by Duke University Medical Center, couples live significantly longer than single people. The Duke investigators found that individuals who never married were more than twice as likely to die during midlife as individuals who were married throughout their adult life. Other studies have shown that married couples have lower levels of cancer and heart disease. Close, trusting relationships don't only protect us at home, they protect us at work too.

In cultures like the Marine Corps, in which the bonds of trust run deep, the "intangibles," as the Marines call them, actually help maintain the strength of the system and its high level of integrity. It is much harder to become addicted to dopamine in a system in which trust and love run rampant. The more oxytocin there is, the stronger the bonds of trust will be, the greater the risks people will take to do the right thing, the more they will look out for each other and the better the group will ultimately perform. A Circle of Safety is kept strong by those who live and work within it.

Ask anyone who has made it through any sort of setback—depression, loneliness, failure, getting fired, a death in the family, the loss of a relationship, addiction, legal conflict, victimization by crime, anything—how they made it through. In nearly 100 percent of the cases, they will say something to the effect that "I could not have done it without the support of _____" as they go on to say the name of a family member, close friend or sometimes even a giving stranger.

Consider that those of us who have ever suffered abominable service on an airline have found solace when we turn to the stranger next to us to talk about how we are being treated. Anyone who has ever been subjected to the ambitions of an egomaniacal boss has found comfort in the person at work who is suffering the same. The person we meet who has a family member suffering from the same disease as someone close to us is someone with whom we bond. It is the group of people with whom we find common interest and common cause that we turn to for support.

Whenever there is a human bond involved—a real, true, honest human bond, where neither party wants anything from the other—we seem to find the strength to endure—and the strength to help. We can put up with a great many hardships when we have a partner to help see us through. In fact, it not only makes the hardships feel easier to endure, but it actually helps us manage the stress and the anxiety. Cortisol can't work its black magic when we have someone by our side. The only reason people like Johnny Bravo, or any Soldier, Sailor, Airman or Marine, are willing to risk their lives for the person to the left or right of them is because they have the utmost confidence that the person at their side would do the same for them.

CHAPTER 26

Shared Struggle

Want Not, Waste Anyway

WE IN THE developed world are generally not working to survive. We have more than enough of everything we need. So much so that we can actually afford to waste it. According to a 2004 study by Timothy Jones, an anthropologist at the University of Arizona in Tucson, as much as 50 percent of ready-to-harvest food will never be eaten. In fact, the average American household wastes 14 percent of food purchases, 15 percent of which are products that have not yet expired. Translated into dollars, the average American family is throwing out nearly $600 per year in meat, fruits, vegetables and grain products. Simply learning to preserve or freeze more food could save families nearly $43 billion per year.

The developing world also loses about the same as the United States, but not because they throw stuff out. According to the Stockholm International Water Institute, as much as 50 percent of postharvest food grains will never be eaten simply because of spoilage and improper storage. The developing world loses 50 percent of its food supply because people aren't looking after it properly, while we, the developed world, lose 50 percent of our food because we throw it out unnecessarily.

This is the burden of having too much. It's easy to spend or dispose of what we don't need when there is plenty more available. Our prodigal ways are not a new phenomenon. That's how our Paleolithic ancestors lived. One of the theories as to why *Homo sapiens* started farming was that they weren't very careful about the resources they had available to them in the first place. One could say we've been wasting what we have since the beginning and that we adapt only when we can't afford to waste anymore. These days, too many leaders of organizations seem to be wasting the good will of people. I wonder how long that can last until they can't afford to do it anymore.

If we simply measure the amount of food or energy Americans throw out, how much money we spend wantonly, that should give us an indication of how little we actually need. And that may be our biggest challenge: the fact that, as a society, we feel no burden. Feeling a shared common burden is one of the things that brings us together. Less hardship means less of a need to cooperate, which means less oxytocin. Few of us volunteer to help people in need before the natural disaster—only after it.

In this day and age there is an abundance of food, resources and choices. The number of products on offer at a supermarket or the availability of something like electricity are things our society takes for granted. This is what commoditization is. It is when a resource becomes so ubiquitous that it loses its perceived value. Computers used to be amazing, special tools. Companies like Dell built huge businesses on the remarkable value of these machines. However, as supplies increased and prices came down, the product became commoditized. And with it, our appreciation for how remarkable these tools are in our lives diminished. Abundance destroys value.

It is not when things come easily that we appreciate them, but when we have to work hard for them or when they are hard to get that those things have greater value to us. Be it a diamond deep in the ground, career success or a relationship, it is the struggle it takes to make it work that helps give that thing its value.

. . . .

It is not the work we remember with fondness, but the camaraderie, how the group came together to get things done.

. . . .

Our Best Days at Work

WHEN ASKED, "WHAT was one of your best days at work?" very few of us recount the time everything went smoothly and the big project we were working on came in on time and under budget. Considering how we work so hard to make things go well, that example should count as a pretty good day at work. But strangely, the days everything goes smoothly and as planned are not the ones we remember with fondness.

For most of us, we have warmer feelings for the projects we worked on where everything seemed to go wrong. We remember how the group stayed at work until 3 a.m., ate cold pizza and barely made the deadline. Those are the experiences we remember as some of our best days at work. It was not because of the hardship, per se, but because the hardship was shared. It is not the work we remember with fondness, but the camaraderie, how the group came together to get things done. And the reason is, once again, natural. In an effort to get us to help one another during times of struggle, our bodies release oxytocin. In other words, when we share the hardship, we biologically grow closer.

You may be getting sick of my saying this over and over, but our bodies are trying to incentivize us to repeat behavior in our best interest. And in hard times, what better way to protect the tribe, organization or species than to make us feel good for helping one another? Our "best days at work" were the ones when we helped each other endure or overcome hardship. And if those days do not come with fond memories, it is probably because the team didn't come together, and backstabbing and selfishness prevailed. When we work in a culture in which we are left to fend for ourselves, even a "good day at work," from a biological perspective, is still a bad day at work.

Those in the military often speak with fondness of their time deployed. It seems strange that a group living in austere conditions, with real threats of danger, would have fond memories of these times. They probably won't say they enjoyed it; they might even say they hated it. But a surprisingly high number will say they were grateful for the experience. This is the result of the oxytocin we feel knowing that we made it through thanks to the help of others. And those relationships help us manage the hardships when we come back too. Contrary to popular belief, those who deployed actually commit suicide at slightly lower rates than those who stayed back. One theory is that the ones who did not deploy often have a hard time coping with being alone while their team goes off to face external dangers together.

In times when resources are scarce and danger is looming, we naturally come together. This is why the four major uniformed services work so well together in a combat situation, but bicker like spoiled children back at the Pentagon. In combat, when uncertainty is high and the external threats are real, they work together to increase the chances of survival and success. In contrast, back at the Pentagon, where losing huge sums of money is the biggest threat they face, the leaders of each service all too often work against one another in the name of protecting or advancing their own interests. Common are the stories in combat of a person who sacrifices themselves to help another person, regardless of uniform. Rare are the stories in the Pentagon of one service sacrificing to help another uniformed service get what they need.

If our species thrives when we are forced to work together to manage through hardship, then what we need to do is redefine hardship for our modern age of abundance. We need to learn how to readapt. To understand how to operate as we were designed within these complicating conditions. To the relief of many readers, we do not need to give up our abundance and live a monk's life to do this. Our challenge is that our visions of the future are confined to our means. We need to reframe our visions to outsize the resources we have to realize them.

Redefining the Struggle

IT IS NO accident that small businesses so often run innovation circles around large corporations. Though almost all large corporations today started small and innovative, they seem to lose their ability to innovate when they get big. About the only way big companies, flush with resources, seem to innovate these days is when they buy the smaller companies that have the big ideas. Have none of the leaders of large corporations stopped to wonder why smaller, less resourced companies, staffed by a small group of people struggling together, are the ones that usually come up with all the latest innovations? Size and resources are not necessarily the advantage.

Sharing a struggle for limited resources and working with people who are intent on building something out of nothing is a good formula for a small business. But recreating those conditions is extremely difficult for organizations that have already suffered together and succeeded. This is one of the reasons we find Apple such a fascinating company. It has repeated its success multiple times, from the Apple I and II to the Macintosh and the iMac, from the iPod and iTunes to the iPhone. Instead of just looking for new ways to sell old products (which is largely what most successful companies do), they invented new products and competed in new industries.

We know that our species is not built for abundance and that our internal systems can short-circuit when we are in environments of abundance. We know that we are at greater risk of succumbing to the addictive qualities of short-term, dopamine-driven incentive structures in our companies if the chemicals that influence our behavior are out of balance. We also know that we won't pull together until the oxytocin and serotonin are able to flow more easily.

Leaders of successful organizations, if they wish to innovate or command loyalty and love from their people, must reframe the struggles their companies face not in absolute terms but in terms relative to their success. In other words, the dangers and opportunities that exist outside the Circle of Safety should be exaggerated to suit the size of the organization itself. Let me explain.

A small company struggles because it does not have the resources to guarantee it will stay alive. Survival is a very real concern. It is how well the people pull together to outthink their problems that often makes the difference between success and failure. Trying to buy one's way out of problems is less effective and unsustainable.

A larger, more successful company, in contrast, doesn't fear for its life because it is flush with resources. Survival is not the motivator, growth is. But we already know that growth is an abstract and non-specific destination that doesn't ignite the human spirit. What ignites the human spirit is when the leaders of our organizations offer us a reason to grow. Aiming for the quarter or the year just isn't that compelling, it doesn't offer much of a struggle. That's not to say it's easy—it may or may not be. But the resources are readily available for the company to accomplish such goals . . . or come close.

To really inspire us, we need a challenge that outsizes the re-sources available. We need a vision of the world that does not yet exist. A reason to come to work. Not just a big goal to achieve. This is what leaders of great organizations do. They frame the challenge in terms so daunting that literally no one yet knows what to do or how to solve it.

Bill Gates set Microsoft on a path to put a PC on every desk. What happened to that vision? Though Microsoft may have largely achieved its goal in the developed world, that goal is still a long, long way from being accomplished. Like a small busi-ness, if a large organization can frame their challenge relative to their existing capacity, the people will figure it out—that's where innovation comes from. (Sadly, due in large part to the poor leadership of Steve Ballmer, an inclination to throw money at problems and sacrifice people when necessary, the leaders of Microsoft sabotaged the very conditions required to drive the innovation they sought.)

Steve Jobs set out, in his words, to "put a dent in the uni-verse." More practically stated, he believed that the only way for us to truly capture the full value of technology is to adapt the technology to fit the way we live our lives instead of requiring that we adapt our lives to fit the way the technology works. This explains why intuitive interfaces and simplicity were key to helping him advance his vision.

If the leaders of organizations give their people something to believe in, if they offer their people a challenge that outsizes their resources but not their intellect, the people will give everything they've got to solve the problem. And in the process, not only will they invent and advance the company, they may even change an industry or the world in the process (just as an early version of Microsoft did). But if the resources are vastly greater than the problem before us, then the abundance works against us.

Though it may take small steps to make a big leap, it is the vision of the big leap and not the action of the small steps that inspires us. And only after we have committed ourselves to that vision can we look back at our lives and say to ourselves that the work we did mattered.

The Value of Purpose

STANLEY MILGRAM'S AUTHORITY and obedience experiment from the 1960s showed that those with a belief in a higher authority were much less likely to follow orders they suspected could harm others than those who did not. In every variance of the experiment, it was the volunteers who did not see the scientist as the ultimate authority who refused to go all the way. It was their adherence to a higher purpose that gave them the strength not to follow orders blindly.

In the case of our businesses, neither our bosses nor our clients are the ultimate authorities over us. And in the case of public companies, nor are the shareholders or Wall Street analysts. And believe it or not, a small company does not answer ultimately to its investors either. All these "authorities" are Milgram's scientists in white lab coats. Authorities in the situation, perhaps, but not ultimate authorities over the decisions we make. Just as Milgram's study would have us predict, those leaders and companies with a strong sense of why, a strong sense of purpose and courage enough to stand up to the pressure of Wall Street or abstract shareholders are the ones that do better in the long term.

Bob Chapman works hard to ensure his company remains profitable and continues to grow, but he sees profit as simply the means by which he can serve the people who work at Barry-Wehmiller. Profit, in his mind, is a fuel, not a destination. Chapman answers to a higher authority and feels a responsibility to look after the sons and daughters who are in the care of his company. Chapman has the courage to ignore those who would demand he make short-term decisions simply to make the numbers work.

Human beings have thrived for fifty thousand years not because we are driven to serve ourselves, but because we are inspired to serve others.

James Sinegal, of Costco, believed he had a greater responsibility to the people who worked for his company than to those who simply profited from their labor. A leader of Marines is taught to put the Marines in their charge before themselves. Every CEO of Southwest Airlines has known that their first responsibility is to their people. Serve them and they will serve the customer, who will ultimately drive the business and benefit the stakeholders. In that order.

These remarkable leaders and all those who work in their organizations believe they serve a cause rather than an outsider with selfish motives. And that cause is always human. Everyone knows why they come to work.

When a company declares that its cause is to become a global leader or to become a household name or to make the best products, those are selfish desires with no intended value to anyone beyond the company itself (and often not even everyone in the company). Those causes can't inspire humans because those causes aren't causes. No one wakes up in the morning inspired to champion that. In other words, none of them is a cause bigger than the company.

Human beings have thrived for fifty thousand years not because we are driven to serve ourselves, but because we are inspired to serve others. That's the value of Step Twelve. All we need are leaders to give us a good reason to commit ourselves to each other.

CHAPTER 27

We Need More Leaders

Johnny Bravo, the A-10 pilot who believed that his greatest asset was the empathy he had for the men on the ground, learned what it really takes to be a leader a few years after his experience in Afghanistan. It was after he landed his plane following a training mission in the Nevada desert. His crew chief, the airman assigned to look after his aircraft, came over to greet him and help him out of the jet. On that day, the crew chief was off his game and distracted, and Johnny Bravo snapped at him. He expects the people around him to be at their best so he can be at his best and support those on the ground.

His crew chief apologized. He was tired because he didn't get enough sleep, he explained. He was going to night school and he and his wife had a new baby who kept them up at night. And it was at that moment that Johnny Bravo realized that empathy is not something we give to the nameless, faceless people we aim to serve. Empathy is not something we offer to our customers or our employees from nine to five. Empathy is, as Johnny Bravo explains, "a second by second, minute by minute service that [we] owe to everyone if [we] want to call [ourselves] a leader."

Leadership is not a license to do less; it is a responsibility to do more. And that's the trouble. Leadership takes work. It takes time and energy. The effects are not always easily measured and they are not always immediate. Leadership is always a commitment to human beings.

People like me write these polemics with the hope that we can somehow influence some change for the greater good, which includes the good of society's commercial interests. And though many of you who read these books and articles may even agree with them, leaders of organizations are not clamoring to challenge the status quo.

The data prove that when we lead our organizations like Charlie Kim, Bob Chapman, James Sinegal, Captain David Marquet or Representatives Robert Goodlatte and Stephanie Herseth Sandlin, the tangible, measurable benefits are actually greater than the norm. Yet the theories espoused by the likes of Milton Friedman and pioneered by executives like Jack Welch continue to be the gospel.

Many leaders today prefer Jack Welch's approach to running a business over James Sinegal's theory on how to lead people simply because it offers more of a thrill. (Please refer back to the chart on page 219 that compares GE's stock performance with Costco's.) Sinegal's style may not come with a roller coaster, but it is stable and sets up the company to succeed in a more steady way. In contrast, Welch's style is much more like gambling. Ups and downs, wins and losses. Thrilling, exciting. Bright lights, high intensity. Vegas. If you have enough money to keep playing through the lows, then you could hit the jackpot. But if you can't afford to play for long, if you are not sure you can time your exit just right or if you are looking for something sustainable and stable, then you would probably prefer to invest in a company with a strong Circle of Safety. Having a few roller-coaster companies in an economy is fine and good. But when there are a high number of leaders who put the thrill of a dopamine hit over the hard work of looking after people, the entire economy becomes unbalanced.

Everything about being a leader is like being a parent. It is about committing to the well-being of those in our care and having a willingness to make sacrifices to see their interests advanced so that they may carry our banner long after we are gone.

Sir Isaac Newton, the seventeenth-century English physicist, offered as his Second Law of Motion the formula $f = ma$. Force equals mass times acceleration. When the mass we aim to move is great, we must apply more force. If we wish to change the direction of a large company or solve a large problem, we need to apply a huge force. And this is often what we do. We have a big repositioning or a big reorg. The trouble with applying large force to anything, however, is it rattles us. We fear it may cause more harm than good. It undermines the Circle of Safety.

However, there is another variable that we often neglect. The "a," for acceleration. Who says the change has to be sudden or instantaneous? Bob Chapman, Charlie Kim, Captain David Marquet and others did not march in with new theories and start dismantling their organizations. They tinkered. They applied small changes. They experimented. Some of their experiments worked. Some didn't. And in time, momentum built, the changes added up and the organizations and the people within them were transformed.

Leadership, true leadership, is not the bastion of those who sit at the top. It is the responsibility of anyone who belongs to the group. Though those with formal rank may have authority to work at greater scale, each of us has a responsibility to keep the Circle of Safety strong. We must all start today to do little things for the good of others . . . one day at a time.

Let us all be the leaders we wish we had.

....

If this book inspired you, please pass it on to someone you want to inspire.

APPENDIX

A Practical Guide to Leading Millenials

What We Can Do

EVERY GENERATION HAS its own flavor, its own way of seeing the world. Some of those unique characteristics and perspectives are positive, some are negative and some are nothing of particular note. The Millennial Generation has some unique personality characteristics that seem to confound their employers. Whether or not this is the same or to a higher degree than previous generations, I cannot say. Regardless, wherever I go, no matter the organization size or industry, managers are looking for guidance on how to lead their Millennials. Exasperated, many have resorted to simply asking their Millennials what they want. Requests from their young workforce range from open plan seating, to more flexibility as to when they work, to providing their meals or a laundry service for them. Many executives find that even when some or all of those requests are granted, they still struggle to inspire engagement or loyalty and many Millennials remain unable to find the sense of job satisfaction or fulfillment they crave.

That is the main reason we expanded the content of chapter 24 and added this section from the book's original release. Based on everything I learned when I wrote *Start with Why* and *Leaders Eat Last*, I wanted to offer some perspective for three reasons. One, to remind employers to practice empathy. There is nothing "wrong" with this generation. Leaders of companies must remember to take their people as they are and respect that their unique experiences growing up impact how they approach the world. This is not something we must consider or practice only for Millennials; we should be practicing empathy with everyone with whom we work. Two, to let Millennials themselves know that some of the negative feelings they may have about themselves are not unique and not their fault. They are shared by many others who grew up the way they grew up. I want those Millennials to take a deep breath and feel the weight taken off their shoulders. There is catharsis in admitting how we actually feel. Lying, hiding and faking only serve to exaggerate some of the insecurities we have. Only when they (or any of us, for that matter) can accept their lot can we begin the hard work to grow and work at our natural best. And third, I wanted to share some of the tactics I've learned so that Millennials and those who employ them can take real steps to grow and help each other. Millennials can take some real steps to growing and finding what they are looking for. And companies can take the steps to create and build Circles of Safety. Good for all employees, a healthy work environment like the one I've outlined in this book will very likely have an even more positive impact in the lives of Millennial-aged employees.

....

Based on how they grew up, there are many characteristics that make Millennials, as a generation, better than the rest of us. They are a remarkably accepting generation. In general, they seem to be more inclusive and more accepting of people who are different from them. They seem more accepting of others' sexuality or gender identity, for example, than older generations. Though not against money or capitalism, they seem to have a heightened desire that money and capitalism be used for good. Unlike the more-for-me mentality of the 1980s, they are drawn to companies that give profits or resources to others less fortunate. And my personal favorite, they are very loud about their desire to make an impact and for companies to have a sense of purpose, cause or belief. We all want to work for a company with a clear sense of Why and have our work be worth more than the money we are paid to do it. Whereas many from older generations return to a job they don't love, day after day, sometimes suffering in silence, it is the Millennials, as a generation, that have the courage and wherewithal to leave a job they don't like more quickly, embrace entrepreneurial paths more readily and demand that the companies they do work for give them more of what they need. And they're right.

Whether they like it or not, leaders of companies do have to make some changes to the way they operate to accommodate some of the unique qualities of their youngest workers. For those who stamp their feet and say that Millennials have to take all the responsibility and have to shut up and do their work, I would like to submit that such a strategy won't help the company grow for very long. True, Millennials share some of the burden to do the heavy lifting to overcome some of the challenges they may face. But companies can and must adjust their strategies and philosophies to keep up with the times, too.

Leaders of companies must appreciate that many Millennials may have lower self-esteem than they let on. They are impatient to get all the things they want . . . including overcoming some of their challenges. And, like so many of us, many suffer from an addiction to their phones and social media which contributes to their struggle to form deep meaningful relationships. I think most of us could do with some sort of digital addiction treatment lest we do damage to our ourselves, our families and our relationships, too. This is the great irony of what it takes to lead Millennials. All they need is good, old-fashioned leadership.

. . . .

In these pages are included some practical, actionable steps for leaders of Millennials, Millennials themselves and parents to combat and overcome some of the challenges our younger generations face in this modern world.

What Companies Can Do

LEADERS EAT LAST outlines a philosophy and strategy to lead, build trust and inspire our people to take care of and support each other. The specific ideas and tactics I offer here pick up from where chapter 24 left off and address the specific challenges Millennials face. In practice, most are good, general leadership concepts that will help everyone in an organization grow.

Keep Conference Rooms Free of Cell Phones

It seems like something small and insignificant. The same can be said for brushing our teeth for two minutes. It is useless unless we do it consistently. Every time we interact with each other at work it is an opportunity to connect as human beings and slowly build trusting relationships. When we are on our phones before meetings, we take away opportunities to simply chat. Whether we talk about work, ask about each other's weekends . . . or even sit in silence together . . . we are doing little things that go a long way over time. If companies simply ban cellphones in all conference rooms, in time they will start to feel improvements in the quality of relationships their people enjoy.

Encourage Notetaking on Paper Instead of Computers

According to a study published in *Psychological Science*, those who take notes on paper are better at processing and retaining information. Though computer note takers may capture more data, those who use paper are forced to discern which information is more important. This learnable, practicable skill significantly impacts critical thinking and decision making. And for those who *have to have* notes captured digitally, then assign one person to take digital notes or simply transcribe the handwritten notes after the meeting.

Teach Leadership

I visited a large bank and asked if they had a leadership training program. "We do," the executive answered excitedly. When I probed for specific courses they teach, I was told they teach compliance. "That's not leadership training," I said, "that's how to follow the law." He continued to share more of the courses on offer, but there wasn't a single class on actual leadership. How can we expect people to lead if we don't teach them how to do it? The best companies I know have a robust curriculum to include human skills like effective confrontation, active listening and communication skills.

Teach How to Give and Receive Feedback

Many Millennials in the workforce say they want more feedback. In practice, I've learned that what they seem to want is more positive feedback, more affirmation when they do well. Stories abound that too many of them aren't actually that good at receiving negative feedback. Giving and receiving feedback are learnable, practicable skills. Getting better at giving feedback is not simply about giving more feedback, it's learning how to give it, positive and negative. Similarly, receiving feedback is not simply about demanding feedback, it's learning how to receive it, positive and negative, then knowing how to act on that feedback when it's offered.

There are many ways to do this. For example, our company has developed its own 360 review system. Once a year, each person on a team is asked to write down their top three strengths or areas they believe they've most improved and their three biggest weaknesses or areas they feel they need the most growth. Everyone's answers are consolidated into one document and shared with every member of their team. We then take whatever time it takes—half a day or a full day, depending on the size of the team—to go through it all.

Each person must first read their weaknesses. Then anyone who wants to can add to or comment on that list. At this time, the person sharing their list may not speak. They are prohibited from defending themselves or offering excuses. Their job is to listen. Immediately after, the person reads their strengths. And again, anyone else can add to or comment on the list. Again, the person being reviewed may only listen. At most, we allow clarifying questions. Someone takes responsibility to run the meeting to ensure that anything outside these parameters is quickly shut down.

It is an amazing experience. The most junior person on my team had the opportunity to tell me how I let her down and how I make her feel when I say or do certain things. It was completely eye-opening for me and it was empowering for her to feel heard. We don't use this process as part of our formal evaluations but rather as a growth tool. We are all also members of smaller coaching pods that meet for an hour once a week or once every other week throughout the year to help each other build on what we learned in the review session.

Take Advantage of Your Millennials

More companies would benefit directly by taking advantage of the unique skills and perspectives Millennials bring to the table thanks to their upbringing. For example, Millennials grew up on social media. They have literally spent their entire lives curating their personal brands. They intuitively understand how branding works. Take advantage of it!

Instead of complaining that Millennials aren't showing up or aren't engaged, use them as a barometer of how you are doing as a leader or to gauge the kind of culture the company is building. Consider that older generations may not, in fact, be more engaged in their work (the data supports this), but rather that they are just better at faking it. Use the fact that Millennials are more willing to speak out when they are feeling uninspired, disengaged or dissatisfied as an accurate accounting of how everyone in the company feels. If given something that inspires them to engage or stick around, Millennials will fully engage for a long, long time.

Growing up in a world of instant gratification has its liabilities. It also offers a huge advantage. Millennials are comfortable with change and quicker to pivot than older generations. I am amazed by how many of them are so comfortable with the thought of quitting their jobs to freelance, join a start-up, or start a company themselves. I've met so many Millennials who quit a job they didn't like without another job lined up. I've never met someone of an older generation who's ever done that. Older generations seem to prefer stability over uncertainty. If there is a project or opportunity that requires lots of quick turns, snap decisions, even risks—throw Millennials at it. Let your older employees support them with experience and know-how. Building on that, although Millennials admit that they struggle to form deep meaningful relationships, they excel at first impressions. They are very impressive at a first engagement. Though they may struggle with issues of self-confidence, they give off an air of confidence that is valuable for networking or sales. Put them on the front line to sell and let the more experienced employees support them to help build deeper relationships with prospects. It will make for a more balanced team dynamic and both generations will learn from each other.

....

Here are a few more general thoughts to keep in mind if you want to take full advantage of all the gifts Millennial employees offer:

- **Mentor and support them** (acknowledging that sometimes they may not have the courage to ask for it). A true mentor is never too busy to mentor.

- **Lead by example.** Leaders in companies can be better role models than the athletes and movie stars Millennials look up to now. Show them heroism and leadership in their daily lives, so they don't just associate those qualities with billionaires and celebrities.

- **Talk about your failures.** It's easy to talk about our achievements, but being frank about our failures helps Millennials understand the realities of the journey that is their life and career. Doing so also contributes directly to building a Circle of Safety, helping create a culture in which everyone feels more comfortable to admit mistakes, fears and misgivings.

- **Give them the opportunity to fall.** There is a lot of talk about "embracing failure" in the business press. But the problem with the word "failure" is that it can be an invaluable lesson or it could mean total destruction of a company. We should continue to remind people that failure is bad and should be avoided when possible. What we can embrace is falling. Millennials should be given more opportunities to fall. Opportunities to have a lot of responsibility on smaller projects. And if they screw up we say, "good fall, now try it again."

- **Offer more opportunities to develop "human" skills.** Because an excess of technology can negatively affect how some Millennials connect, it's up to us to bridge the gap. Lead by example by connecting in more human ways. Reduce e-mail use, make more calls instead. Roam the halls more to talk to your people and ask more questions. If we want them to engage better, let us better engage with them.

- **Help them love themselves.** Help Millennials build their self-confidence. Think about how you would want another leader to treat your children. As Bob Chapman from Barry-Wehmiller says, let's work to treat all our people, each of them someone else's son or daughter, the same way.

- **Take a chance on them.** They may surprise you.

- **They are the leaders of the future, but we are the leaders right now.** We are the ones with the authority and an ability to exert far more influence on their lives than they can on ours. We must preach our own causes. We must reconnect with our own Why. We must become the kind of idealist we were when we were younger . . . then build our companies and lead our people to join us.

What Millennials Can Do

I BELIEVE THAT leaders of companies bear some responsibility to move their corporate cultures away from the dog-eat-dog philosophies of yesteryear to more trusting, Circle of Safety–style environments. And that must happen if we want to help Millennials in the workforce work at their natural best. However, as a Millennial, you too have some work to do if you want to reap all the benefits of a good culture. As great as handholding feels in the moment, if your desire is truly to find fulfillment in work and make an impact in the world, there's going to be some heavy lifting, hard truths to face and much patience required. So . . . if you're game, read on.

Solve Your Own Problem

If you're assigned to do something, big or small, and you don't know how to do it or even how to start, ask for help. If your boss doesn't give you an answer or the guidance you need, find the answer somewhere else. Some bosses won't help because they're assholes, but others won't help because they want you to figure it out yourself and trust that you're smart enough to do so. Either way, you need to figure it out because it's good for you. Google probably won't help either. The opportunity for growth here is to reach out to other people you know. Friends, old bosses, other people at the company, the bosses of your friends are all viable choices. This is an opportunity to develop interpersonal skills. In other words, this has to be more than an e-mail request. The most valuable advice will not come from an e-mail response with a list of suggestions or instructions; the real goal of leaving you to figure it out is to push you to cultivate a relationship. Go to someone in the company you may not know, knock on their door and ask for their help. If you're in a small company, look outside the company. Again, the goal isn't to simply have a person other than your boss give you step-by-step instructions, but to learn to develop a relationship with someone who knows more to guide you or act as a sounding board as you figure it out yourself.

Push to Completion

Responsibility or accountability isn't about starting a task or a project. It happens when we carry it to completion. For example, every now and then I ask someone to help me find something or get a hold of someone. A few days go by and I don't hear back, so I follow up on my request. "I looked it up but couldn't find anything" is the answer I get, or "I e-mailed him but haven't gotten a reply back yet." Those who are brilliant at pushing to completion do all the things the rest of us do to start a task and when they run into a roadblock, figure out all the other ways they can continue to make progress. They don't simply repeat what they've done. When asked about their progress they don't reply, "I'll try to e-mail him again." The really gifted Completers start thinking about what workarounds they can use if whatever they tried before isn't working well enough or quickly enough. Even if they never end up having to use that next step, it's already been considered. The gift of this practice is that the next time a similar challenge comes up, ideas are already generated, and new relationships already exist thanks to the way they handled things the previous time. This is what makes them so resourceful. It's not how they solved one problem, it's how prepared they are to solve the next problem.

Beg for Criticism

There is no question positive reinforcement is extremely valuable in any organization. Being recognized for our strengths and contributions does wonders for our self-confidence and our feelings of belonging. However, being told only what we are good at reduces our opportunity to grow. We don't learn much when everything goes well and we get all the answers right. Real learning happens when things go wrong or when we screw up. What we should all want is a balance of feedback. At the end of every project, I ask my team what I could have done better. At the end of most meetings, we tell each other what little mistakes we should watch out for next time. Find the people whom you respect and admire, the ones you want to be more like or know how they are good at something you could be better at, regardless of their rank or responsibility, and ask them what you can do better next time. In time, you will find yourself much more receptive to negative feedback and much better at giving feedback, positive and negative, to others.

Unless your company offers a class on how to give and receive feedback, don't assume those around you, including your boss, know how to give negative feedback. They may be too aggressive. Too blunt. Maybe even a little mean. Perhaps they are bad at giving feedback because no one ever taught them how. Or perhaps they've had bosses who were bad at giving them feedback. Try to brush aside the stuff that offends or upsets you to really try to hear what they are saying you can do better next time. And if they only tell you things like, "don't let that happen again," then work to figure out what you can do better next time, so that it doesn't actually happen again. Preparing to solve a problem for next time feels better than getting upset about our failure to solve it this time.

Sacrifice Credit

Like feedback, giving credit where credit is due goes a long way to building a Circle of Safety and creating an environment of mutual respect between boss and employee. Of course leaders should publicly acknowledge the hard work that specific people contributed to a project. However, there is more to work than getting the credit for it. Like almost every tip in this section, it's about balance. There is something quite magical about learning to be a shadow player who helps make others look good, whose silent impact makes projects turn out better. There is a humble magic in feeling an immense sense of joy and pride in seeing someone we supported, worked with and helped get the public praise.

Much in the same way parents find real joy in the success of their kids and great leaders feel pride when their people achieve things others didn't think they could, so too can we all learn to feel joy in the contributions we make to see those around us thrive. I know what some of you are thinking: if I did the work, I want the credit. I agree. But the short-term burst of goodness you feel for the extrinsic reward won't last. More important, it won't help you develop the muscle responsible for long-term feelings of fulfillment. What's more, the more others see you experience real joy in being the shadow player, the more they will seek you out for help. The more they will rely on you and trust you. When that happens, take intense pride and joy in the success of the project and start working hard to celebrate each other.

This book, for example, has an acknowledgments section. I didn't have to write it, and most people won't read it. But it's not for you—it's for the people who helped me. It's my little tip of the hat to say thank you. And here's the best part—because of the relationship we've built, almost all of them take immense personal pride when they hear someone say how much they enjoyed this book, without knowing their contribution to its creation. They are the real reason things like this can happen.

Cold Turkey Your Phone

Many of you won't like this one and will think of all kinds of excuses to ignore or avoid doing it. For example, here's a suggestion: stop keeping your phone by your bed when you sleep, charge your phone in another room. You already have your excuse, don't you: but it's my alarm clock!

I don't need to offer an alternative option for you—you've already read Solve Your Own Problem and Push to Completion and know what to do.

Just as an alcoholic removes the alcohol from their house because they can't rely on their willpower not to drink, you need to find ways to keep yourself away from the addictive power of your devices. You are simply not strong enough to deny yourself that hit of dopamine goodness. You have to cut yourself off. I'm not suggesting we abandon our phones or social media altogether, I'm suggesting we regain balance. What I've learned is that if we start with some more dramatic strategies, we can actually beat the habit and overcome our urge to jump every time our phones buzz, bing, flash or beep. Beat the addiction, lose the craving. That's how it works. So . . . what can we do in the short and medium term to help us overcome the urge to constantly check and check in?

1. From this moment on, no cell phones at any meal table. If you're out for lunch or dinner with a friend, family, colleague or client, turn your ringer off and put your phone away and out of sight. Upside down on the table doesn't count. A bottle of vodka with the cap on it won't help the alcoholic beat the craving. It has to be out of sight altogether! If the person you're with takes their phone out—you can say politely, "Hey, let's have a meal together, without our phones." You can make exceptions: if you happen to be waiting for an important message, just inform the people you're with why you need your phone out. Once that message comes in, put the phone away. You get the idea.

You'll probably hate it the first or even dozen times you do it. Too many of us are addicts, remember. Taking away the thing that makes us feel good doesn't feel good. Give it some time and you'll start to feel the effect. We actually enjoy the company of our friends more. We have an even better time when we go out with them. We have livelier conversations. We learn more about them and they learn more about us. We learn to trust and rely on them more just as they learn to trust and rely on us more. This is one simple step you can take to build deep, meaningful relationships with the people in your lives.

2. On the same note, if you have a spouse or significant other, the next time you go out on a date with them, agree to leave both your phones at home. Or, if you need a phone for kids, to call a car—or take a picture of your food—take just one phone and let the other person carry it. If you are carrying your date's phone, you won't feel the craving to check it and vice versa. The quality of the time you spend together will, in short order, significantly improve. And when you come home to texts from people asking you why you took so long to respond, some of you may start to enjoy replying, "I was out with the person I love and we left our phones at home."

What We Can Do as Parents

Digital-Free Family Vacation

A fourteen-year-old boy I know was furious at his mother for taking over a week to replace his broken cell phone. In the course of that time, his girlfriend broke up with him because he failed to respond to her texts. It's worth noting that the kids go to the same school and live in the same neighborhood. Disturbed by their son's addiction to his phone, the parents came up with what they thought was a radical idea. They took a family vacation and took only one phone with them. With their phones taken away, their two children became agitated and short-tempered. It's safe to say it was starting off looking like the worst family vacation ever. Then, after a few days, something changed.

They started to talk and laugh and really bond. It ended up being the best vacation they've ever had together.

Sign the Contract

Cell phone companies make us sign contracts filled with terms and conditions to have our phones, so why shouldn't our kids have to sign a contract to have theirs? Delany Ruston is a psychologist and filmmaker who produced a great documentary called *Screenagers*, in which she tackles whether or not to buy her young teenage daughter a cell phone. In the film, she demonstrates a unique and effective idea—if their daughter wanted the smart phone, she had to sign a contract and agree to certain conditions. I've heard of other parents trying the same thing, too. They are writing up contracts that include terms such as:

- The phone can never be used or even kept in the child's bedroom.

- The child cannot have the phone at any meal table.

- If friends come over, ALL the children have to forfeit their phones while they are together. (If the friends' parents complain, saying they want their kids to have their phones on them at all times, call those parents and give them the house number to call if they need to get hold of their kids at any time.)

- Restrict the times when they are allowed to use their phones.

- If any of these terms are violated, the child loses their phone for a week.

Spin the Password

One family I met would change the password to the Wi-Fi every day. Only when their kids had completed their chores or their homework would they be given the new password. And even then, it was only enabled for a limited time before being disabled again.

Lead by Example

I frequently hear from parents complaining that their kids are constantly on their phones. However, I also hear from kids that their parents are always on their phones. If we truly believe that our families are more important than our work, we need to prove it. I have met too many parents who actually tell me that they have to have their phones at the family dinner table in case of work calls or e-mails. Unless you're an emergency surgeon on call to save someone's life, unless you're a first responder who has to run out the door at any moment, you need to question whether you *really have to* have your phone at the family dinner table. We can make our kids feel that we don't care about them as much as we say we do simply by having our phones out at the dinner table.

Being a Parent Is Hard Work

It breaks my heart when I go to restaurants and I see entire families on their devices. I was in a restaurant recently where I noticed a mom and grandmother with heads down in their phones. One kid, probably around six or seven, was playing a game on another phone and another kid, probably around nine or ten, had headphones on watching a movie. I saw them while I was eating a few tables away. Over the course of my dinner, nothing changed. When I finally got up to leave, not a single one of them had changed positions.

Another time I was out for brunch and was seated next to what looked like two or three families all out for brunch together. The parents sat at one table and all the kids, six or seven of them, all sat at an adjacent table. Not a single adult had a phone out, but every single kid had their own device and was head down for the entire brunch. I understand the temptation. Sometimes it is so nice to take a little vacation from our kids. But not every time. I honestly believe it would do less long-term damage to a kid to put them up for adoption than to hand them a device every single time we don't want to deal with them. Kids are annoying and loud and they fight and distract us from the things we like doing. That's because they're kids. And being a parent is hard work. Find shortcuts, take breaks from them, put them in front of the TV now and then. But don't fill them up with so much dopamine as impressionable children that you end up doing serious damage to them as adults. If you do let them engage with you or each other more often, you'll find that they say really funny or profound things that remind you that all that annoying stuff is really worth putting up with.

. . . .

There is an entire section in the bookshop called "self-help." What we really need is a section called "help others." If we all agree to practice even some of these suggestions, we will be pioneering the help-others industry together. Inspire on!

—SIMON SINEK
February 20, 2017

ACKNOWLEDGMENTS

I felt an intense sense of accomplishment when I completed this book. It was easily one of the most difficult things I have ever done. There were many sleepless nights, weekends lost, family events missed, periods of despair and feelings that I couldn't do it. It was only because of the love, support and friendship of some remarkable people that I was able to finish it. And so I thought it only appropriate to share a little serotonin with those who stood by me. I hope I made them proud.

First and foremost is my incredible publisher, Adrian Zackheim. He took a risk on me with *Start with Why,* then another risk on me with this book. He offered me his patience (of which he needed a great deal) and helped make my ideas better. It was over lunch together that the concept of the Circle of Safety came to life. (I wish I had kept that scrap of paper.) Thank you, Adrian.

Danielle Summers was about the best research assistant I could have ever asked for. With a nerdy love for the science and a genuine curiosity for what I was trying to figure out, there is no way I could have learned as much as I did without her tireless energy to help me understand it all. She is off becoming a nurse now, which is great for those she will serve, but I miss her. Thank you, Danielle.

When writing my first book, I discovered that I was more productive when I was on a plane. I took multiple flights to random cities across the country, showing up at the airport with nothing more than my laptop. But not for this one. For this book, I discovered that I was immensely more productive when I had someone here with me to keep me on task. Thank you to Sarah Haarmann for making sure I got my work done. I am confident that this book would have taken two or three times longer to complete if Sarah weren't there to push me and look after me. Thank you, Sarah.

There are some friends who seem to show up when you need them most. Jenn Hallam has been a rock throughout this process. From the beginning she helped me keep my ideas straight. When I had hundreds of pages of random thoughts, she showed up to help make sense of it all. Near the end of the project when I couldn't keep going, she was there. Even at the last minute, when it took fifteen-, sixteen- or seventeen-hour days to pull this off, Jenn was there. Thank you, Jenn. You are something remarkable.

I want to give special recognition to my amazing team, Kim Harrison, Monique Helstrom, David Mead, Lauren Hadeed, Mikaila Robert, Laila Soussi, and Diane Hare. You guys were so supportive and so patient throughout this process. I get the strength to do what I do because of you.

Thank you to Lt. Col. Matt Whiat and Maj. Charles Throckmorton for looking after me on our trip to Afghanistan. It was that experience, more than any other, that taught me the definition of service. I am so grateful I experienced it with the two of you. You are my brothers.

To Lt. Col. Paul Mullis, USAF. Thank you for all the stories you shared of remarkable people. You were the first one to tell me about JB's story. And I can't thank you enough for being there for me when I needed you most. Your courage to do what you signed up to do inspired me to keep going (and still does). Thank you, JQ.

Thank you to my agent, Richard Pine, and my editor, Maria Gagliano, for helping me bring my crazy ideas to life. Thank you.

There are a few friends who so graciously gave me their time to hear what I was writing to make sure it all made sense. Thank you Julia Hurley, who was not only the first person to lay eyes on a manuscript, but who did so much work to make sure all the facts in the book are true. Thank you to Courtney Keller and

Christina Houghton for your eyes and ears. To Kendra Fitzgerald, who made sure to remind me on a regular basis that I wasn't alone. She was always there to give me a boost of inspiration to help me through the process. A special thank you to Sarah Salisbury, who not only sat and listened, but who also suffered through the stress of the project with me. Thank you, Sarah.

There are four people who have had more influence on my understanding of leadership and service than anyone else. Bob Chapman. I am proud to call you my mentor and my friend. I will forever carry your name in my right pocket and carry your torch into the future. Lt. Gen. George Flynn, USMC (Ret.). Sir— from the first phone call, there was a connection. You are my teacher, my friend and now my partner as we work together to change the world. Semper Fi, George. Charlie Kim. You are generous like few others I know. Thank you for the rapid-fire ideas and for pushing me. You have made your father proud. And Capt. David Marquet, USN (Ret). I'm still a groupie. Your understanding of what leadership is and how it works is clearer than that of anyone else I know. Thank you for being the other half of my brain and such an amazing friend.

To all the people who made themselves available for interviews and an exchange of ideas—even if our specific conversations didn't end up in the final manuscript, what you taught me was instrumental to my understanding of the subject. Scott Belsky, Megan Bezdichek, Matthew Bishop, Tom Brokaw, Dr. Loretta Breuning, Nayam Busa, Ashley Bush, Pierce Bush, John T. Cacioppo, Susan Cain, David Copperfield, Kelly Dane, Dr. Charles Denham, Peter Docker, Col. Michael Drowley, USAF, David Ekstein, Jo Frost, Seth Godin, Adrian Grenier, Kristen Hadeed, Lt. Col. DeDe Halfhill, USAF (you earned this one, Deeds), Scott Harrison, Ken and Teri Hertz, Elissa Hogan, Joey, Gen. Ray Johns, USAF (Ret.), Lt. Gen. Darrell Jones, USAF, the amazing people at the Kipp School, Ted Koppel, Jim Kwik, Leland Melvin, Summer Rayne Oakes, Cameron Parker, Shrage Posen, Peter Roskam, Craig Russell, Stephanie Herseth Sandlin,

Jules Shell, Rhonda Spencer, Dr. Lynn Stout, Matt Tenney, Dr. William Ury, Peter Whybrow, Cami Yoder, Paul Zak and the remarkable Marines I met from Parris Island, Camp Lejeune and Marine Corps Base Quantico.

Then there is Laurie Flynn. Laurie joined me for what was supposed to be a two- to three-month assignment to help me clean up the book at what I thought was the end of the project. Twelve months later, we finished the book. She, more than anyone, shared all that cortisol with me as we worked to figure this one out. We worked many, many fourteen-hour days together . . . many of them. Yet we always found ourselves giggling at the end. Not only do I really love working with Laurie, I just plain love her. Laurie, I would gladly write a hundred books with you. Thank you, Laurie.

Then there is one other group to thank. Perhaps the most important group of all. You. To the people who took the time to read my ramblings and to hear my thoughts, to those who raised their hands and volunteered to lead in the spirit of *Leaders Eat Last*. Thank you for the courage you have to be the leaders we need in this world. I will do all I can to share your stories and support you as you work to serve those who serve others. It is because of you that, together, I know we will change our world for the better.

Inspire on!

NOTES
....

Some names and identifying details have been changed to protect those individuals who continue to work in organizations where their leaders do not afford them much protection.

PART ONE: OUR NEED TO FEEL SAFE

3   **Flying over the thick clouds:** Mike Drowley, "There Are Some Fates Worse than Death," TED Talk. Recorded May 2012. TEDx: http://tedx talks.ted.com/video/TEDScottAFB-Mike-Drowley-There. Mike Drowley, author's interview, April and June 2013.

10   **Before there was empathy:** Mike Merck and Ron Campbell, personal interviews, April 2013.

10   **But things would change after Bob Chapman:** Bob Chapman, author's interviews, June 2012.

18   **80 percent of people are dissatisfied:** John Hagel III and John Seely Brown, "Measuring the Forces of Long-Term Change—the 2010 Shift Index," Deloitte Center for the Edge.

23   **George's mind raced:** Primary research was through an author's visit to Marine boot camp, April 2012. "George" is a composite character of the men and women I met that day. Stephen M. Buckley, "Military, Marine Recruit Training," Stephen M. Buckley's home page, Boston College, https://www2.bc.edu/~bucklesg/PI.htm.

24   **A lion used to prowl:** Aesop, "The Four Oxen and the Lion," chapter 52 in *Harvard Classics Volume 17: Folklore and Fable, 1909*, ed. Charles W. Eliot (Seattle: Amazon Digital Services Inc., 1909).

27   **Spartans:** Steven Pressfield, *Gates of Fire: An Epic Novel of the Battle of Thermopylae* (New York: Bantam, 1999), 47.

33   **A 2011 study:** P. Butterworth et al., "The Psychosocial Quality of Work Determines Whether Employment Has Benefits for Mental Health: Results from a Longitudinal National Household Panel Survey," *Occupational & Environmental Medicine* 11 (2011): 806–12.

33 **Another study, conducted by researchers at University College London:** Anna Hodgekiss, "Hating Your Job and Unemployment Are Equally Bad for Your Health," *Daily Mail*, November 23, 2012. http://www.dailymail.co.uk/health/article-2237371/Hating-job -bad-health-unemployed-researchers-warn.html.

34 **According to a Gallup poll:** "State of the American Workplace," Gallup (2013). http://www.gallup.com/strategicconsulting/163007/state -american-workplace.aspx.

34 **Whitehall Studies:** "The Whitehall II Study," International Centre for Health and Society, Department of Epidemiology and Public Health, University College London, 2004. http://www.ucl.ac.uk /whitehallII/pdf/Whitehallbooklet_1_.pdf. M. G. Marmot et al., "Health Inequalities Among British Civil Servants: The Whitehall II Study," Department of Epidemiology and Public Health, University College and Middlesex School of Medicine, London, 1991. http: //www.ncbi.nlm.nih.gov/pubmed/1674771. University College London Research Department of Epidemiology and Public Health, "Whitehall II History." Last modified July 30, 2013. http://www.ucl .ac.uk/whitehallII/history.

35 **It even has a name: "executive stress syndrome":** "Executive Stress," Simma Lieberman Associates, http://www.simmalieberman.com /executive-stress.html.

35 **Researchers found:** Gary D. Sherman et al., "Leadership Is Associated with Lower Levels of Stress," *Proceedings of the National Academy of Sciences of the United States of America* (2012). http://www .pnas.org/content/early/2012/09/19/1207042109.abstract.

35 **Researchers at Harvard and Stanford:** Max McClure, "More Authority Means Less Stress, Say Stanford and Harvard Psychologists," *Stanford University News Service*, September 24, 2012. http://news .stanford.edu/pr/2012/pr-leadership-stress-levels-092412.html.

36 **"The more senior you are in the employment hierarchy":** "The Whitehall II Study," International Centre for Health and Society, Department of Epidemiology and Public Health, University College London, 2004. http://www.ucl.ac.uk/whitehallII/pdf/Whitehallbooklet _1_.pdf.

37 **Human resources consultancy Mercer LLC:** "One in Two US Employees Looking to Leave or Checked Out on the Job, Says What's Working Research," Mercer press release, June 20, 2011. http://www .mercer.com/press-releases/1418665.

38 **A study by two researchers:** "The Importance of an After-Work Smile," *Harvard Business Review, The Magazine*, October 2011. http://hbr.org/2011/10/the-importance-of-an-after-work-smile/ar/1.

PART TWO: POWERFUL FORCES

49 **"You can't laugh and be afraid":** Stephen Colbert, interview by James Kaplan, *Parade,* September 23, 2007, 6-7.

49 **"I hope you're all Republicans":** Reagan Ronald to the chief surgeon upon entering the operating room following the assassination attempt, March 30, 1981. http://edition.cnn.com/TRANSCRIPTS/1308/10/cotc.01.html.

52 **That one day, "little black boys":** Martin Luther King, Jr., "I Have a Dream . . ." Address, March on Washington, Lincoln Memorial, Washington, D.C., August 28, 1963. http://www.archives.gov/press/exhibits/dream-speech.pdf.

57 **"you like me . . .":** Sally Field, 57th Academy Awards, speaking to the audience, March 25, 1985. http://www.hollywoodreporter.com/video/video-sally-field-oscar-speech-101595.

64 **people who claim to be happy:** Sharon Jayson, "Happy? You May Live 35% Longer, Tracking Study Suggests," *USA Today,* October 31, 2011. http://yourlife.usatoday.com/mind-soul/story/2011-10-31/Happy-You-may-live-35-longer-tracking-study-suggests/51016606/1. Andrew Steptoe and Jane Wardle, "Positive Affect Measured Using Ecological Momentary Assessment and Survival in Older Men and Women," *Proceedings of the National Academy of Sciences of the United States of America* (2011).

71 **The National Counterterrorism Center:** "2011 Report on Terrorism," National Counterterrorism Center, March 12, 2012. http://www.fas.org/irp/threat/nctc2011.pdf.

71 **According to FBI statistics:** "Murder in America," *Wall Street Journal.* http://projects.wsj.com/murderdata/?mg=inert-wsj.

71 **Compare those numbers to the 600,000:** Donna L. Hoyert and Jiaquan Xu, "National Vital Statistics Reports," *Centers for Disease Control and Prevention, National Center for Health Statistics*, no. 6 (2012): 17. http://www.cdc.gov/nchs/data/nvsr/nvsr61/nvsr61_06.pdf.

72 **Charlie Kim could sense the tension:** Charlie Kim, author's interview, October 2012.

80 **A 2010 study:** Francesca Gino, Michael Norton, and Dan Ariely, "The Counterfeit Self: The Deceptive Costs of Faking It," *Psychological*

Science, no. 5 (2010): 712–20. http://www.people.hbs.edu/mnorton /ginonortonariely.pdf.http://www.people.hbs.edu/mnorton/ginonor ton ariely.pdf.

81 **"The cost of leadership":** Lieutenant General George Flynn, author's interview, November 2011.

85 **"We would never dream of":** Bob Chapman, author's interview, January 2011.

86 **"It is better that we all suffer":** Ibid.

PART THREE: REALITY

89 **"How many souls . . .":** Author's interview with confidential FAA source, July 2012.

91 **domestic and passenger flights:** United States Department of Transportation, Bureau of Transportation Statistics, press release. Last modified April 4, 2013. http://www.rita.dot.gov/bts/press_releases /bts016_13.

95 **self-help industry:** "The Market for Self-Improvement Products and Services," Marketdata Enterprises Inc. (2012). http://www.market research.com/Marketdata-Enterprises-Inc-v416/Self-Improvement -Products-Services-7284574/.

96 **therapist:** Ronald W. Dworkin, "The Rise of the Caring Industry," *Policy Review* (Hoover Institution, Stanford University), no. 161. http://www.hoover.org/publications/policy-review/article/5339.

PART FOUR: HOW WE GOT HERE

101 **one commercial radio station:** History Channel, *The Roaring Twenties*. http://www.history.com/topics/roaring-twenties.

102 **"Black Tuesday":** Federal Deposit Insurance Corp., FDIC Learning Bank. http://www.fdic.gov/about/learn/learning/when/1930s.html.

102 **the Great Depression—a period:** Harold Bierman Jr., "The 1929 Stock Market Crash," *Economic History Association*, February 5, 2010. http://eh.net/encyclopedia/article/bierman.crash.

103 **lasted for over a decade:** History Channel, *The Great Depression*. http://www.history.com/topics/great-depression.

103 **America entered World War II:** Sabrina Tavernise, "As Fewer Americans Serve, Growing Gap Is Found Between Civilians and Military," *New York Times*, November 24, 2011. http://www.nytimes.com/2011 /11/25/us/civilian-military-gap-grows-as-fewer-americans-serve .html?_r=0.

103 *The War:* Ken Burns and Lynn Novick, Florentine Films and WETA-TV, 2007. http://www.pbs.org/thewar/.

104 **the whole country came together:** "18-Year-Old," *Life,* November 30, 1942.

106 **U.S. Birth Rate:** U.S. Census. www.census.gov.

106 **In 1946, the number of children born:** Jessica R. Sincavage, "The Labor Force and Unemployment: Three Generations of Change," U.S. Department of Labor, Bureau of Labor Statistics, *Monthly Labor Review* (June 2004): 34–41. http://www.bls.gov/opub/mlr/2004/06/art2full.pdf.

106 **The end of the Boomer:** Ibid.

106 **Boomers added 76 million:** Ibid.

107 **Average U.S. Income:** U.S. Census. www.census.gov.

108 **African Americans:** "Landmark Legislation: The Civil Rights Act of 1964," United States Senate Web site. http://www.senate.gov/artandhistory/history/common/generic/CivilRightsAct1964.htm.

109 **"Me" decade:** Thomas Wolfe, "The 'Me' Decade and the Third Great Awakening," *New York Magazine,* August 23, 1976. http://nymag.com/news/features/45938/ (accessed September 24, 2013).

109 **Gross domestic product:** Bureau of Economic Analysis. www.bea.gov.

112 **"A PC on every desk":** John Naughton, "How Microsoft Spent a Decade Asleep on the Job," *The Observer,* July 20, 2013. http://www.theguardian.com/technology/ 2013/jul/21/microsoft-realignment-steve-ballmer-naughton.

113 **President Ronald Reagan:** History Channel Web site, *This Day in History,* "August 5, 1981: Reagan Fires 11,359 Air-Traffic Controllers." http://www.history.com/this-day-in-history/reagan-fires-11359-air-traffic-controllers.

113 **strike is illegal:** "1947 Taft-Hartley Substantive Provisions," National Labor Relations Board. http://www.nlrb.gov/who-we-are/our-history/1947-taft-hartley-substantive-provisions.

114 **Reagan banned:** Greg Miller, "Clinton Lifts Ban on Fired Air Controllers," *Los Angeles Times,* August 13, 1993.

116 **the more financial analysts . . . less innovative:** Jie (Jack) He and Xuan Tian, "The Dark Side of Analyst Coverage: The Case of Innovation," *Journal of Financial Economics,* vol. 109, no. 3 (September 2013): 856–78. http://www.sciencedirect.com/science/article/pii/S0304405X13001086.

118 **"No one wakes up in the morning":** Bob Chapman, author's interview, February 2013.

PART FIVE: THE ABSTRACT CHALLENGE

122 **Eichmann lived:** Geller Doron, "Israeli Military Intelligence: The Capture of Nazi Criminal Adolf Eichmann," Jewish Virtual Library. http://www.jewishvirtuallibrary.org/jsource/Holocaust/eichcap .html.

123 **Stanley Milgram:** Stanley Milgram, "Some Conditions of Obedience and Disobedience to Authority," The Tavistock Institute. http:// psyc604.stasson.org/Milgram2.pdf (accessed October 10, 2013). S. A. Mcleod, *Simply Psychology: The Milgram Experiment,* 2007, retrieved from http://www.simplypsychology.org/milgram.html; http://psycnet.apa.org/index.cfm?fa=search.displayRecord&uid=1964 -03472-001.

128 **In 2009, the** *New York Times:* Sabrina Tavernise, "Charges Filed in Peanut Salmonella Case," *New York Times,* February 21, 2013. http:// www.nytimes.com/2013/02/22/business/us-charges-former-owner -and-employees-in-peanut-salmonella-case.html?_r=0.

130 **Jamie Dimon:** Duff McDonald, "It's Time to Stop Blaming the Lenders," *CNN Money,* October 15, 2010. http://finance.fortune.cnn.com /2010/10/15/its-time-to-stop-blaming-the-lenders/.

130 **in 1970, six years before:** Milton Friedman, "The Social Responsibility of Business Is to Increase Its Profits," *New York Times Magazine,* September 13, 1970.

131 **Apple Inc. managed to sidestep:** Nelson D. Schwartz and Charles Duhigg, "Apple's Web of Tax Shelters Saved It Billions, Panel Finds," *New York Times,* May 20, 2013. http://www.nytimes.com/2013/05 /21/business/apple-avoided-billions-in-taxes-congressional-panel -says.html?pagewanted=all.

132 **"Unfortunately, the tax code":** Brian Patrick Eha, "Lessons in Persuasion from Apple CEO Tim Cook," *NBC News,* May 25, 2013. http://www.nbcnews.com/id/52001345/ns/business-small_busi ness/t/lessons-persuasion-apple-ceo-tim-cook/.

132 **By the time the** *Titanic:* Chris Berg, "The Real Reason for the Tragedy of the *Titanic,*" *Wall Street Journal Online,* April 12, 2012. http://online .wsj.com/article/SB10001424052702304444604577337923643095442 .html. John Mersey, Charles Bigham, and Somerset Arthur Gough-Calthorpe, "Loss of the Steamship 'Titanic,'" Senate Document, 62nd Congress, no. 933 (1912). http://archive.org/stream/loss steamshipti00 titgoog#page/n1/mode/2up. "Regulatory Failure of Titanic Proportions,"

ABC, *The Drum*, April 11, 2012. http://www.abc.net.au/unleashed /3940980.html.

133 **It may be worth noting:** "The U.S. Federal Budget: A Closer Look at Revenues," Congressional Budget Office (accessed September 22, 2013).

136 **"The death of one man is a tragedy":** http://www.goodreads.com /quotes/232468-the-death-of-one-man-is-a-tragedy-the-death. I recognize that the source of this quote is disputed: Eoin O'Carroll, "Political Misquotes: The 10 Most Famous Things Never Actually Said," *Christian Science Monitor*. http://www.csmonitor.com/USA/Politics /2011/0603/Political-misquotes-The-10-most-famous-things-never -actually-said/The-death-of-one-man-is-a-tragedy.-The-death-of -millions-is-a-statistic.-Josef-Stalin.

136 **the country of Syria:** Alan Cowell, "War Deaths in Syria Said to Top 100,000," *New York Times*, June 26, 2013. http://www.nytimes.com /2013/06/27/world/middleeast/syria.html?_r=0. http://www.cbo.gov /sites/default/files/cbofiles/attachments/BS_Revenues_print.pdf.

137 **Cami Yoder:** Cami Yoder, San Clemente, California, author's interview, March 2013.

140 **One quarter of all teenagers:** Elizabeth Landau, "When Bullying Goes High Tech," CNN, April, 13, 2013. http://www.cnn.com/2013/02/27 /health/cyberbullying-online-bully-victims/index.html (accessed September 22, 2013).

140 **But if social media is the end-all:** "BlogWorld Moves Western U.S. Event Back to Las Vegas," *PR Newswire*, April 19, 2012. http://www .prnewswire.com/news-releases/blogworld-moves-western-us -event-back-to-las-vegas-148079795.html and www.nmxlive.com.

141 **In 1958, Bill Gore:** "About Gore," Creative Technologies Worldwide. http://www.gore.com/en_xx/aboutus/.

142 **Bill Gore:** Jack Browne, "Gore Celebrates 50 Years of PTFE," *Microwaves and RF*, February 13, 2008. http://mwrf.com/materials/gore -celebrates-50-years-ptfe.

142 **It turned out, Bill Gore was onto something:** Lois Brown Easton, *Professional Learning Communities by Design: Putting the Learning Back into PLCs* (Thousand Oaks, Calif.: Corwin, 2011), 252. "Don't Believe Facebook; You Only Have 150 Friends," *All Things Considered*, National Public Radio, June 5, 2011. http://www.npr.org/2011/06/04 /136723316/dont-believe-facebook-you-only-have-150-friends.

142 Robin Dunbar: "Don't Believe Facebook; You Only Have 150 Friends," *All Things Considered,* National Public Radio, June 5, 2011. http://www .npr.org/player/v2/mediaPlayer.html?action=1&t=1&islist=false&id= 136723316&m=136957910.

144 If you were to sit down: Rick Lax, "Dunbar's Number Kicked My Ass in Facebook Friends Experiment," *Wired,* March 2, 2012. http:// www.wired.com/underwire/2012/03/dunbars-number-facebook/.

146 In 2010, Adam Grant: Adam M. Grant and Devin T. Mathias, "Recruiting and Motivating Fundraising Callers: How Making a Difference . . . Makes a Difference," Wharton School, University of Pennsylvania. http://moredonors.com/motivating.pdf. Adam M. Grant, "How Customers Can Rally Your Troops," *Harvard Business Review, The Magazine,* June 2011. http://hbr.org/2011/06/how-customers-can-rally-your -troops/ar/1. Susan Dominus, "Is Giving the Secret to Getting Ahead?," *New York Times,* March 27, 2013. http://www.nytimes.com/2013/03/31 /magazine/is-giving-the-secret-to-getting-ahead.html?pagewanted= all&_r=0.

147 The loan department of Wells Fargo: Adam M. Grant, "How Customers Can Rally Your Troops," *Harvard Business Review, The Magazine,* June 2011. http://hbr.org/2011/06/how-customers-can-rally -your-troops/ar/1.

147 Further proof of how much: Yehonatan Turner, M.D., "The Effects of Including a Patient's Photograph to the Radiographic Examination," Presented at RSNA Conference, December 3, 2008. http:// rsna2008.rsna.org/event_display.cfm?em_id=6008880.

PART SIX: DESTRUCTIVE ABUNDANCE

159 "Long-term greedy": Nelson Schwartz, "Public Exit from Goldman Raises Doubt Over a New Ethic," *New York Times,* March 14, 2012. http://www.nytimes.com/2012/03/15/business/a-public-exit-from -goldman-sachs-hits-a-wounded-wall-street.html and http://dealbook .nytimes.com/2010/03/22/reining-in-greed-at-goldman/.

159 Given their reputation these days: David Smith, "Into the Belly of the Beast (Part 1—How Goldman Sachs Became the Most Hated Bank on Earth)," *Economy Watch,* January 26, 2012. http://www .economywatch.com/economy-business-and-finance-news/into-the -belly-of-the-beast-part-one.26-01.html.

159 Goldman could do no wrong: Suzanne McKee, *Chasing Goldman Sachs: How the Masters of the Universe Melted Wall Street Down . . .*

and Why They'll Take Us to the Brink Again (New York: Crown Books, 2010).

160 **Goldman's IPO:** Lawrence Lessig, "What's Really Wrong with Goldman Sachs," CNN, March 15, 2012. http://www.cnn.com/2012 /03/15/opinion/lessig-goldman-sachs.

161 **William Cohan highlights this:** William D. Cohan, *Money and Power: How Goldman Sachs Came to Rule the World* (New York: Anchor Books, 2011).

161 **By 2010, with Goldman Sachs' role:** "Wall Street and the Financial Crisis," Web site of U.S. Senator Carl Levin. http://www.levin.senate .gov/issues/wall-street-and-the-financial-crisis.

161 **Its CEO, Lloyd Blankfein:** Graham Bowley, "$500 Million and Apology from Goldman," *New York Times,* November 17, 2009. http: //www.nytimes.com/2009/11/18/business/18goldman.html?_r=0.

162 **The employees of WestJet:** "Meet Our Team, WestJetters," WestJet. http://www.westjet.com/guest/en/media-investors/2011-annual-report /meet-our-team/index.shtml.

163 **As Goethe:** http: //josephsoninstitute.org/quotes/quotations.php?q= Character.

164 **On March 14, 2012, the *New York Times*:** Greg Smith, "Why I Am Leaving Goldman Sachs," *New York Times,* March 14, 2012. http:// www.nytimes.com/2012/03/14/opinion/why-i-am-leaving-goldman -sachs.html.

165 **Taj Mahal Palace Hotel:** Rohit Deshpandé, "The Ordinary Heroes of the Taj," *Harvard Business Review,* December 2011. http://hbr.org /2011/12/the-ordinary-heroes-of-the-taj. Alix Spiegel, "Heroes of the Taj Hotel: Why They Risked Their Lives." NPR, last modified, December 23, 2011 (accessed October 2, 2013). http://www.npr.org/2011/12 /23/144184623/mumbai-terror-attacks-the-heroes-of-the-taj-hotel. Marie Brenner, "Anatomy of a Siege," *Vanity Fair,* November 2009.

166 **Kim Stewart:** Kim Stewart (not her real name), personal interview, February 2013.

167 **Citi issued:** Aaron Elstein, "Citigroup's Layoff of 52,000 Makes History," *Crain's New York Business,* November 17, 2008. http://www .crainsnewyork.com/article/20081117/FREE/811179995.

168 **Post-it Notes:** "About Post-it Brand," Post-it Products. http://www .post-it.com/wps/portal/3M/en_US/Post_It/Global/About/.

168 **3M:** Gerard J. Tellis, *Unrelenting Innovation: How to Create a Culture for Market Dominance* (San Francisco: Jossey-Bass, 2013), 171. *A*

Century of Innovation: The 3M Story, 3M Company, 2002. http ://multimedia.3m.com/mws/mediawebserver?6666660Zjcf6lV s6EVs666IMhCOrrrrQ-.

168 **The development of Post-it Notes:** "The History of Post-it," Post-it Products. http://www.post-it.com/wps/portal/3M/en_US/Post_It/Global /About/History/.

169 **"At 3M we're a bunch of ideas":** Tellis, *Unrelenting Innovation,* 171.

169 **"Innovation from interaction":** Ben Paynter, "How a Superbulb Massively Brightened 3M's Innovation Pipeline," *Fast Company,* March 21, 2013. http://www.fastcompany.com/3003229/innovation-agents/how -superbulb-massively-brightened-3ms-innovation-pipeline.

169 **One sure sign that all this collaborating:** 3M officials, personal interview, September 2013.

172 **Stanley O'Neal:** *Time* lists: "25 People to Blame for the Financial Crisis: Stan O'Neal . . ." http://www.time.com/time/specials/packages/article /0,28804,1877351 _1877350_1877344,00.html. David Ellis, "O'Neal Out at Merrill," *CNN Money,* October 31, 2007. http://money.cnn.com/2007 /10/30/news/companies/merrill_oneal/. Bethany McLean and Joe Nocera, "The Blundering Herd," *Vanity Fair, Business,* November 2010. http://www.vanityfair.com/business/features/2010/11/financial-crisis -excerpt-201011. Greg Farrell, "Crash of the Titans: The Rise and Fall of Stan O'Neal," *CNN Money,* November 4, 2010. http://finance.fortune .cnn.com/2010/11/04/crash-of-the-titans-the-fall-of-merrill-lynch /. Gretchen Morgenson, "How the Thundering Herd Faltered and Fell," *New York Times,* November 8, 2008. http://www.nytimes.com/2008/11 /09/business/09magic.html. Norm Brodsky, "Stan O'Neal Failed the First Rule of Leadership," *Inc.,* October 29, 2007. http://www.inc.com /ask-norm/2007/10/stan_oneal_failed_the_first_rule_of_leadership .html. Devin Leonard, "How Merrill Went into the Toilet," *Bloomberg Businessweek,* December 9, 2010. http://www.businessweek.com /magazine/content/10_51/b4208098627853.htm.

173 **O'Neal laid off thousands:** "America Attacked: The Changing Employment Picture," *Washington Post,* July 25, 2002. http://www .washingtonpost.com/wp-srv/business/legacy/layoff_article.htm.

174 **In October 2007, the company announced it had lost:** Bradley Keoun, "Merrill Lynch Reports Loss on $8.4 Billion Writedown," *Bloomberg News,* October 24, 2007. http://www.bloomberg.com /apps/news?pid=newsarchive&sid=axuWCcMYMdA0.

174 **severance package:** Rob Wile, "These CEOs Got Paid $100 Million+ Each to Quit," *Business Insider,* January 15, 2012. http://www.busi nessinsider.com/the-21-largest-golden-parachutes-of-the-new-mil lenium-2012-1?op=1.

175 **Saddam Hussein:** Mark Bowden, "Tales of the Tyrant," *Atlantic,* May 1, 2002. http://www.theatlantic.com/magazine/archive/2002 /05/tales-of-the-tyrant/302480/.

176 **David Marquet:** David Marquet, *Turn the Ship Around! A True Story of Turning Followers into Leaders* (New York: Portfolio, 2013). http://www .amazon.com/Turn-Ship-Around-Turning-Followers/dp/1591846404.

176 **David Marquet was a career submariner:** author's interviews, 2012–2013.

185 **The Foxhole Test:** author's visit to Quantico, June 2011.

187 **"Integrity," said the CEO:** Mike Duke, president and CEO of Wal-Mart Stores, Inc. "Walmart's Enduring Values," Walmart Shareholders' Meeting 2012. http://news.walmart.com/news-archive/2010/06/04/walmart -ceo-mike-duke-outlines-strategies-for-building-the-next-generation -walmart. Gretchen Morgenson, "Moving the Goal Posts on Pay," *New York Times,* national ed., May 7, 2011. http://www.nytimes .com/2011/05/08/business/08gret.html?pagewanted=all (accessed October 2, 2013).

190 **Jackie Goebel:** James Covert, "How Walmart Makes It Easy for Boss to Bag Bonus," *New York Post,* April 17, 2010. http://nypost.com /2012/04/17/how-walmart-makes-it-easy-for-boss-to-bag-bonus and http://www.youtube.com/watch?v =yOf16irzrVs.

190 **Jackie Goebel, a Walmart employee:** Jackie Goebel, Walmart employee and union activist from Kenosha, Wisconsin, personal interview, October 2013.

191 **the general manager of Ralph Lauren's Argentinian subsidiary:** James O'Toole, "Ralph Lauren Admits Bribery at Argentina Subsidiary," *CNN Money,* April 22, 2013. http://money.cnn.com/2013/04 /22/news/companies/ralph-lauren-bribery/index.html. Jonathan Green and James L. Athas, "Ralph Lauren Outed Its Subsidiary's Bribery and Set an Example for All," *Forbes,* April 26, 2013. http://www.forbes.com /sites/forbesleadershipforum/2013/04/26/ralph-lauren-outed-its -subsidiarys-bribery-and-set-an-example-for-all/.

193 **Bank of America:** Jennifer Liberto, "BofA Chief: We Have a 'Right to Make a Profit,'" *CNN Money,* October 5, 2011. http://money.cnn

.com/2011/10/05/news/economy/bank_of_america_moynihan/index .htm. Susanna Kim and Matt Gutman, "Bank of America Cancels $5 Fee," *ABC News*, November 1, 2011. http://abcnews.go.com/Business /bank-america-drops-plan-debit-card-fee/story?id=14857970.

194 **Bank of America leaders refused:** "Bank of America Will Not Implement Debit Usage Fee," *Bank of America Newsroom*, November 1, 2011. http://newsroom.bankofamerica .com/press-release/consumer -banking/bank-america-will-not-implement-debit-usage-fee.

194 **"The economics of offering a debit card":** Blake Ellis, "Bank of America to Charge $5 Monthly Debt Card Fee." *ABC News,* September 29, 2011. http://money.cnn.com/2011/09/29/pf/bank_of_america _debit_fee/index.htm.

198 **Newt Gingrich:** Katharine Q. Seelye, "Gingrich's Life: The Complications and Ideals," *New York Times,* November 24, 1994. http://www .nytimes.com/1994/11/24/us/gingrich-s-life-the-complications-and -ideals.html?pagewanted=all&src=pm.

199 **Charles Gibson:** Charles Gibson, "Restoring Comity to Congress," Discussion Paper Series, Joan Shorenstein Center on the Press, Politics and Public Policy, Harvard University, 2011. http://shorensteincenter .org/wp-content/uploads/2012/03/d60_gibson.pdf.

201 **PowerPoint presentation shown:** Ryan Grim and Sabrina Siddiqui, "Call Time for Congress Shows How Fundraising Dominates Bleak Work Life," *Huffington Post,* January 8, 2013. http://www.huffing tonpost.com/2013/01/08/call-time-congressional-fundraising_n _2427291.html.

202 **Olympia Snowe:** Kevin Miller, "Olympia Snowe Quits Senate Race," *Bangor Daily News,* February 29, 2012. http://bangordailynews.com /2012/02/28/politics/olympia-snowe-quits-senate-race/.

202 **Gallup poll in January 2013:** Frank Newport, "Congress Begins 2013 with 14% Approval," *GALLUP Politics.* http://www.gallup.com /poll/159812/congress-begins-2013-approval.aspx.

202 **That's lower than the approval rating:** Biography Channel, *Genghis Khan.* http://www.biography.com/people/genghis-khan-9308634. "Genghis Khan the GREEN: Invader Killed So Many People That Carbon Levels Plummeted," *Daily Mail Online,* January 25, 2011. http://www.dailymail.co.uk/sciencetech/article-1350272/Genghis -Khan-killed-people-forests-grew-carbon-levels-dropped.html.

203 **the 112th Congress:** "Congressional Activity," U.S. House of Representatives Web site, Office of the Clerk. http://library.clerk.house.gov

/resume.aspx. Amanda Terkel, "112th Congress Set to Become Most Unproductive Since 1940s," *Huffington Post*, December 28, 2012.

204 **Stephanie Herseth Sandlin:** author's interview, 2013.

206 **William Ury:** author's interview, 2013.

208 **When we understand the history:** Michael C. Jensen and William Meckling, "Theory of the Firm: Managerial Behavior, Agency Costs and Ownership Structure," *Journal of Financial Economics*, no. 4 (1976): 305–60. http://www.sfu.ca/~wainwrig/Econ400/jensen-meckling.pdf.

209 **Though Milton Friedman first proposed:** Ibid.

209 **In 2012, Professor Lynn Stout:** Lynn Stout, *The Shareholder Value Myth: How Putting Shareholders First Harms Investors, Corporations, and the Public* (San Francisco: Berrett-Koehler Publishers, 2012).

210 **the boom years of the 1980s and 1990s:** Joe Nocera, "Down with Shareholder Value," *New York Times*, August 10, 2012. http://www.nytimes.com/2012/08/11/opinion/nocera-down-with-shareholder-value.html. Roger Martin, "The Age of Customer Capitalism," *Harvard Business Review, The Magazine*, January 2010. http://hbr.org/2010/01/the-age-of-customer-capitalism. Justin Fox, "What Good Are Shareholders?," *Harvard Business Review, The Magazine*, July–August 2012. http://hbr.org/2012/07/what-good-are-shareholders/ar/1. Alan Murray, "Should I Rank My Employees?," *Wall Street Journal*, April 7, 2009. http://guides.wsj.com/management/recruiting-hiring-and-firing/should-i-rank-my-employees/.

210 **Every year, Welch would fire:** Jack Welch, *Jack: Straight from the Gut* (New York: Business Plus, 2003).

210 **While he was running things:** "Past Leaders," General Electric Web site. https://www.ge.com/about-us/leadership/past-leaders.

211 **"Anybody could run a business in the 1990s":** Francesco Guerrera, "Welch Denounces Corporate Obsessions," *Financial Times*, UK edition, March 13, 2009. http://www.ft.com/cms/s/0/3ca8ec2e-0f70-11de-ba10-0000779fd2ac.html.

212 **"Teams led by a directive leader":** Natalia Lorinkova, Matthew Pearsall, and Henry Sims, "Examining the Differential Longitudinal Performance of Directive Versus Empowering Leadership in Teams," *Academy of Management Journal* (2012). Jesse Eisinger, "Challenging the Long-Held Belief in 'Shareholder Value,'" *New York Times*, *DealBook*, June 27, 2012. http://dealbook.nytimes.com/2012/06/27/challenging-the-long-held-belief-in-shareholder-value/.

214 **"There's a growing body of evidence":** Justin Fox and Jay W. Lorsch, "What Good Are Shareholders?," *Harvard Business Review, The Magazine*, July–August 2012. http://hbr.org/2012/07/what-good-are-shareholders/ar/1.

215 **As it turns out, BP had a long:** "Deep Water: The Gulf Oil Disaster and the Future of Offshore Drilling," National Commission on the BP Deepwater Horizon Oil Spill and Offshore Drilling, Report to the President, January 2011. http://docs.lib.noaa.gov/noaa_documents /NOAA_related_docs/oil_spills/DWH_report-to-president.pdf. "The State of the Offshore U.S. Oil and Gas Industry," Quest Offshore Resources Inc., for the American Petroleum Industry, December 2011. http://www.api.org/policy/exploration/upload/quest_2011_december _29_final.pdf. Steven Greenhouse, "BP Faces Record Fine for '05 Refinery Explosion," *New York Times*, October 30, 2009. http://www .nytimes.com/2009/10/30/business/30labor.html. Terrence Henry, "BP Settles with OSHA: $13 Million for Texas City Refinery Explosion," *StateImpact*, National Public Radio, July 12, 2012. http://stateimpact .npr.org/texas/2012/07/12/bp-settles-with-osha-13-million-for-texas -city-refinery-explosion/. Pierre Thomas et al., "BP's Dismal Safety Record," *ABC News*, May 27, 2010. http://abcnews.go.com/WN/bps -dismal-safety-record/story?id=10763042. Abrahm Lustgarten, "Furious Growth and Cost Cuts Led to BP Accidents Past and Present," *Propublica*, October 26, 2010. http://www.propublica.org/article/bp -accidents-past-and-present.

219 **The cofounder of Costco, Sinegal:** Steven Greenhouse, "How Costco Became the Anti-Wal-Mart," *New York Times*, July 17, 2005. http:// www.nytimes.com/2005/07/17/business/yourmoney/17costco.html. Brad Stone, "Costco CEO Craig Jelinek Leads the Cheapest, Happiest Company in the World," *Bloomberg Businessweek*, June 6, 2013. http:// www.businessweek.com/articles/2013-06-06/costco-ceo-craig-jelinek -leads-the-cheapest-happiest-company-in-the-world.

219 **Back in 2005, when Sinegal:** Steven Greenhouse, "How Costco Became the Anti-Wal-Mart," *New York Times*, July 17, 2005. http:// www.nytimes.com/2005/07/17/business/yourmoney/17costco.html.

219 **GE vs. Costco:** Yahoo Finance.

221 **Costco is the second largest retailer:** Brad Stone, "Costco CEO Craig Jelinek Leads the Cheapest, Happiest Company in the World," *Bloomberg Businessweek*, June 6, 2013. http://www.businessweek.com

/articles/2013-06-06/costco-ceo-craig-jelinek-leads-the-cheapest
-happiest-company-in-the-world. Omar Akhtar et al., "World's Most
Admired Companies," *CNN Money,* 2013. http://money.cnn.com
/magazines/fortune/most-admired/2013/snapshots/2649.html.

221 **"Wall Street is in the business":** Alan B. Goldberg and Bill Ritter,
"Costco CEO Finds Pro-Worker Means Profitability," *ABC News,* August 2, 2006. http://abcnews.go.com/2020/Business/story?id=1362779.

221 **"Instead of minimizing wages":** Bonnie Kavoussi, "Costco CEO:
Raise the Minimum Wage to More Than $10 Per Hour," *Huffington
Post,* March 6, 2013. http://www.huffingtonpost.com/2013/03/06/cost
co-ceo-minimum-wage-craig-jelinek_n_2818060.html.

222 **"We should be figuring out":** Brad Stone, "Costco CEO Craig Jelinek
Leads the Cheapest, Happiest Company in the World," *Bloomberg
Businessweek,* June 6, 2013. http://www.businessweek.com/articles
/2013-06-06/costco-ceo-craig-jelinek-leads-the-cheapest-happiest
-company-in-the-world.

PART SEVEN: A SOCIETY OF ADDICTS

227 **Case 1. Mrs. _____ was confined:** Oliver Wendell Holmes and
Charles William Eliot, *The Contagiousness of Puerperal Fever* (Cam-
bridge, Mass.: Harvard Classics, 1909).

229 **"Doctors are not the cause":** Richard W. Wertz and Dorothy C.
Wertz, *Lying-in: A History of Childbirth in America* (New Haven,
Conn.: Yale University Press, 1989).

230 **This is how Jon felt:** AA member, confidential interview, January
2013.

235 **The Act was later replaced:** C. H. Sterling, "Deregulation," Museum
of Broadcast Communications. http://www.museum.tv/archives/etv
/D/htmlD/deregulation/deregulation.htm. Dan Fletcher, "A Brief
History of the Fairness Doctrine," *Time,* February 20, 2009. http://
www.time.com/time/nation/article/0,8599,1880786,00.html.

236 **"We were sort of driven":** Ted Koppel, author's interview, March
2012.

236 **"the loss leader that permitted":** Ted Koppel, "Olbermann, O'Reilly
and the Death of Real News," *Washington Post,* November 14, 2010.
http://www.washingtonpost.com/wp-dyn/content/article/2010/11
/12/AR2010111202857.html.

236 **"It never occurred to the network":** Ibid.

236 **Not long after, ABC News debuted:** ABC News, "Timeline: Nightline 30th Anniversary." http://abcnews.go.com/Nightline/fullpage ?id=8984599.

238 **What the Committee for the Fair Broadcasting of Controversial Issues:** Fletcher, "A Brief History of the Fairness Doctrine."

240 **Before the stock market crashed in 1929:** "Glass-Steagall Act (1933)," *New York Times.* http://topics.nytimes.com/top/reference /timestopics/subjects/g/glass_steagall_act_1933/index.html.

240 **half of them went out of business:** "FDIC Learning Bank: The 1930s," Federal Deposit Insurance Corporation (FDIC). http://www .fdic.gov/about/learn/learning/when/1930s.html.

240 **In 1933, Congress passed the Glass-Steagall Act:** "FDIC Learning Bank: The 1930s," Federal Deposit Insurance Corporation (FDIC). http://www.fdic.gov/about/learn/learning/when/1930s.html.

240 **In addition to the introduction of the Federal Deposit Insurance Corporation (FDIC):** "About FDIC: Who Is the FDIC?," Federal Deposit Insurance Corporation (FDIC). http://www.fdic.gov/about/learn /symbol/.

240 **as then Treasury Secretary Lawrence Summers:** Stephen Labaton, "Congress Passes Wide-Ranging Bill Easing Bank Laws," *New York Times,* November 5, 1999. http://www.nytimes.com/1999/11/05 /business/congress-passes-wide-ranging-bill-easing-bank-laws.html.

242 **In an interview with Bloomberg Television:** Jonathan Erlichman and David Mildenberg, "Ex-Merrill CEO Komansky Regrets Helping Kill Glass-Steagall," Bloomberg, May 5, 2010. http://www .bloomberg.com/news/2010-05-05/merrill-s-ex-chief-komansky -regrets-backing-glass-steagall-s-1999-repeal.html.

242 **John Reed:** "Culture Clash Means Banks Must Split, Says Former Citi Chief," *Financial Times,* September 8, 2013.

243 **This Be the Verse:** "This Be the Verse" from *The Complete Poems of Philip Larkin* by Philip Larkin, edited by Archie Burnett. Copyright © 2012 by the Estate of Philip Larkin. Reprinted by permission of Farrar, Straus and Giroux, LLC.

246 **threats to the traditional ways of doing things:** Adam Thierer, "Why Do We Always Sell the Next Generation Short?," *Forbes,* January 8, 2012. http://www.forbes.com/sites/adamthierer/2012/01 /08/why-do-we-always-sell-the-next-generation-short/#7600 1920582b.

246 **Many of those children of the 1930s and 1940s:** Glen H. Elder, Jr., *Children of the Great Depression: Social Change in Life Experience,* 25th Anniversary Updated Edition (Boulder, Colo.: Westview, 1998).

247 **greater respect for others:** "Millennials: Confident. Connected. Open to Change, Executive Summary," Pew Research Center, February 24, 2010. http://www.pewsocialtrends.org/2010/02/24/millennials-confident -connected-open-to-change/.

247 **Millennials are founding their own businesses:** "BNP Paribas Global Entrepreneurs Report 2016," BNP Paribas, November 18, 2015. https://group.bnpparibas/en/news/bnp-paribas-global-entre preneurs-report-2016.

248 **poised to be the most educated generation in history:** "Millennials: Confident. Connected. Open to Change, Executive Summary," Pew Research Center, February 24, 2010. http://www.pewsocialtrends .org/2010/02/24/millennials-confident-connected-open-to-change/.

250 **early exposure to animals, plants, dirt and microbes:** Martijn J. Schuijs et al., "Farm Dust and Endotoxin Protect Against Allergy Through A20 Induction in Lung Epithelial Cells," *Science,* vol. 349, no. 6252 (September 4, 2015).

250 **parents of Millennials admit they may have been overprotective:** "Choose Your Parents Wisely," *Economist,* July 25, 2014. http://www .economist.com/news/united-states/21608779-there-large-class -divide-how-americans-raise-their-children-rich-parents-can.

250 **Jessica Lahey, talking about her own children:** Jessica Lahey, *The Gift of Failure: How the Best Parents Learn to Let Go So Their Children Can Succeed* (New York: HarperCollins, 2015).

251 **Julie Lythcott-Haims, a former Stanford dean:** Julie Lythcott-Haims, *How to Raise an Adult: Break Free of the Overparenting Trap and Prepare Your Kid for Success* (New York: St. Martin's Press, 2015).

251 **"scanning the sidelines for Mom and Dad":** ibid.

251 **In a *Time* magazine interview:** Mary C. Mazzio, "Can Entrepreneurship Be Taught? Richard Branson's Mother Says Yes," *Time,* May 9, 2012. http://business.time.com/2012/05/09/can-entrepreneurship -be-taught-richard-bransons-mother-says-yes/.

252 **"fall on their faces from time to time":** ibid.

252 **In his 1969 book:** Nathaniel Branden, *The Psychology of Self-Esteem: A Revolutionary Approach to Self-Understanding That Launched a*

New Era in Modern Psychology, 32nd Anniversary Edition (San Francisco: Jossey-Bass, 2001).

252 **the "Self-Esteem Movement" was born:** Amanda Ripley, *The Smartest Kids in the World: And How They Got That Way* (New York: Simon & Schuster, 2013).

253 **The thinking behind participation awards:** Sunny Chen, "Participation Awards: Good or Bad," Novak Djokovic Foundation, November 1, 2015. https://novakdjokovicfoundation.org/participation-awards-good-or-bad/. Ashley Merryman, "Losing Is Good for You," *New York Times*, September 24, 2013. https://learning.blogs.nytimes.com/2013/09/26/do-we-give-children-too-many-trophies/. "Should Every Young Athlete Get a Trophy?," Room for Debate, *New York Times*, October 6, 2016. Lisa Belkin, "Does Rewarding Children Backfire?," *New York Times*, November 14, 2008. https://parenting.blogs.nytimes.com/2008/11/14/does-rewarding-children-backfire/?_r=0. Jean M. Twenge, *Generation Me, Revised and Updated* (New York: Atria, 2014).

253 **complacency and overconfidence:** https://novakdjokovicfoundation.org/participation-awards-good-or-bad/; and https://learning.blogs.nytimes.com/2013/09/26/do-we-give-children-too-many-trophies/.

254 **What we call "entitlement":** Jean M. Twenge, *Generation Me: Why Today's Young Americans Are More Confident, Assertive, Entitled—and More Miserable than Ever Before*, Revised and Updated (New York: Atria, 2014).

256 **"accept that we can multitask very well":** *Digital Nation* (transcript), produced by Rachel Dretzin, February 2, 2010. http://www.pbs.org/wgbh/pages/frontline/digitalnation/etc/script.html.

256 **According to brain researchers:** Bob Sullivan and Hugh Thompson, "Brain Interrupted," *New York Times*, May 3, 2013. http://www.nytimes.com/2013/05/05/opinion/sunday/a-focus-on-distraction.html.

256 **It takes time for our brains to reset and return:** Jim Taylor, Ph.D., "Technology: Myth of Multitasking," *Psychology Today*, March 30, 2011. https://www.psychologytoday.com/blog/the-power-prime/201103/technology-myth-multitasking. "Multitasking: Switching Costs," American Psychological Association, March 20, 2006. http://www.apa.org/research/action/multitask.aspx.

257 **"shifting between tasks can cost as much as 40 percent of someone's productive time":** "Multitasking: Switching Costs," American

Psychological Association, March 20, 2006. http://www.apa.org
/research/action/multitask.aspx.

257 **twenty-three minutes to return to their original task:** "Worker, Interrupted: The Cost of Task Switching," interview with Gloria Mark,
July 28, 2008. https://www.fastcompany.com/944128/worker-inter
rupted-cost-task-switching.

257 **self-interruption:** Gloria Mark, Daniela Gudith, and Ulrich Klocke,
"The Cost of Interrupted Work: More Speed and Stress," *Proceedings of
the SIGCHI Conference on Human Factors in Computing Systems*, 2008.
https://www.ics.uci.edu/~gmark/chi08-mark.pdf. Laura Dabbish, Gloria Mark, and Víctor M. González, "Why Do I Keep Interrupting
Myself?: Environment, Habit and Self-Interruption," *Proceedings of the
International Conference on Human Factors in Computing Systems*,
2011. https://www.ics.uci.edu/~gmark/Home_page/Research_files/CHI
%202011%20Self-interruption.pdf.

257 **chronic multitaskers make more mistakes and remember less:**
Eyal Ophir, Clifford Nass, and Anthony D. Wagner, "Cognitive Control in Media Multitaskers," *Proceedings of the National Academy of
Sciences*, vol. 106, no. 37, July 20, 2009. http://www.pnas.org/con
tent/106/37/15583. "Multitasking May Not Mean Higher Productivity," interview with Dr. Clifford Nass, *Talk of the Nation*, NPR,
August 28, 2009. http://www.npr.org/templates/story/story.php?
storyId=112334449&ft=1&f=5.

257 **MIT professor David Jones:** *Digital Nation* (transcript), produced
by Rachel Dretzin, February 2, 2010. http://www.pbs.org/wgbh/pages
/frontline/digitalnation/etc/script.html.

257 **The number of children and young people diagnosed with attention
deficit hyperactivity disorder (ADHD):** Erin Spain, "Diagnosis of
ADHD on the Rise," *Northwestern Now* (Northwestern University),
March 19, 2012. http://northwestern.edu/newscenter/stories/2012/03
/adhd-diagnosis-pediatrics.html.

257 **continued to rise between 2011 and 2014:** "Understanding ADHD:
General Prevalence," CHADD, National Resource Center on ADHD.
http://www.chadd.org/understanding-adhd/about-adhd/data-and
-statistics/general-prevalence.aspx.

258 **The Centers for Disease Control:** "Facts About ADHD," Centers for
Disease Control and Prevention, last modified July 16, 2013. http://
www.cdc.gov/ncbddd/adhd/facts.html.

259 **still forming brains and neural pathways:** "The Teenage Brain: Under Construction," American College of Pediatrics, April 2016. https://www.acpeds.org/the-college-speaks/position-statements /parenting-issues/the-teenage-brain-under-construction.

259 **More than 40 percent of children who discover alcohol before age fifteen will become alcoholics later in life:** Bridget F. Grant and Deborah A. Dawson, "Age at Onset of Alcohol Use and Its Association with DSM-IV Alcohol Abuse and Dependence: Results from the National Longitudinal Alcohol Epidemiologic Survey," *Journal of Substance Abuse*, vol. 9 (1997): 103–10. http://www.inbalancecontinuum .com/outpatient/about/statistics. https://www.acpeds.org/the-college -speaks/position-statements/parenting-issues/the-teenage-brain -under-construction.

259 **same percentage of adult alcoholics:** "The Teenage Brain: Under Construction," American College of Pediatrics, April 2016. https:// www.acpeds.org/the-college-speaks/position-statements/parenting -issues/the-teenage-brain-under-construction.

259 **88 percent of teenagers age thirteen to seventeen had access to cell phones or smart phones:** Amanda Lenhart, "Teens, Social Media & Technology: Overview, 2015," Pew Research Center, April 9, 2015. http://www.pewinternet.org/2015/04/09/teens-social-media-tech nology-2015/.

259 **In both China and South Korea, Internet addiction is recognized:** Natalya Kadyrova, *China's Digital Detox*, May 20, 2016. https://rtd .rt.com/films/chinas-digital-detox/. *Digital Nation* (transcript), produced by Rachel Dretzin, February 2, 2010. http://www.pbs.org/wgbh /pages/frontline/digitalnation/etc/script.html.

260 **"How a young person chooses to spend their time":** *Digital Nation* (transcript), produced by Rachel Dretzin, February 2, 2010. http://www.pbs.org/wgbh/pages/frontline/digitalnation/etc/script .html.

260 **In the best-case scenario, their brains will change:** "The Teenage Brain: Under Construction," American College of Pediatrics, April 2016. https://www.acpeds.org/the-college-speaks/position-statements /parenting-issues/the-teenage-brain-under-construction.

260 **rely on our friends to cope with the stress:** "Friendships—Helping Your Child Through Early Adolescence," U.S. Department of Education, last modified September 11, 2003. https://ed.gov/parents /academic/help/adolescence/part9.html.

262 **2015 Deloitte Millennial Survey:** "Mind the Gaps: The 2015 Deloitte Millennial Survey—Executive Summary," Deloitte, 2015. www.deloitte.com/MillennialSurvey.

262 **Many of them donate and volunteer:** "Cause, Influence & the Workplace. The Millennial Impact Report Retrospective: Five Years of Trends," compiled by ACHIEVE with support from the Case Foundation, November 2016. www.TheMillennialImpact.com.

263 **More than seventeen million people:** "ALS Ice Bucket Challenge—FAQ," ALS Association. http://www.alsa.org/about-us/ice-bucket -challenge-faq.html.

263 **including an exceptionally high number of Millennials:** James Surowiecki, "What Happened to the Ice Bucket Challenge," *New Yorker*, July 25, 2016. http://www.newyorker.com/magazine/2016/07/25/als-and-the -ice-bucket-challenge.

263 **two and a half million people:** "ALS Ice Bucket Challenge—FAQ," ALS Association. http://www.alsa.org/about-us/ice-bucket-challenge -faq.html.

264 **the year before the original campaign:** John Bonifield, "One Year Later, Your ALS Ice Bucket Money Goes To . . . ," CNN, July 15, 2015. http://www.cnn.com/2015/07/15/health/one-summer-after-the-als -ice-bucket-challenge/.

267 **Teenagers are socializing less:** Riley Griffin, "Social Media Is Changing How College Students Deal with Mental Health, for Better or Worse," *Huffington Post*, July 21, 2015, updated July 22, 2015. http:// www.huffingtonpost.com/entry/social-media-college-mental-health _us_55ae6649e4b08f57d5d28845. Tyler Kingkade, "College Freshmen Are More Depressed and Alone Than Ever," *Huffington Post*, February 5, 2015, updated February 9, 2015. http://www.huffingtonpost .com/2015/02/05/college-students-depressed-ucla_n_6624012.html.

267 **social media usage among eighteen- to twenty-nine-year-olds:** "Social Networking," Pew Research Center, last updated April 2015. http:// www.pewresearch.org/data-trend/media-and-technology/social -networking-use/.

267 **a 2014 survey done by UCLA:** Kevin Eagan et al., "The American Freshman: National Norms Fall 2014," CIRP (Los Angeles: Higher Education Research Institute, UCLA, 2014). https://www.heri.ucla .edu/monographs/TheAmericanFreshman2014.pdf.

267 **2015 survey by Common Sense Media:** "The Common Sense Census: Media Use by Tweens and Teens," Common Sense, 2015. https://www

.commonsensemedia.org/research/the-common-sense-census -media-use-by-tweens-and-teens.

268 **"Social media is a really easy way to feel excluded":** Riley Griffin, "Social Media Is Changing How College Students Deal with Mental Health, for Better or Worse," *Huffington Post*, July 21, 2015, updated July 22, 2015. http://www.huffingtonpost.com/entry/social-media -college-mental-health_us_55ae6649e4b08f57d5d28845.

268 **2013 study by social scientists at the University of Michigan:** Ethan Kross et al., "Facebook Use Predicts Declines in Subjective Well-Being in Young Adults," *PLoS ONE* vol. 8, no. 8 (August 14, 2013). http://jour nals.plos.org/plosone/article?id=10.1371/journal.pone.0069841.

268 **it's easy to become envious:** "If Facebook Causes Envy, Depression Could Follow," News Bureau, University of Missouri, February 3, 2015. http://munews.missouri.edu/news-releases/2015/0203-if-facebook -use-causes-envy-depression-could-follow/.

269 **Universities today are experiencing:** Gregg Henriques, Ph.D., "The College Student Mental Health Crisis," *Psychology Today*, February 15, 2014. https://www.psychologytoday.com/blog/theory-knowledge /201402/the-college-student-mental-health-crisis.

269 **one in six:** American College Health Association, *National College Health Assessment II: Spring 2014 Reference Group Executive Summary* (Hanover, Md.: American College Health Association, 2014). http://www.acha-ncha.org/docs/ACHA-NCHA-II_ReferenceGroup _ExecutiveSummary_Spring2014.pdf.

269 **The National Institute of Mental Health reports:** "Major Depression Among Adolescents," Health & Education, National Institute of Mental Health, 2015. https://www.nimh.nih.gov/health/statistics/preva lence/major-depression-among-adolescents.shtml. Ramin Mojtabai, Mark Olfson, and Beth Han, "National Trends in the Prevalence and Treatment of Depression in Adolescents and Young Adults," *Pediatrics*, November 2016. http://pediatrics.aappublications.org/content /early/2016/11/10/peds.2016-1878.

269 **teenagers now suffer depression:** "Major Depression Among Adolescents," Health & Education, National Institute of Mental Health, 2015. https://www.nimh.nih.gov/health/statistics/prevalence/major -depression-among-adolescents.shtml. Ramin Mojtabai, Mark Olfson, and Beth Han, "National Trends in the Prevalence and Treatment of Depression in Adolescents and Young Adults," *Pediatrics*, Novem-

ber 2016. http://pediatrics.aappublications.org/content/early/2016/11/10/peds.2016-1878.

269 **Suicide is already the second:** "Suicide Facts at a Glance 2015," Centers for Disease Control and Prevention (CDC), National Center for Injury Prevention and Control, Division of Violence Prevention. https://www.cdc.gov/violenceprevention/pdf/suicide-datasheet-a.pdf.

269 **the number of young people who attempt suicide:** "Suicide Statistics," American Foundation for Suicide Prevention. https://afsp.org/about-suicide/suicide-statistics/.

269 **In the period between 1999 and 2014:** Sally C. Curtin, Margaret Warner, and Holly Hedegaard, "Increase in Suicide in the United States, 1999–2014," National Center for Health Statistics (NCHS) Data Brief No. 241, April 2016. https://www.cdc.gov/nchs/products/databriefs/db241.htm.

269 **The fact that teenage girls:** "The Common Sense Census: Media Use by Tweens and Teens," Common Sense, 2015. https://www.common sensemedia.org/research/the-common-sense-census-media-use-by-tweens-and-teens.

269 **and have a rate of depression nearly five times:** "Major Depression Among Adolescents," Health & Education, National Institute of Mental Health, 2015. https://www.nimh.nih.gov/health/statistics/prevalence/major-depression-among-adolescents.shtml. Ramin Mojtabai, Mark Olfson, and Beth Han, "National Trends in the Prevalence and Treatment of Depression in Adolescents and Young Adults," *Pediatrics*, November 2016. http://pediatrics.aappublications.org/content/early/2016/11/10/peds.2016-1878.

269 **In the period from 1969 to 1978:** Jessie Klein, *The Bully Society: School Shootings and the Crisis of Bullying in America's Schools* (New York: New York University Press, 2012).

270 **Between 2013 and 2017 alone:** "Guns in Public Places," Everytown for Gun Safety. https://everytownresearch.org/school-shootings/.

270 **all the data show a clear and consistent increase:** Pete J. Blair and Katherine W. Schweit, *A Study of Active Shooter Incidents in the United States Between 2000 and 2013*, Texas State University and Federal Bureau of Investigation (Washington, D.C.: U.S. Department of Justice, 2014). Peter Langman, Ph.D., "Multi-Victim School Shootings in the United States: A Fifty-Year Review," version 1.1, October 31, 2016. www.schoolshooters.info. Jessie Klein, *The Bully*

Society: School Shootings and the Crisis of Bullying in America's Schools (New York: New York University Press, 2012). Katherine S. Newman et al., *Rampage: The Social Roots of School Shootings* (New York: Basic Books, 2004). "Analysis of School Shootings," Everytown for Gun Safety. https://everytownresearch.org/reports/analysis-of -school-shootings/.

270 **A major FBI review of active shooting incidences:** Pete J. Blair and Katherine W. Schweit, *A Study of Active Shooter Incidents in the United States Between 2000 and 2013*, Texas State University and Federal Bureau of Investigation (Washington, D.C.: U.S. Department of Justice, 2014).

270 **Many are victims of bullying, teasing, or social exclusion:** Jessie Klein, *The Bully Society: School Shootings and the Crisis of Bullying in America's Schools* (New York: New York University Press, 2012). Katherine S. Newman et al., *Rampage: The Social Roots of School Shootings* (New York: Basic Books, 2004).

270 **Depression, substance abuse, or psychological disorders:** Katherine S. Newman et al., *Rampage: The Social Roots of School Shootings* (New York: Basic Books, 2004).

PART EIGHT: BECOMING A LEADER

272 **Civilizations don't usually die from murder:** Arnold J. Toynbee, *A Study of History: Abridgement of Volumes 1–6* (Oxford: Oxford University Press, 1947).

272 **Alcoholics Anonymous (AA):** "The Twelve Steps of Alcoholics Anonymous," Alcoholics Anonymous. http://www.aa.org/en_pdfs/smf-121 _en.pdf.

274 **Preliminary findings from a 2012 study:** Cort A. Pedersen et al., "Intranasal Oxytocin Blocks Alcohol Withdrawal in Human Subjects," *Alcoholism: Clinical and Experimental Research*, no. 3 (2013): 484–89. http://www.ncbi.nlm.nih.gov/pubmed/23025690. Maia Szalavitz, "'Cuddle Chemical' Oxytocin Relieves Alcohol Withdrawal," *Time*, October 15, 2012. http://healthland.time.com/2012/10/15/cuddle -chemical-oxytocin-relieves-alcohol-withdrawal/.

275 **According to another 2012 study:** "Marriage Linked to Better Survival in Middle Age; Study Highlights Importance of Social Ties During Midlife," *Science Daily*, January 10, 2013, http://www.science daily.com/releases/2013/01/130110102342.htm.

275 **Other studies have shown that:** Alexandria Sifferlin, "Why Facebook Makes You Feel Bad About Yourself," *Time*, January 24, 2013.

http://healthland.time.com/2013/01/24/why-facebook-makes-you-feel-bad-about-yourself/.

277 **According to a 2004 study:** Timothy Jones, "Study: Nation Wastes Nearly Half Its Food," *University of Arizona, UA News,* November 18, 2004. http://uanews.org/story/study-nation-wastes-nearly-half-its-food.

277 **According to the Stockholm International Water Institute:** Society of St. Andrews, "Food Waste." http://endhunger.org/food_waste.htm.

280 **those who deployed actually commit suicide:** Cynthia Leardmann, "Risk Factors Associated with Suicide in Current and Former US Military Personnel," *Journal of the American Medical Association,* 2013. http://jama.jamanetwork.com/article.aspx?articleid=1724276.

288 **Second Law of Motion:** "Newton's Laws of Motion," Glenn Research Center, NASA Online. http://www.grc.nasa.gov/WWW/k-12/rocket/newton.html.

APPENDIX

292 **According to a study published in *Psychological Science*:** Pam A. Mueller and Daniel M. Oppenheimer, "The Pen Is Mightier Than the Keyboard: Advantages of Longhand Over Laptop Note Taking," *Psychological Science,* 2014, 1–10.

BIBLIOGRAPHY

Breuning, Loretta Graziano. *I, Mammal: Why Your Brain Links Status and Happiness*. Oakland: System Integrity Press, 2011.

Breuning, Loretta Graziano. *Meet Your Happy Chemicals*. Oakland: System Integrity Press, 2012.

Brokaw, Tom. *The Greatest Generation*. New York: Random House, 1998.

Cacioppo, John T., and William Patrick. *Loneliness: Human Nature and the Need for Social Connection*. New York: W. W. Norton, 2009.

Collins, Jim, and Jerry Porras. *Built to Last*. New York: HarperPerennial, 2004.

Freeman, John. *The Tyranny of E-Mail: The Four-Thousand-Year Journey to Your Inbox*. New York: Scribner, 2011.

Hill, R. A., and R. I. Dunbar. "Social Network Size in Humans." *Human Nature* 14, no. 1 (2003): 53–72.

Lane, Robert E. *Loss of Happiness in Market Economies*. New Haven, CT: Yale University Press, 2001.

McClellan, James E., and Harold Dorn. *Science and Technology in World History: An Introduction*. Baltimore: Johns Hopkins University Press, 2006.

Marquet, L. David. *Turn the Ship Around! A True Story of Turning Followers into Leaders*. New York: Portfolio / Penguin, 2012.

Milgram, Stanley. *Obedience to Authority: An Experimental View*. New York: HarperPerennial, 2009.

Olds, Jacqueline. *The Lonely American: Drifting Apart in the Twenty-first Century*. Boston: Beacon Press, 2010.

Rappaport, Alfred. *Creating Shareholder Value: The New Standard for Business Performance*. New York: Free Press, 1986.

Sapolsky, Robert M. *Why Zebras Don't Get Ulcers*. 3rd ed. New York: Holt Paperbacks, 2004.

Schwartz, Mark. "Robert Sapolsky Discusses the Physiological Effects of Stress." *Stanford University News Service*. Accessed February 28, 2012. http://news.stanford.edu/news/2007/march7/sapolskysr-030707.html.

Smith, Lacey Baldwin. *English History Made Brief, Irreverent, and Plea-surable.* Chicago: Academy Chicago Publishers, 2006.

"Social Status and Health: Misery Index." *Economist*, April 14, 2012. Accessed May 4, 2012. www.economist.com/node/21552539/print.

Sorkin, Andrew Ross. *Too Big to Fail: The Inside Story of How Wall Street and Washington Fought to Save the Financial System from Crisis—and Themselves.* New York: Viking, 2009.

Stavrianos, Leften Stavros. *Lifelines from Our Past: A New World History.* Armonk, NY: M. E. Sharpe, 1997.

Stout, Lynn A. *The Shareholder Value Myth: How Putting Shareholders First Harms Investors, Corporations, and the Public.* San Francisco: Berrett-Koehler, 2012.

Turkle, Sherry. *Alone Together: Why We Expect More from Technology and Less from Each Other.* New York: Basic Books, 2011.

Uchitelle, Louis. *The Disposable American: Layoffs and Their Consequences.* New York: Knopf, 2006.

Whybrow, Peter C. *American Mania: When More Is Not Enough.* New York: W. W. Norton, 2005.

Zak, Paul J. *The Moral Molecule: The Source of Love and Prosperity.* New York: Dutton, 2013.

INDEX